797,885 Books
are available to read at

Forgotten Books

www.ForgottenBooks.com

Forgotten Books' App
Available for mobile, tablet & eReader

ISBN 978-1-4400-3793-1
PIBN 10110313

This book is a reproduction of an important historical work. Forgotten Books uses state-of-the-art technology to digitally reconstruct the work, preserving the original format whilst repairing imperfections present in the aged copy. In rare cases, an imperfection in the original, such as a blemish or missing page, may be replicated in our edition. We do, however, repair the vast majority of imperfections successfully; any imperfections that remain are intentionally left to preserve the state of such historical works.

Forgotten Books is a registered trademark of FB &c Ltd.
Copyright © 2015 FB &c Ltd.
FB &c Ltd, Dalton House, 60 Windsor Avenue, London, SW19 2RR.
Company number 08720141. Registered in England and Wales.

For support please visit www.forgottenbooks.com

1 MONTH OF FREE READING

at
www.ForgottenBooks.com

By purchasing this book you are eligible for one month membership to ForgottenBooks.com, giving you unlimited access to our entire collection of over 700,000 titles via our web site and mobile apps.

To claim your free month visit: www.forgottenbooks.com/free110313

* Offer is valid for 45 days from date of purchase. Terms and conditions apply.

English
Français
Deutsche
Italiano
Español
Português

www.forgottenbooks.com

Mythology Photography **Fiction**
Fishing Christianity **Art** Cooking
Essays Buddhism Freemasonry
Medicine **Biology** Music **Ancient Egypt** Evolution Carpentry Physics
Dance Geology **Mathematics** Fitness
Shakespeare **Folklore** Yoga Marketing
Confidence Immortality Biographies
Poetry **Psychology** Witchcraft
Electronics Chemistry History **Law**
Accounting **Philosophy** Anthropology
Alchemy Drama Quantum Mechanics
Atheism Sexual Health **Ancient History**
Entrepreneurship Languages Sport
Paleontology Needlework Islam
Metaphysics Investment Archaeology
Parenting Statistics Criminology
Motivational

THE CONTEMPORARY SCIENCE SERIES.

EDITED BY HAVELOCK ELLIS.

THE ORIGIN OF THE ARYANS.

By the same Author—

WORDS AND PLACES: ETYMOLOGICAL ILLUSTRATIONS OF HISTORY, ETHNOLOGY, AND GEOGRAPHY.

GREEKS AND GOTHS: A STUDY ON THE RUNES.

THE ALPHABET: AN ACCOUNT OF THE ORIGIN AND DEVELOPMENT OF LETTERS.

LEAVES FROM AN EGYPTIAN NOTE-BOOK.

THE ORIGIN
OF THE ARYANS.

AN ACCOUNT OF THE PREHISTORIC
ETHNOLOGY AND CIVILISATION OF EUROPE

BY

ISAAC TAYLOR,
M.A., Litt. D., Hon. LL.D.

ILLUSTRATED.

SCRIBNER & WELFORD,
743 & 745 BROADWAY,
NEW YORK.

1890.

11525a

A.76834

~~A.9321~~

CONTENTS.

CHAPTER I.

	PAGE
THE ARYAN CONTROVERSY	1

CHAPTER II.

THE PREHISTORIC RACES OF EUROPE—

§ 1. The Neolithic Age	54
§ 2. The Methods of Anthropology	63
§ 3. The Races of Britain	66
§ 4. The Celts	81
§ 5. The Iberians	92
§ 6. The Scandinavians	102
§ 7. The Ligurians	110

CHAPTER III.

THE NEOLITHIC CULTURE—

§ 1. The Continuity of Development	125
§ 2. Metals	133
§ 3. Weapons	150
§ 4. Cattle	151
§ 5. Husbandry	163
§ 6. Food	167
§ 7. Dress	171
§ 8. Habitations	174
§ 9. The Boat	177
§ 10. The Ox Waggon	179
§ 11. Trades	180
§ 12. Social Life	182
§ 13. Relative Progress	189

CONTENTS.

CHAPTER IV.

THE ARYAN RACE—   PAGE
- § 1. The Permanence of Race   197
- § 2. The Mutability of Language   204
- § 3. The Finnic Hypothesis   213
- § 4. The Basques   217
- § 5. The Northern Races   226

CHAPTER V.

THE EVOLUTION OF ARYAN SPEECH—
- § 1. The Aryan Languages   251
- § 2. Dialect and Language   261
- § 3. The Lost Aryan Languages.   267
- § 4. The Wave Theory .   269
- § 5. Language and Race   273
- § 6. The Genesis of Aryan Speech   282

CHAPTER VI.

THE ARYAN MYTHOLOGY   299

INDEX   333

LIST OF ILLUSTRATIONS.

	PAGE
1. Diagram of Aryan Migrations	22
2. Diagram of Cephalic and Orbital Indices	66
3. Long Barrow Skull from Rudstone	71
4. Round Barrow Skull from Cowlam	71
5. Side View of Skull from Rudstone	72
6. Side View of Skull from Cowlam	72
7. Long Barrow Skull from Sherburn	74
8. Round Barrow Skull from Flixton	75
9. Skull from a Cave at Sclaigneaux	82
10. Skull from a Tumulus at Borreby	83
11. Skulls from Ilderton and Borreby	83
12. Helvetian Skull	87
13. Roman Skull	89
14. Skull from Gibraltar	96
15. Skull of a Man from Hissarlik, Bronze Age	98
16. Skulls from Hissarlik and Gibraltar	99
17. Skull of St. Mansuy	108
18. Skull of an Auvergnat	111
19. Skull from Hissarlik, Stone Age	114
20. Skull from the Trou de Frontal	117
21. Rhætian Skull	121
22. Iberian and Silurian Skulls	123
23. Copper Celt, from Swiss Lake Dwelling	141
24. Horses, Engraved on Reindeer Antler	158
25. Horseman, from Cyprus	161
26. Hut Urn from Alba Longa	176
27. Ox-Cart from a Thracian Coin	179
28. Skull of a Spanish Basque	220
29. Map	253
30. Diagram of Aryan Languages	269

PREFACE.

THIS series is intended to present in popular form an account of the progress of Contemporary Science, especially in those departments where our knowledge has recently been enlarged, either by the accumulation of fresh facts, or where new theories have taken the place of others hitherto accepted.

This has been notably the case with the subject of the present volume. The last ten years have seen a revolution in the opinion of scholars as to the region in which the Aryan race originated, and theories which not long ago were universally accepted as the well-established conclusions of science now hardly find a defender.

In Germany several works have been devoted exclusively to the subject, but no English book has yet appeared giving an account of the state of the controversy, and embodying the results recently arrived at by philologists, archæologists, and anthropologists.

The present volume does not aim at setting forth new views or speculations. It is rather a summary of the labours of many scholars, and a critical digest of the very considerable literature which has now accumulated on the subject. Its object is to present in condensed form a statement of ascertained facts, and of the arguments which have been based upon them. On the works of four scholars, Cuno, Pösche, Penka, and Schrader,[1] who deal specially with the subject of this book, I have freely drawn, often without specific acknowledgment. I am more especially indebted to Dr. Schrader's admirable work, which forms an almost exhaustive treasury of facts and arguments, set forth in a critical and impartial spirit. To this work, an English translation of which is announced for speedy publication, the student who desires to follow out the subject may be confidently referred.

Of the anthropologists I have relied chiefly on Virchow, the greatest of the Germans, and on Broca, the greatest of the Frenchmen; but without neglecting other writers, such as Rolleston, Huxley, Thurnam, Davis, Greenwell, De Quatrefages, Hamy, and Topinard.

For archæological details constant reference has been made to Helbig's little-known but admirable book on the prehistoric civilisation of Italy, as well as to the works of Keller, De Mortillet, and Boyd Dawkins.

---

[1] Johann Gustav Cuno, *Forschungen im Gebiete der alten Völker-kunde*; Theodor Pösche, *Die Arier*; Karl Penka, *Origines Ariacæ* and *Die Herkunft der Arier*; O. Schrader, *Sprachvergleichung und Urgeschichte*.

I have obtruded my own opinions as little as possible. On the main thesis of the book they are essentially those of Spiegel and Schrader, though in several points I find myself rather in agreement with Cuno, whose ingenious work seems to be almost unknown in this country, if one may judge from the fact that I have seen it quoted in no English book, and found that it was unknown even in the British Museum.

I believe the speculation as to the relations of the Basques and Iberians is new. I have also worked out a pregnant suggestion of Dr. Thurnam's—the identification of the primitive Aryans with the "Turanian" race of the British round barrows, an hypothesis which seems to afford the most probable solution of the problem of the origin of the Aryans, and this I have combined with the philological arguments of Anderson, Weske, and Cuno, the only scholars who have effectively investigated the linguistic affinities of primitive Aryan speech.

In the chapter on mythology I have attempted to work out to its legitimate conclusion a line of argument suggested in the Hibbert lectures of Professor Rhys.

I. T.

SETTRINGTON,
December 1889.

THE ORIGIN OF THE ARYANS.

CHAPTER I.

THE ARYAN CONTROVERSY.

WHEN towards the close of the last century Sanskrit and Zend became known to European scholars, the new science of Comparative Philology came into existence. The first stone of the edifice was laid in 1786, when Sir William Jones made the memorable declaration that the similarities between Sanskrit, Greek, Latin, German, and Celtic could only be explained on the hypothesis that these languages had a common parentage. Hegel hardly exaggerated the consequences of this discovery when he called it the discovery of a new world.

Fifty years elapsed before Bopp succeeded in establishing, as a settled conclusion of science, what had hitherto been little more than a probable hypothesis. His *Comparative Grammar*, published in 1833-35, has been superseded in its details by other works, and it has now only an historical interest. But to Bopp belongs the honour of having discovered the method of the comparison of grammatical forms, which at once placed Comparative Philology on a scientific footing. In this and subsequent works

Bopp showed that Zend and Slavonic, as well as Albanian and Armenian, must be included in what he called the Indo-Germanic family of speech.

The great linguistic family, whose existence was thus established, embraces seven European groups of languages—the Hellenic, Italic, Celtic, Teutonic, Slavonic, Lithuanic or Lettic, and Albanian; in fact, all the existing languages of Europe except Basque, Finnic, Magyar, and Turkish. There are also three closely related Asiatic groups: the Indic, containing fourteen modern Indian languages derived from Sanskrit; secondly, the Iranic group, comprising Zend, Persian, Pushtu or Afghan, Baluchi, Kurdish, and Ossetic; and, thirdly, the Armenian, which is intermediate between Greek and Iranian.

No name, altogether unobjectionable, has been devised for this family of speech. Japhetic, modelled after the pattern of Semitic and Hamitic, involves the assumption of a descent from Japhet. Caucasian is both too narrow and too broad, and, if used at all, is applicable to race rather than to language. Sanskritic gives undue prominence to one member of the group. Indo-Germanic and Indo-European are not only clumsy, but inaccurate. The first, adopted by Bopp, is a favourite term in Germany; but French and Italian scholars see no reason why German should be taken as the type of European speech. Indo-European, which they prefer, is too narrow, since it excludes Iranian and Armenian, and too broad, since the languages in question are spoken only in a part of India and a part of Europe.

ARYAN, a term invented by Professor Max Müller, is almost as objectionable as Sanskritic, since it properly designates only the Indo-Iranian languages, in which sense it is used by many continental scholars. Moreover, it tacitly implies or suggests that the ancient Ariana, the district round Herat, was the cradle of the Aryan languages, and thus begs the whole question of their European or Asiatic origin. However, since the term has the great merit of being short and compact, and since it is almost universally adopted by English writers, and is increasingly used in France and Germany, it will, in spite of its manifold demerits, be employed in the ensuing pages.

We have already seen that Comparative Philology, as a science, dates from the publication of Bopp's *Comparative Grammar* in 1835. But this great achievement was not without its nemesis. When Bopp had demonstrated that the greater number of the languages of Europe and some languages of Asia must be referred to a common ancestral speech, there was a tendency to assume, as a matter of course, that the speakers of these languages were also themselves descended from common ancestors. From a primitive unity of speech scholars hastily inferred a primitive unity of race.

Professor Max Müller, owing to the charm of his style, to his unrivalled power of popular exposition, and to his high authority as a Sanskrit scholar, has done more than any other writer to popularise this erroneous notion among ourselves. Thus, in his *Lectures on the Science of Language*, delivered in 1861, instead of speaking only of a primitive Aryan language, he speaks of an "Aryan race," an "Aryan family," and asserts that there was a time "when the first ancestors of the Indians, the Persians, the Greeks, the Romans, the Slaves, the Celts, and the Germans were living together within the same enclosures, nay, under the same roof," and he argues that because the same forms of speech are "preserved by all the members of the Aryan family, it follows that before the ancestors of the Indians and Persians started for the South, and the leaders of the Greek, Roman, Celtic, Teutonic, and Slavonic colonies marched towards the shores of Europe, there was a small clan of Aryans, settled probably on the highest elevation of Central Asia, speaking a language not yet Sanskrit or Greek or German, but containing the dialectical germs of all."[1]

Than this picturesque paragraph more mischievous words have seldom been uttered by a great scholar. Professor Max Müller's high reputation has been the means of impressing these crude assumptions, which he would now doubtless repudiate, upon his numerous disciples.[2] In England, at all events, such misconceptions are still widely prevalent, and our popular writers persistently ignore the labours of those French and German scholars who, during the last quarter of a century, have been offering more scientific explanations of the great fact of the fundamental unity of the Aryan languages. They have shown conclusively that the assumption of the common ancestry of the speakers of Aryan languages is a mere figment, wholly contrary to the evidence, and as improbable as the hypothesis that a small Aryan clan in Central Asia could have sent out great

[1] Max Müller, *Lectures*, 1st Series, pp. 211, 212.
[2] These opinions are still held by writers of repute. Thus, in 1884, Canon Cook affirmed that "it is a fact, scientifically demonstrated, that the ancestors of all the families belonging to this (the Aryan) race must have dwelt together as one community after their separation from the Semitic and Hamitic branches."—Cook, *Origins of Religion and Language*, p. 312.

colonies which marched four thousand miles to the shores of Europe.

It cannot be insisted upon too strongly that identity of speech does not imply identity of race, any more than diversity of speech implies diversity of race. The language of Cornwall is the same as the language of Essex, but the blood is Celtic in the one case and Teutonic in the other. The language of Cornwall is different from that of Brittany, but the blood is largely the same. Two related languages, such as French and Italian, point to an earlier language, from which both have descended; but it by no means follows that French and Italians, who speak those languages, have descended from common ancestors. The most inexperienced eye can distinguish between a Spaniard and a Swede, and yet both speak Aryan tongues, and even in Northern and Southern Germany there is a manifest difference of race, though the language is the same.

The old assumption of the philologists, that the relationship of language implies a relationship of race, has been decisively disproved and rejected by the anthropologists. The ultimate unity of the human race may be admitted, but Professor Max Müller has maintained a nearer kinship of all speakers of Aryan languages. He has asserted that the same blood runs in the veins of English soldiers "as in the veins of the dark Bengalese," and has had the courage to affirm that "there is not an English jury nowadays which, after examining the hoary documents of language, would reject the claim of a common descent and a legitimate relationship between Hindu, Greek, and Teuton."[1] Coming from such a source, this

[1] Max Müller, *Survey of Languages*, p. 29.

statement cannot be passed over as it might be if it came from a less eminent authority. It will be admitted that the language spoken by the negro in Alabama resembles the language spoken by the New Englander of Massachusetts far more nearly than the language spoken by the English soldier resembles that of the Bengal sepoy with whom he is brigaded, and the evidence derived from the documents of language—in this case not hoary—which might be put before an English jury as to a "common descent," and a "legitimate relationship" between the negro and the Yankee, would be far more intelligible to the twelve English tradesmen in the box than the more obscure evidence which applies to the case of the Teuton and the Hindu. Such rash assertions are calculated to discredit, and have discredited, the whole science of Comparative Philology, and those who have given them the authority attached to influential names must be charged with having retarded for twenty years in England the progress of the science of Comparative Ethnology.[1]

To the French anthropologists, and more especially to Broca, belongs the credit of raising a needful protest against the overweening claims of the philologists. He observes that "races have frequently within the historic period changed their language without having apparently changed the race or the type. The Belgians, for instance, speak a neo-Latin language; but of all the races who have mingled their

[1] Thus in a recent work Professor Rawlinson quotes the foregoing appeal to the English jury, "from the greatest of modern ethnologists," as the "result of advanced modern inductive science," which has "proved beyond all reasonable doubt" the common origin of the nations which speak Aryan languages.—Rawlinson, *Origin of Nations*, p. 176.

blood with that of the autochthones of Belgium it would be difficult to find one which has left less trace than the people of Rome." Hence, he continues, "the ethnological value of comparative philology is extremely small. Indeed, it is apt to be misleading rather than otherwise. But philological facts and deductions are more striking than minute measurements of skulls, and therefore the conclusions of philologists have received undue attention."[1]

These warning words are still neglected, the speakers of Aryan languages are assumed to constitute an Aryan race, and the question is debated, where did this Aryan race originate?

It is now contended that there is no such thing as an Aryan race in the same sense that there is an Aryan language, and the question of late so frequently discussed as to the origin of the Aryans can only mean, if it means anything, a discussion of the ethnic affinities of those numerous races which have acquired Aryan speech; with the further question, which is perhaps insoluble—among which of these races did Aryan speech arise, and where was the cradle of that race?

To the same effect, Topinard, a distinguished follower of Broca, remarks that it has been proved that the anthropological types in Europe have been continuous, and if the Aryans came from Asia they can have brought with them nothing but their language, their civilisation, and a knowledge of metals. Their blood has disappeared. In France, he continues, we are Aryans only by speech. By race we are mainly Cymry in the north, and Celts in the central region.[2]

Thirty years ago this question as to the cradle of

[1] Broca, *La Linguistique et l'Anthropologie*, p. 259.
[2] Topinard, *L'Anthropologie*, p. 444.

the Aryan race was deemed a reasonable question to ask, and a possible one to answer. It was even believed that it had received a final and definite solution. European scholars, with hardly an exception, were agreed that the cradle of what they were pleased to call the Aryan race must be sought in Central Asia on the upper waters of the Oxus.

There is hardly a more instructive chapter in the whole history of scientific opinion than that which deals with the arguments on which this conclusion was based, and with the counter arguments which have led, during the last few years, to its general abandonment.

At the beginning of the present century, and even so recently as thirty years ago, the chronology of Archbishop Usher was accepted without question, the origin of the human race being assigned to the year 4004 B.C. It was believed that the primeval language spoken by our first parents was Hebrew,[1] and that the origin of the languages of Europe must be referred to the family of Japhet, who set forth from the plains of Shinar in the year 2247 B.C.

This theory, based on the belief that the human race originated in Asia at a comparatively recent period, and that the diversity of human speech dates from the confusion of tongues at Babel, was universally accepted. It was maintained, for instance, by Vans Kennedy[2] in 1828, by Dr. Kitto[3] in 1847, and by Canon Cook[4] as late as 1884, as well as by a host of less influential writers.

[1] Gill, *Antiquity of Hebrew*, p. 44.
[2] Kennedy, *Researches into the Origin and Affinity of the principal Languages of Europe and Asia.*
[3] In Knight's *Pictorial Bible*, vol. i. p. 38.
[4] Cook, *Origins of Religion and Language*, p. 314.

In a somewhat modified form this opinion is still held. Mommsen, in 1874, adhered to the valley of the Euphrates as the primitive seat of the Indo-Germanic race,[1] and the same theory was advocated in 1888 by Dr. Hale in a paper read before the Anthropological Section of the American Association for the Advancement of Science.[2]

Adelung, the father of Comparative Philology, who died in 1806, placed the cradle of mankind in the valley of Cashmere, which he identified with Paradise. To Adelung we owe the opinion, which has prevailed so widely, that since the human race originated in the east, the most westerly nations, the Iberians and the Celts, must have been the first to leave the parent hive.

As soon as the archaic character of Zend, and its close relation to Sanskrit, had been recognised, it was seen that the Cashmere hypothesis of Adelung was untenable, and that the Indians and Iranians must at one time have occupied in common some northern region, from which the Indians penetrated into the Punjab. The hypothesis, which for half a century was generally accepted, that Central Asia was the cradle of the Indo-European race, was first propounded in 1820 by J. G. Rhode. His argument was based on the geographical indications contained in the first chapter of the Vendidad, which pointed not obscurely to Bactria as the earlier home of the Iranians.

In view of the enormous extension of time which is now demanded for the evolution and differentiation of the Aryan languages, these arguments lose their

---

[1] Mommsen, *Romische Geschichte*, vol. i. p. 30.
[2] *Popular Science Monthly*, vol. xxxiv. p. 674, March 1889.

cogency; but they were sufficient to obtain the accession of W. von Schlegel, who nearly at the same time declared himself an adherent of Rhode's hypothesis. But the general acceptance of this theory by European scholars was chiefly due to the great authority of Pott. The reasoning of this eminent scholar is an instructive example of the way in which the imagination can be influenced by a mere metaphor. Pott's argument, if it can be called an argument, is based upon the aphorism—*ex oriente lux*. The path of the sun must be the path of culture. In Asia, he declares, or nowhere, was the school-house where the families of mankind were trained. He fixes on the region watered by the Oxus and the Jaxartes, north of the Himalaya and east of the Caspian, as the true cradle of the Indo-European race. Klaproth and Ritter supported this conclusion by a futile attempt to identify the names of the European nations with certain frontier tribes mentioned by Chinese historians. In 1847 Lassen declared his adherence to the view of Pott on the ground that the Sanskrit people must have penetrated into the Punjab from the north-west through Cabul, and that the traditions of the Avesta point to the slopes of the Belurtag and the Mustag as the place of their earlier sojourn. That before their separation the Indo-Iranians were nomad herdsmen, inhabiting the steppes between the Oxus and the Jaxartes, is not improbable; but in view of the philological arguments which establish the comparatively late date of the separation of the Indian and Iranian stems, it is now seen that the admission of a Bactrian home for the Indo-Iranians has little bearing on the question.

In the following year (1848) this opinion received

the powerful support of Jacob Grimm, who calmly lays it down as an accepted conclusion of science, which "few will be found to question," that "all the nations of Europe migrated anciently from Asia; in the vanguard those related races whose destiny it was through moil and peril to struggle onwards, their forward march from east to west being prompted by an irresistible impulse, whose precise cause is hidden in obscurity. The farther to the west any race has penetrated so much the earlier it must have started on its pilgrimage, and so much the more profound will be the footprints which it impressed upon its track."[1]

In 1859 Professor Max Müller, in his *History of Ancient Sanskrit Literature*, adopted, with sundry poetic embellishments, Grimm's theory of the "irresistible impulse." "The main stream of the Aryan nations," he says, "has always flowed towards the north-west. No historian can tell us by what impulse those adventurous nomads were driven on through Asia towards the isles and shores of Europe. . But whatever it was, the impulse was as irresistible as the spell which in our own times sends the Celtic tribes towards the prairies, or the regions of gold across the Atlantic. It requires a strong will, or a great amount of inertness, to be able to withstand such national or rather ethnical movements. Few will stay behind when all are going. But to let one's friends depart and then to set out ourselves— to take a road which, lead where it may, can never lead us to join those again who speak our language and worship our gods—is a course which only men of strong individuality and great self-dependence

[1] Grimm, *Deutsche Sprache*, pp. 6, 162.

are capable of pursuing. It was the course adopted by the southern branch of the Aryan family—the Brahmanic Aryans of India and the Zoroastrians of Irân."

On this passage Professor Whitney somewhat maliciously observes that a less poetic and more exact scientific statement would have been preferable, and that the paragraph seems to have been suggested by Kaulbach's famous picture "representing the scattering of the human race from the foot of the ruined Tower of Babel, where we see each separate nationality, with the impress of its after character and fortunes already stamped on every limb and feature, taking up its line of march towards the quarter of the earth which it is destined to occupy."[1]

Pictet, in his *Origines Indo-Européennes*, of which the first volume was published in 1859, constructed an elaborate theory of the successive Aryan migrations from Central Asia. He brought the Hellenes and Italians by a route south of the Caspian through Asia Minor to Greece and Italy, and the Celts south of the Caspian through the Caucasus to the north of the Black Sea, and then up the Danube to the extreme west of Europe; the Slaves and Teutons marching north of the Caspian through the Russian steppes. Pictet's arguments, derived mainly from philological considerations as to the animals and plants with which he supposed the various races to have been acquainted, vanish on examination.

In the same year Pictet's view was endorsed by a far greater name—that of one of the most acute and profound scholars of the century. So rapidly has science progressed that it seems difficult to

[1] Whitney, *Oriental and Linguistic Studies*, p. 95.

believe that so recently as 1862 Schleicher could have propounded, in its crudest form, the theory of the successive migrations of the Aryan races from the east. "The home of the original Indo-Germanic race," he writes in his *Compendium*, "is to be sought in the central highlands of Asia." "The Slavo-Teutonic races first began their journeyings towards the west; then followed the Græco-Italo-Celtic peoples; of the Aryans who remained behind, the Indians travelled south-eastward, and the Iranians spread in a south-westerly direction."

The general acceptance in this country of the Central Asian hypothesis is undoubtedly due to the confidence with which, in words already quoted,[1] it was propounded by Professor Max Müller in his deservedly popular *Lectures on the Science of Language*, delivered in 1861. Stamped with the hall-mark of the approval of the most eminent scholars in Europe—Pott, Lassen, Grimm, Schleicher, and Max Müller—the theory rapidly made its way into all the text-books as an accepted conclusion of linguistic science. Thus Professor Sayce writes in 1874—"When the Aryan languages first make their appearance it is in the highlands of Middle Asia, between the sources of the Oxus and Jaxartes."[2] It would be tedious to enumerate all the books in which this theory was accepted. Suffice it to say that it was approved by Link, Justi, Misteli, and Kiepert on the Continent, and by Sayce, Muir, Richard Morris, and Papillon in this country.

Before giving an account of the singular revulsion of opinion which has recently taken place, it may be

---

[1] See p. 3, *supra*.
[2] Sayce, *Principles of Philology*, p. 101.

well to examine briefly the arguments which induced the most eminent European scholars, with hardly a dissentient voice, to approve a theory which is now almost as universally rejected.

In 1880, when two daring sceptics, Benfey and Geiger, had already ventured to state the difficulties in the way of the accepted hypothesis, Professor Sayce summed up more forcibly than had been done by any previous writer the reasons why he thought it "best to abide by the current opinion which places the primeval Aryan community in Bactriana, on the western slopes of the Belurtag and the Mustag, and near the sources of the Oxus and Jaxartes."[1]

He argues that "Comparative Philology itself supplies us with a proof of the Asiatic cradle of the Aryan tongue." This "proof" consists in the allegation that "of all the Aryan dialects Sanskrit and Zend may, on the whole, be considered to have changed the least; while, on the other hand, Keltic in the extreme west has changed most." Hence it would appear that the region now occupied by Sanskrit and Zend must be the nearest to the primitive centre of dispersion. This conclusion, he adds, is confirmed by the assertion in the Avesta that the first creation of mankind by Ahuramazda (Ormuzd) took place in the Bactrian region. Professor Sayce admits that "this legend is at most a late tradition, and applies only to the Zoroastrian Persians," but he thinks it agrees with the conclusions of Comparative Philology, which teach us that the early Aryan home was a cold region, "since the only two trees whose names agree in Eastern and Western Aryan are the birch and the pine, while winter was

[1] Sayce, *Science of Languages*, vol. ii. p. 123.

familiar, with its snow and ice." He locates it in the neighbourhood of the Sea of Aral, to which the universal Aryan myth of the wanderings of Odysseus may refer.

It is fortunate that we should have from such a competent authority a summary of the arguments which, after sixty years of discussion, were considered, only nine years ago, sufficient to establish the Asiatic origin of the Aryan languages.

According to Professor Sayce, the first and most conclusive "proof" is the assumption that Sanskrit and Zend are the most archaic of the Aryan languages, and that therefore the cradle of the Indo-Iranians must also be the cradle of the Aryans.

It is now recognised that the archaic character of Sanskrit and Zend is mainly due to the fact that our knowledge of these languages is derived from documents more ancient than those belonging to any of the languages with which they are to be compared. But if we confine our attention to contemporary forms of speech, and compare, for instance, modern Lithuanian with any of the vernacular dialects of India which have descended from Sanskrit, we find that the Lithuanian is immeasurably the more archaic in its character. It may be surmised that if we possessed a Lithuanian literature of a date contemporary with the oldest literature of India, it might be contended with greater reason that the cradle of the Aryan languages must have been in the Lithuanian region. In like manner it is not fair to compare ancient Zend with modern German. But if a comparison is made between modern Persian and the vernacular Icelandic, the latter is seen to have preserved the more archaic forms, so that if the argument from archaism be admissible, and the argument is confined to these contemporary languages, it would be more reasonable to place the Aryan cradle in Iceland than in Bactria.

But, it will be said, we know Iceland has been colonised within the historic period. True; but we know also that the Indo-Iranians were nomad herdsmen at a time when the European Aryans were no longer nomads, and therefore they might easily have wandered with their herds to Bactria; while the archaic character of the Indo-Iranian speech is explained by the parallel case of the Tartar tribes, which exhibit the conservative influence on language of a wandering pastoral life.

Against the traditions of the Avesta, which are so late as to be valueless, may be placed certain synchronous traditions of the European Aryans that they were themselves autochthonous. The Deucalion legend of the Greeks has as much, or as little value, as the traditions of the Avesta.

The philological deductions, as to latitude and climate apply with as much force to Europe as to Asia; and if the birch and the pine were known to the primitive Aryans, so also, it may be urged, was the beech, which, unlike the birch and the pine, is confined to Europe, while the ass and the camel, which were certainly unknown to the undivided Aryans, are especially characteristic of the fauna of Central Asia. As for the Sea of Aral, and the wanderings of Odysseus, they are disposed of by the fact that the words both for sea and salt are not common to the European and Asiatic Aryans, while if a sea is required, the Baltic, for that matter, would serve as well as the Sea of Aral.

It is very instructive to learn how extremely shadowy are the arguments which sufficed to convince all the greatest scholars in Germany and England, Pott, Lassen, Grimm, Schleicher, Mommsen, and Max Müller, that the origin of the Aryans must be sought in Asia, whence, in successive migrating hordes, they wandered to the West. In spite of the intrinsic probabilities of the case, in spite of the enormous difficulties of any such migration, this opinion was universally accepted, on no solid grounds whatever; at first merely from the general impression that Asia was necessarily the cradle of the human race, and afterwards on the authority of a late Iranian legend, aided by the belief, which now proves to be baseless, of the more archaic character of Zend and Sanskrit. There is no more curious chapter in the whole history of scientific delusion. The history of the general abandonment, within the last ten years, of conclusions which had prevailed for half a century, as the first fruits of the new science of Comparative Philology, must now be sketched.

First among the causes which have led to this change of opinion must be placed the evidence as to the antiquity and early history of man supplied by the new sciences of Geology, Anthropology, Craniology, and Prehistoric Archæology. The assumption that man was a comparatively recent denizen of the earth, the traditional belief that Asia was the cradle of the human race, and the identification of the Aryans with the descendants of Japhet, had to be reconsidered when it was recognised that man had been an inhabitant of Western Europe at a time anterior to the oldest traditions, probably before the close of the last glacial epoch.

The geographical centre of human history has now been shifted from the East to the West. The earliest existing documents for the history of mankind come not from Asia, but from Western Europe. The most ancient records of any actual events which we possess are no longer the slabs with cuneiform writing disinterred from Babylonian mounds, but the immeasurably older memorials of successful hunts, preserved in the caverns of the Dordogne, which were inscribed by the contemporaries of the mammoth on the bones and tusks of extinct animals, compared with which the records on Babylonian tablets, or in Egyptian tombs, much more the traditions preserved in the Avesta, are altogether modern. The Iranian traditions may take us back for three, or, happily, for four thousand years, the Babylonian and Egyptian records for four or six thousand at the outside. The new science of Comparative Philology has made possible another science, the science of Linguistic Archæology, which takes us back to a period older than all written records, to an age before the invention of writing or the discovery of metals, when the first rude plough was a crooked bough, and the first ship a hollow log propelled by poles.

From another new science, that of Craniology, we learn that those who now speak the Aryan languages do not belong to one race, but to several, and that the same races which now inhabit Europe have inhabited it continuously since the beginning of the neolithic period, when the wild horse and reindeer roamed over Europe.

The sciences of Prehistoric Archæology and Geology have extended still further the history of the human race, and have shown that in Western Europe man was the contemporary of the mammoth, the woolly rhinoceros, and other extinct pachyderms, and have brought to light from the gravels of Abbeville evidences of his handiwork, dating from a period when the Somme flowed three hundred feet above its present level, and England was still united to the Continent. Man must have inhabited France and Britain at the close of the quaternary period, and must have followed the retreating ice of the last glacial epoch, to the close of which Dr. Croll and Professor Geikie assign on astronomical grounds an antiquity of some 80,000 years.

When it was recognised that Europe had been continuously inhabited from such remote ages, it was at once asked whether there is any evidence at all for those great successive migrations from Central Asia which have been so confidently assumed. Is there any reason for supposing that the present inhabitants of Europe are not in the main the descendants of the neolithic races whose rude implements fill our museums? If not, what became of these primitive people? And when the anthropologists succeeded in proving that the skulls of the present inhabitants of Central France are of the same peculiar type as the skulls of the cave-men and dolmen builders who inhabited the same region at the beginning of the neolithic period, when they proved that the skulls of the Spanish Basques belonged to another neolithic type, when they proved that the neolithic skulls from Sweden belong to a third type which is that of the Scandinavians and Northern Teutons, when similar discoveries were made in Denmark, in England, and in Eastern Europe, the conclusion seemed inevitable that the present inhabitants of Spain, France, Denmark, Germany, and Britain are to a great extent the descendants of those rude savages who occupied the same regions in neolithic or possibly in palæolithic times.

It is the anthropologists who have been the chief apostles of the new doctrine, but it must be acknowledged that the first protest against the old assumption of the philologists was raised, before anthropology became a science, by a man who was himself a philologist. To the late Dr. Latham belongs the credit of having been the first to call in question the prevalent belief. As early as 1851, in his edition of the *Germania* of Tacitus, he ventured to assert that no valid argument whatever had been produced in favour of the Asiatic origin of the Aryans. He maintained, on the other hand, that a European origin was far more probable. His argument was twofold. He urged, firstly, that Lithuanian is closely related to Sanskrit, and no less archaic. Sanskrit must either have reached India from Europe, or else Celtic, German, Lithuanian, Slavonic, Greek, and Latin must have reached Europe from Asia. He says he finds no argument whatever in favour of the latter hypothesis, but merely a "tacit assumption" that the human species, and the greater part of our civilisation, originated in the East. But if this tacit assumption be rejected, what, he asked, is the most probable conclusion? We find the main body of the Aryans in Europe, and a small detached body in Asia. Which, he argued—and his argument has never been answered—is *à priori* the more probable, that the smaller body broke away from the larger, or the larger from the smaller? The species comes from the genus, and not the genus from the species. To derive the Aryans of Europe from those of Asia would be as reasonable as to bring the Germans from England, instead of bringing the English from Germany; or to derive the reptiles of England from those of Ireland. We find, he argues, two bodies of Aryans, one nearly homogeneous, and of small geographical extent, the other spread over a vast region, and exhibiting numerous varieties. It is more reasonable to suppose that the small homogeneous body branched off from the larger than to assume that the larger parted from the smaller. If we found in Australia a single family of Campbells, and in Scotland a whole clan, it is antecedently more probable that the Australian family emigrated from Scotland than that the Scotch clan came from Australia, leaving only one family behind them.

Latham's argument, extended as it has been by subsequent researches, may be represented graphically by the diagram on the next page.

Linguistically the Slaves are closely related to the Letts, and the Letts to the Teutons, as has been shown by Bopp, Zeuss, Schleicher, Fick, and Schmidt. The Teutons again have been connected with the Celts by Ebel, Lottner, and Rhys; while the relation between the Celts and Latins has been shown by Newman, Schleicher, and Lottner. Again, Mommsen, Curtius, Förstemann, Fick, Schleicher, and Schmidt have shown the connection between Latin and Greek; while the connection between Greek and Indo-Iranian has been established by Grassmann, Benfey, Sonne, and Kern. Again, Schmidt, Ascoli, Leskien, and Miklosich have proved the connection between Indo-Iranian and Slavonic. Lastly, Schmidt has shown the absence of cross connections, such as between Greek and Slavonic, or between Indo-Iranian and either Latin or Teutonic.

Hence the European Aryans form a closely-united circular chain of six links; but there is one vacant place—one link is missing from the chain. This missing link is discovered far away in Asia, where we find the Indo-Iranians, who are very closely united

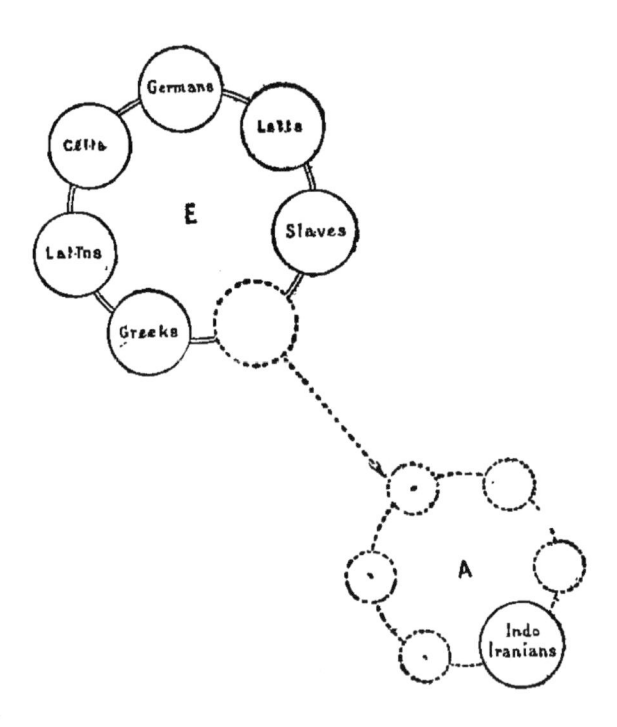

with each other, but whose affinities with the European Aryans are chiefly with the Slaves on the one hand, and with the Greeks on the other. They clearly constitute the missing link in the chain, which would be complete in its continuity if they had at some former period occupied the vacant post.

Only two hypotheses are possible. The Aryan languages must either have all originated in Europe around the spot marked E; one member, the Indo-Iranian, separating from the rest, and migrating to its present position, or they must all have originated in Asia, and have been grouped originally round the spot marked A, and then have migrated severally to E, preserving in their new homes the precise relative positions which their mutual connections prove must have originally existed. Which is the more probable hypothesis—that of a single migration, the migration of a people whom we know to have been nomads at no very distant time, or six distinct migrations of six separate peoples, as to which there is no evidence whatever that they ever migrated at all, and whose traditions assert that they were autochthons?

Latham's argument was more conclusive than any that had been advanced on the other side; but it was unheeded. The assumption as to the Asiatic origin of the European peoples was so firmly rooted, and, more than all, was upheld by the authority of such great names, that no one thought it worth while to take the trouble even to reply. His voice was a *vox clamantis in eremo*. He was met, not with argument, but with mockery; and more than twenty years after his book had appeared a learned German thus characterised the fruitful suggestion which has revolutionised the science of Ethnology —"And so it came to pass that in England, the native land of fads, there chanced to enter into the head of an eccentric individual the notion of placing the cradle of the Aryan race in Europe."[1]

After Latham's views had lain unheeded before the

[1] "Da geschah es (Hehn wrote in 1874), dass in England, dem Lande der Sonderbarkeiten, ein originelles Kopf es sich einfallen liess, den Ursitz der Indo-germanen nach Europa zu verlegen."

world for sixteen years, they received the qualified support of Professor Whitney, who ventured to call in question the Central Asian theory, denying that the traditions in the Avesta had any bearing on the direction of the earliest Aryan migrations, and maintaining that neither language, history, nor tradition had as yet thrown any light on the cradle of the Aryan race.

This was a useful protest, as scholars had not then realised the fact, now generally admitted, that the differentiation of the Aryan languages must have taken place at a period immeasurably more remote than could possibly be reached by the oldest Aryan traditions.

Whitney's position, however, was merely that of an agnostic; he saw that the arguments produced in favour of an Asiatic origin were valueless, but he did not perceive that arguments not without force might be adduced in favour of another solution.

It was only in 1868, after seventeen years of contemptuous neglect, that Latham found his first real disciple—a disciple who did not confine himself to the merely sceptical standpoint of Whitney, and a disciple, moreover, of such eminence that his opinions could not be treated with contempt as merely an amusing illustration of the customary eccentricity of the English. In 1868 appeared the first edition of Fick's *Vergleichendes Wörterbuch der Indogermanischen Sprachen*, accompanied by a preface by Benfey, containing the germ of an argument which has subsequently been greatly developed by other scholars. In this memorable preface Benfey may be said to have originated the science of Linguistic Palæontology. He suggested that the investigation of the vocabulary common to the whole of the Aryan languages might yield a clue to the region inhabited by the Aryans before the linguistic separation. He contended that certain animals, such as the bear and the wolf, and certain trees, such as the beech and the birch, with which the primitive Aryans must have been acquainted, are all indigenous to the temperate zone, and, above all, to Europe, whereas the characteristic animals and trees of Southern Asia, such as the lion, the tiger, and the palm, were known only to the Indians and the Iranians. He urged that the absence from the primitive Aryan vocabulary of common names for the two great Asiatic beasts of prey, the lion and the tiger, or for the chief Asiatic beast of transport, the camel, is difficult to explain on the theory of the migration of the Aryans from the region eastward of the Caspian. That the Greeks called the lion by its Semitic name, and the Indians by a name which cannot be referred to any Aryan root, argues that the lion was unknown in the common home of Greeks and Indians.

Some of these conclusions have been contested, but Benfey's merit was, not only that he indicated a fresh region for research, but that he pointed out the battle-field on which the whole question has since been fought. The great archæological discoveries which took place between 1860 and 1865, especially those of the flint implements in the gravels of the Somme, the Danish shell mounds, the Swiss Lake Dwellings, and the caves in Aquitaine, together with the publication of such works as Lubbock's *Prehistoric Times* in 1865, and of Lyell's *Antiquity of Man* in 1873, could not fail to modify the ethnological assumptions which had been hitherto unquestioned.

Benfey saw clearly that the conclusions of the philologists, by whom alone the question had hitherto been discussed, would have to be revised in accordance with the teachings of the new sciences of geology, archæology, and anthropology. "Since," he says, "the investigations of the geologists have established the fact that from immemorial times Europe has been the abode of man, the whole of the arguments which have been adduced in favour of the migration of the Aryans from Asia fall to the ground." Written, be it remembered, in 1868, this was indeed a prophetic utterance. The revolution in opinion has been brought about by the anthropologists, the philologists merely following tardily in their train.

Benfey's declaration speedily bore fruit, and Geiger forthwith ranged himself in the same camp,[1] but placing the cradle of the Aryans, not as Benfey had done, in the region to the north of the Black Sea, but more to the north-west, in Central and Western Germany. Geiger's contribution to the argument was not without its value. He bases his conclusions largely on the tree names which belong to the primitive Aryan vocabulary. In addition to the fir, the willow, the ash, the alder, and the hazel, he thinks the names of the birch, the beech, and the oak are specially decisive. Since the Greek φηγός, which denotes the oak, is the linguistic equivalent of the Teutonic *beech* and of the Latin *fagus*, he draws the conclusion that the Greeks migrated from a land of beeches to a land of oaks, transferring the name which denoted the tree with "eadible" fruit from the

[1] Geiger, *Zur Entwickelungsgeschichte der Menschheit*, pp. 113-150. (Stuttgart, 1871.)

one tree to the other. This argument is as valuable as it is ingenious. The characteristic forest tree of Greece is the evergreen oak, the beech not being found south of Dodona, in the centre of Epirus. The oldest Greek legends are connected with Dodona, where the earliest prophetic utterances were obtained from the rustling of the leaves of this sacred tree. Hence we may believe that the Hellenes entered the peninsula from the North-West, through the valleys of Epirus, a route which will explain how the old Aryan word, which originally meant the beech, was transferred to designate the tree which flourished on the hill-slopes of the territory into which they moved.[1]

[1] This explanation of the transference of the name seems more probable than the well-known suggestion of Professor Max Müller, that the word originally denoted the oak, and was transferred to the beech at the time when the oak forests of Jutland were replaced by beeches. This would not account for the word *fagus* meaning "beech" in Latin, for the Umbrians had already reached Italy before the age of bronze, while in the bronze age of Denmark, which was later than the bronze age in Italy, the oak was still the prevailing tree, the beech only appearing sporadically. Moreover, the replacement of the oak by the beech in Jutland occupied a long period. Had the people of Denmark no name for the beech when it first appeared, and what did they call the oak during the many centuries while it was being gradually replaced by the beech? On the other hand, a people migrating, as the Greeks did, from a land of beeches to a land of oaks, would readily transfer the name of the one tree to the other, as in the case of the United States, where the English names of the robin, the maple, and the hemlock have been applied to denote wholly different species. The question as to whether the word originally meant the oak or the beech is not unimportant, as if it denoted the beech it is difficult to avoid the conclusion that the cradle of the Aryans was west of the beech line. The beech, which is a lover of chalk soils, is not only absent from Hellas proper, but is not found east of a line drawn from the south of Norway to the Swedish coast near Gottenburg, and then from Königsberg through Poland and Podolia across the Russian steppes to the Crimea, and terminating in the Caucasus. Now the name

The objection that the Greeks must have had a name for the oak before they entered Greece is met by the fact that the word which means "tree" in Sanskrit and Teutonic is used to denote the oak in Greek and Celtic. Hence it was only the evergreen oak or ilex to which the name of the beech was transferred. Geiger also maintained that the undivided Aryans must have lived in a cold northern region, since the name of the birch is common to all the Aryan languages, and he contended that the cereals originally known were barley and rye, but not wheat. The word "rye" is common to the Teutonic, Lettic, and Slavonic languages, and has been identified by Grimm with the Sanskrit *vrîhi*, rice. But that the primitive meaning was "rye," and not "rice," appears from the agreement of the North European languages with each other, and with the Thracian βρίζα. The zone which comprised barley and rye, but not wheat, must be sought somewhere to the north of the Alps, the limit of wheat having doubtless been extended northward since primitive times.

of the beech, transferred by the Greeks to the oak, is common to the languages of the European Aryans, but is absent from the Indo-Iranian languages. Either they lost the name, because, like the Greeks, they had lost the tree, or else their portion of the common home lay east of the beech line. But if, on the other hand, the cradle of the European Aryans, more especially of the Teutonic and Italic families, had been in Central Asia, where the beech is unknown, it is extremely difficult to explain how the ancestors of the Latins, Celts, and Teutons, migrating, as Pictet contends, at separate times, and by different routes, to lands where the beech abounds, should have called it by the same primitive name, but modified according to the phonetic laws of Latin and German, the German *b* corresponding to the Latin *f*, and the German *k* to the Latin *g*. The Slavonic name for the beech is a loan word from the German, a fact which indicates that the primitive seat of the Slaves was east of the beech line, just as that of the Latins, Greeks, and Germans must have been to the west of it.

Geiger also argued that the undivided Aryans were acquainted with woad and its use, that they were familiar with snow and ice, and had common words for winter and spring, but none for summer and autumn—facts which all point to a northern habitat. He maintains that no proof has ever been adduced of any Aryan migration from the East to the West, and that on all these grounds the cradle of the Aryans is more probably to be sought in Europe than in Asia. He concludes by saying, "Of the two opposed theories (a European or an Asiatic origin) one only is supported by any reasons; for the migration from the East not a single argument has been adduced. It is improbable in itself, and well-nigh impossible, if we are to suppose it took place by successive waves." To suppose that a small Aryan tribe first migrated to Europe, and that the various Aryan languages were subsequently developed, is practically equivalent to a European origin.

To Geiger's argument it was replied by Piètrement that there are regions in Asia whose Fauna and Flora conform to the linguistic conditions. Such a region, he thought, might be found in the neighbourhood of Lake Balkash and the Alatau. But it was rejoined that this region has always, so far as we know, been the home of Mongolic races, and that the hypothesis of an early Aryan population was purely gratuitous and supported by no evidence, no vestiges of any Aryan population having been discovered in this region, which is too barren and inhospitable to have been the cradle of such a numerous race.

In the same year that Geiger's book was published a noteworthy contribution to the discussion was made by Cuno,[1] who contended that the undivided Aryans, instead of being a "small clan," must have been a numerous nomad pastoral people inhabiting an extensive territory. A long period—several thousand years—he considered, must have been occupied in the evolution of the elaborate grammatical system of the primitive speech, while the dialectic varieties out of which the Aryan languages were ultimately evolved could not have arisen except through geographical severance. The necessary geographical conditions were, he thought, a vast plain, undivided by lofty mountain barriers, by desert tracts, or impassable forests, together with a temperate climate, tolerably uniform in character, where a numerous people could have expanded, and then, in different portions of the territory, could have evolved those dialectic differences which afterwards developed in the several Aryan languages.

There is only one region, he contends, on the whole surface of the globe which presents the necessary conditions of uniformity of climate and geographical extension. This is the great plain of Northern Europe, stretching from the Ural Mountains over Northern Germany and the north of France as far as the Atlantic. In this region, he thinks, and no other, the conditions of life are not too easy, or the struggle for existence too hard, to make possible the development of a great energetic race such as the Aryans. At the beginning of the historic period we find this region occupied by the Celtic, Teutonic, Lithuanic, and Slavonic races, whom he regards as autochthonous. At some earlier time he considers that the

---

[1] Cuno, *Forschungen im Gebiete der alten Völkerkunde.* (Berlin, 1871.)

Italic and Hellenic races had extended themselves to the South across the mountain chain of Central Europe, and the Indo-Iranians had wandered with their herds further to the East, subduing and incorporating non-Aryan tribes.

To this it might be replied that the steppes of Central Asia, extending eastward of the Caspian for more than a thousand miles beyond Lake Balkash, also offer the necessary conditions, and that here the great Turko-Tartaric race has grown up, presenting an actual picture of what the Aryan race must have been in the early nomad stage of its existence. But it must be conceded to Cuno that the conditions of climate, of soil, of greater geographical extension, and of proximity to the regions now occupied by the Aryans, are arguments for selecting the European rather than the Asiatic plain as the probable cradle of the Aryan race.

It will hereafter be shown that Craniology, Archæology, and Linguistic Palæontology, sciences with which Cuno had a very limited acquaintance, have supplied remarkable confirmations of his hypothesis.

Cuno was not only the first to propound what must be regarded as the most probable solution of the problem, but he was also the first to insist on what is now looked on as an axiom in ethnology—that race is not co-extensive with language. The existing extension of Aryan speech is, he contends, largely the result of conquest and of the incorporation of unwarlike tribes by the more energetic northern races. By reason of their language, he says, we now class the Spaniards among the Latin races, and yet how small is the trace of Roman blood in Spain. It is the same in France,

Belgium, and Roumania. In these regions neo-Latin languages prevail, but there is very little Latin blood, in some cases practically none. How much common blood, he asks, is there in the veins of Teutons and Hindus, or of Celts and Persians, or of Russians and Spaniards, and yet all these nations speak closely-related languages, which we call Aryan.

The southern and eastern extensions of Aryan speech may therefore be due to Aryan conquest, or to the gradual expansion of Aryan civilisation over contiguous tribes, and there is therefore no difficulty in regarding the great plain of Northern Europe as the region in which the Aryan race originated.

Cuno then goes on to note that a large portion of North-Eastern Europe is now, or has been in historical times, occupied by Finns. Between Finnic and Aryan speech the relations are intimate and fundamental. They show themselves not so much in vocabulary as in the pronouns, the numerals, the pronominal suffixes of the verb, and the inner morphological structure of language. The extreme members of the Ural-Altaic family, such as the Finns and the Mongols, are separated by differences almost as wide as those which divide Finnic from Aryan speech.

The conclusion he draws is not, however, the obvious conclusion that the Finnic tongues may represent a form of speech out of which the Aryan languages might have been evolved, but that the Finns and Aryans must have been originally in contact, so that if we bring the Aryans from Central Asia we must also find room for the Finns in the same region.

What Cuno failed to notice, though it lay ready to his hand, is the probability that the dialectic differences in Aryan speech may be largely due, not, as he thought, merely to geographical separation, but to the imperfect acquirement of a strange language by those non-Aryan tribes which were Aryanised by conquest. This pregnant suggestion is due, as we shall presently see, to another writer.

Cuno's most important contribution to the controversy was his demolition of the assumption that Aryan blood must be co-extensive with Aryan speech. Another gratuitous assumption, the whole theory of the successive migrations of Aryan tribes from the East, was swept away in the following year by Johannes Schmidt in a pamphlet of sixty-eight pages.[1] A pebble from the sling of a shepherd boy smote down the Philistine giant, and in like manner this little essay, by a young and almost unknown writer, made an end of the huge structure which had been painfully reared by some of the giants of philology. If, as had been hitherto supposed, the ancestors of the Aryan nations—Celts, Teutons, Lithuanians, Slaves, Latins, and Greeks—had, one after the other, left the parent hive, and had marched in successive or associated swarms from Central Asia to find new homes in Europe, it would manifestly be possible to construct a pedigree in the form of a genealogical tree, representing graphically the relationships and affiliations of the Aryan languages, and their connection, more or less remote, with the parent speech. For twenty years philologists had occupied themselves in the construction of such trees, but no two of their schemes agreed. Bopp, Pott, Grimm, Lottner, Schleicher, Pictet, Zeuss,

[1] Schmidt, *Die Verwantschaftsverhältnisse der Indogermanischen Sprachen.* (Weimar, 1872.)

Fick, Förstemann, Grassmann, Sonne, Curtius, Max Müller, Pauli, Spiegel, Justi, Ebel, were hopelessly at variance as to the ramifications of the supposed Aryan tree, a matter which, if an Aryan family had really existed, ought to have been susceptible of exact determination. There was a fundamental difference of opinion as to whether Slavonic was to be classed with the European or the Asiatic languages, whether it was a sister tongue of German or of Zend, and there was a similar dispute as to the relationship of Greek, some scholars considering it to be most closely allied to Latin; and others maintaining that the relationship was with Sanskrit, while opinions were divided as to whether the separation of the Celts was very early or very late, and whether their nearest affinities were with Latin or Teutonic. There was also a fundamental difference of opinion as to whether the earliest cleavage was between the Northern and the Southern languages, or between the Eastern and the Western, and also, as has been said, as to whether Greek and Slavonic must be classed among the Eastern or the Western tongues.

This *stammbaum* controversy, as it was called, which seemed to be interminable, received a solution as complete as it was unexpected. Schmidt's pamphlet placed the whole matter on a new footing. The disputants were shown that none of their apparently irreconcilable opinions as to the affinities of the Aryan languages were necessarily wrong, but that the method of representing those affinities by a genealogical tree must be given up. Schmidt asserted that the relationship could not be represented by the branches of a tree, but were analogous to the waves caused by disturbances in a pond. He supposes that at some early period the geographical continuity of the primitive Aryan speech was unbroken. At certain points in this area local centres of disturbance arose, and new linguistic formations, or new phonetic variations, began to manifest themselves, and then spread, like waves, in every direction from the point where they originated, the disturbances growing feebler the further they extended, in the same way that concentric wave-circles arise when stones are dropped into still water at parts more or less remote. These waves would spread in concentric circles round the centres of disturbance, till at length they interfere. In this way, he thought, the difficulties could be explained, and the opposite contentions at last be reconciled.

The two chief points which had been disputed between the partisans of rival "trees" were, as we have seen, whether Slavonic was a branch from the Iranian or the Teutonic stem, and whether Greek had bifurcated from Latin or from Sanskrit. Schmidt showed that Greek was in some respects as closely united with Sanskrit as it was in others with Latin, while Slavonic shared certain peculiarities only with Teutonic, and others only with Iranian. Schmidt also showed that the more geographically remote were any two of the Aryan languages, the fewer were the peculiarities they possessed in common. Thus, while there are fifty-nine words and roots peculiar to Slavo-Lithuanian and Teutonic, and sixty-one to Slavo-Lithuanian and Indo-Iranian, only thirteen are peculiar to Indo-Iranian and Teutonic. Again, while one hundred and thirty-two words and roots are peculiar to Latin and Greek, and ninty-nine to Greek and Indo-Iranian, only twenty are peculiar to

Indo-Iranian and Latin. Hence Slavonic forms the transition between Teutonic and Iranian, and Greek the transition between Latin and Sanskrit. Schmidt successfully contended that the notion of a genealogical tree must be entirely given up. There must at one time, he thought, have been an inclined plane of language, sloping continuously over the whole domain of Aryan speech from East to West—from Sanskrit to Celtic. At various points dialectic differences arose, and then, owing to political, social, or religious causes, certain local dialects obtained predominance and developed into languages, exterminating the weaker intermediate dialects. In like manner Attic exterminated the other Greek dialects, and the dialect of Rome absorbed Oscan, Umbrian, and the other Italic dialects. Thus, he thought, the inclined plane of Aryan speech was broken up into steps, and converted into a staircase.

Schmidt's theory of the origin of the Aryan languages resembled Darwin's theory of the origin of species. Languages were due to some unknown tendency to variation, coupled with the extermination of intermediate varieties, and the survival of the prepotent. This principle has recently been ably developed by Professor Paul in his *Principien der Sprachgeschichte.*

Schmidt's argument was plainly fatal to the old theory of successive separations and migrations from the East. It was manifest that the linguistic differences must have arisen *in situ*, at a time when the Aryan nations occupied much the same relative geographical positions as they do now.

Leskien improved on Schmidt's theory by introducing the element of relative time. It was not necessary, he maintained, to suppose that all the disturbances were simultaneous. One disturbance, for instance, might have affected the Teutonic region and spread to the contiguous Slaves, and then, after the Slaves and Teutons had become separated, another disturbance might have affected the Slaves and spread to the Iranians. Penka afterwards suggested a *vera causa* for these disturbances, which Schmidt had considered to be arbitrary or accidental.

Combining Cuno's theory with Schmidt's, he argued that as the primitive Aryans must have incorporated many non-Aryan races, the dialectic differences may be due to these incorporations. For instance, the peculiarities shared by Lithuanians and Slaves may be due to the incorporation of Finnic tribes, and those common to Slaves and Iranians to the incorporation of Ugrians. That there may be some truth in this explanation is shown by the fortunes of the neo-Latin languages. It is highly probable, for instance, that some of the differences which distinguish French and Spanish may be due to the fact that in one case Latin was a foreign language acquired by Celts, and in the other by Iberians.

The loss of inflections in French and Persian was largely due to the difficulty felt by Frankish and Arab conquerors in acquiring a foreign tongue. English has been similarly affected—first by the coalescence of Saxon and Anglian speech, and then by the influence of the Danish and Norman conquests and the preaching of the Franciscan monks. In the process it has lost its genders and four of its five cases, while of the six ways of forming the plural all were lost but one. In like manner, when we find that Latin lost three of the old tenses, and formed a new future, a new perfect, a new imperfect, and a new passive, we have to take into account the possibility of the incorporation by Aryan invaders of a non-Aryan population.

But the influence of these theories was more far-reaching than their advocates had supposed. The ultimate result has been to bring about a conviction not only that there is no such thing as any pure Aryan race, but that the existence of a primitive Aryan language is doubtful.

In 1880 Delbrück,[1] after discussing the Stammbaum theory, and the theories of Schmidt and Leskien, came to the conclusion that there had never been, as had been universally assumed, any uniform primitive Aryan speech. The development of the inflections must have occupied, he thinks, many thousand years, and the Aryans, before the grammar was fully developed, must have become a very numerous people, occupying an extended territory, within which vast region diversities of speech must have originated. These diversities were the germs of some of the differences which now separate the families of Aryan speech. In short, the primitive Aryan speech had begun to break up into dialects before it was fully formed.

The publication in 1871 of the books of Geiger and Cuno marked the beginning of a new era in the controversy. Up to this time the Asiatic origin of the Aryans had been the orthodox view which it was a scientific heresy to doubt. The Asiatic or the European origin now became an open question, and the ensuing decade was a period of unceasing strife between the partisans of the rival theories. Year by

[1] Delbrück, *Einleitung in das Sprachstudium*, pp. 131-137.

year the adherents of the old hypothesis became fewer and less confident; while the European theory found fresh advocates among the younger generation of scholars.

Höfer repeated the old argument that since the most archaic forms of Aryan speech are preserved in the Rig Veda and the Avesta, the cradle of the Aryans must have been in the region where Sanskrit and Zend were spoken—an argument already answered by Whitney with the remark that among existing languages Icelandic and Lithuanian preserve the primitive forms of Aryan speech more faithfully than the Armenian or the Kurd.

Piètrement revived once more the argument from the geographical traditions of the Avesta, which may be valid for the later migration of the Iranians, but not for those of any other race, or even for the earlier migrations of the Iranians.

Kiepert and Hehn followed with the contention that Asia is the true *officina gentium*, and that the analogy of other migrations from East to West makes it difficult to believe that the earliest and greatest of all took place in the opposite direction. Is it credible, says Hehn, that the oldest forms of Aryan speech are to be sought in the woods and swamps of Ger many rather than in the literary monuments of India and Bactria?

To this it might be replied—if indeed mere rhetoric requires a reply—that if Ghengiz Khan marched from Bactria to Europe, Alexander marched from Europe to Bactria; and that if Tamerlane led his army westward to Galatia, the Galatians themselves had marched eastwards from Gaul to Galatia; while, if Germans and Slaves at one time extended their border to the West, they have now for several centuries been extending it to the East.

The logical weakness of the Asiatic hypothesis cannot be better shown than by the fact that a zealous and able advocate like Hehn was driven to resort to such feeble analogies in lieu of solid argument.

Perhaps the strongest argument that has been adduced in favour of the Asiatic origin of the Aryans is that which has been drawn by Hommel, Delitzsch, and Kremer, from certain supposed primitive relations between Aryan and Semitic speech. That the Semites originated in Asia may be admitted; and if any fundamental connection could be shown between the Aryan and Semitic languages there would be reason to suppose that the cradles of the two races must be sought in contiguous regions. Hommel adduces six culture words which, he thinks, establish such a primitive connection. But six words are not enough to base a theory on; the phonetic resemblances may be accidental, or the words may be very early loan words due to Phœnician commerce. This is probably the case with the names of silver, gold, and wine, which, as will hereafter be shown, there is reason for believing, on archæological grounds, to have been unknown to the early Aryans.

Delitzsch goes deeper. He claims to have identified one hundred Semitic roots with Aryan roots. But even if these identifications be accepted, it would not suffice, as it would be also necessary to show an agreement of grammatical formative elements; and it is universally admitted that in grammatical structure the Semitic and Aryan languages differ fundamentally. The agreement of certain primitive verbal roots, if they do agree, may, possibly, be otherwise explained. The speakers of Aryan languages are not all of Aryan race. It will hereafter be shown that the Mediterranean race of Southern Europe was probably Berber or Hamitic. A remote connection between the Semitic and Hamitic families is generally admitted, and there are numerous verbal roots which seem to be common to the Hamitic and Semitic languages. If the Southern Aryans are only Aryanised Hamites, it would account for fundamental differences in Semitic and Aryan grammar co-existing with certain coincidences of Semitic and Aryan roots.

In spite of these objectors, possibly because their objections were so feeble, the new doctrine continued to gain adherents. In 1873 Friedrich Müller admitted the force of the arguments for a European origin which had been adduced by Benfey and Geiger from the names of animals and plants common to the Aryan languages. About the same time Spiegel also combated the arguments drawn from the traditions in the Avesta, and urged that it was impossible to believe, with Monier Williams, that a region so lofty, so barren, and so inhospitable as the Pamir could have produced such vast swarms of men as the theory of an Aryan migration would demand, or that they could have vanished without leaving a trace behind; and he declares his adhesion to the view that the cradle of the Aryans must be sought in Europe between the 45th and 60th parallels of latitude.

In this region, he maintains, is a land well suited for the development of the primitive Aryan race. Here we may find room for their expansion, both to the East and to the West, an expansion in which migration, properly so-called, played a very insignificant part.

The Aryan race, he continues, must constantly have extended itself, including within its domain other races, owing to whose absorption there arose dialectic varieties of speech, which, in course of time, aided by geographical severance and the absence of a literature, gradually developed into separate languages. No more rational theory, it may be affirmed, than this of Spiegel has yet been advanced to account for the origin of the Aryan languages.

Pösche, in a monograph devoted to the controversy,[1] was the first to bring forward the anthropological argument, which has since been developed by Penka. He maintained that anthropology and archæology must supplement and correct the conclusions of philology. He urged, as Broca had urged before, that while there may be Aryan languages, there is no such thing as an Aryan race, and that language is only one, and that the least important factor in the inquiry, and that while Aryan languages are spoken by races wholly unrelated, there is only one race, the tall, blue-eyed, fair-skinned German race, with abundant beard and dolichocephalic skull, which can claim to be genuine Aryans by blood as well as by language.

Pösche identified this race with that whose skeletons are found in the Alemannic "row-graves" of Southern Germany, and he contended that it has existed in Europe since the neolithic period. This argument was discredited by his theory, which has not found favour with anthropologists, that the Aryan race originated in the great Rokitno swamp, between the Pripet, the Beresina, and the Dnieper. Here depigmentation or albinism is very prevalent, and here

[1] Pösche, *Die Arier. Ein Beitrag zur historischen Anthropologie.* (Jena, 1878.)

he considers the fair, white race originated. In this swamp, he thinks, lived the pile-dwellers who afterwards extended themselves to the Swiss lakes and the valley of the Po. The archaic character of the neighbouring Lithuanian language induced him to believe that the Lithuanians were a surviving relic of this oldest Aryan race.

The obvious objections to this theory are that the Rokitno swamp is not sufficiently extensive for the cradle of such a numerous people, and that the Aryans, an athletic and energetic race, exceeded in vital force by no other people, could hardly have originated in an unhealthy region, where the conditions of existence are depressing, while the sickly, tow-haired albinism which prevails in the Rokitno swamp is quite different from the tawny hair and the ruddy, healthy, lily and carnation tint of his typical Aryans. Moreover, there is good reason for believing that the primitive Aryans were nomad herdsmen, an occupation unsuited to the conditions of the Rokitno swamp.

Two years later the European hypothesis received the adherence of Lindenschmit, who considers that "we must give up the idea of an Aryan migration from the East as an old delusion derived from historical traditions."[1] He comes to the conclusion that there is no specially oriental character in the common vocabulary of the primitive Aryans, and he agrees with Benfey in thinking that the absence of primitive Aryan designations for the elephant and the camel, the lion and the tiger, is a strong argument against an Asiatic origin. He also combated, with well-chosen instances, Hehn's argument, that the direction of

[1] Lindenschmit, *Handbuch der deutschen Alterthumskunde*, 1880, p. 5.

conquest and migration has always followed the movement of the sun from east to west.

He argues that the vital energy and the power of expansion of the European Aryans is unique. They are long-lived, and possess great muscular force, and hence the cradle of such a tall, powerful, energetic race is not likely to have been in Asia, which has not, so far as we know, developed great physical capacity. He thinks the case of the Goths, the Scandinavians, the Normans, the Scotch, the English, the Germans, and the Dutch, who have overrun the South, who have colonised America, and ruled vast territories in Asia, teaches us that it is in Northern Europe only that we find, in its highest development, the characteristics of the energetic Aryan race. Where these characteristics are now chiefly developed is probably the region where they originated.

Fligier followed in 1881 with a repetition of Cuno's argument as to the primitive connection of the Finnic and Aryan languages, from which he drew the conclusion that the true *vagina gentium* is to be sought in Eastern Europe.

A new epoch in the discussion opened in 1883 with the publication of two remarkable books, which have brought the whole question again into prominence, and have exerted a decisive influence on public opinion. The first of these was a slashing but somewhat one-sided work by Karl Penka,[1] somewhat feeble from the philological side, but in which the anthropological arguments advanced by Pösche were re-stated with considerable force. The second, by far the most important book which has yet been written on the subject, was the exhaustive treatise by Dr.

---

[1] Penka, *Origines Ariacæ*. (Wien, 1883.)

Schrader,[1] which contains a cautious and judicial statement of the whole case.

As many of the arguments and facts adduced by these writers will be reproduced in the following chapters, it will only be necessary, in this historical summary, briefly to state the conclusions at which they have arrived.

In his *Origines Ariacæ*, and in a subsequent work[2] in which he replied to his critics, and brought forward fresh facts and arguments in support of his views, Penka maintained that Aryan blood is far from being coextensive with Aryan speech. He proved that those who employ Aryan languages belong to several distinct anthropological types. The primitive Aryans must, however, have been of only one race. Either the physical types must have been developed subsequently to the linguistic separation, or Aryan speech must have been acquired by races not of Aryan blood. The former supposition is most improbable, knowing, as we do, the persistency of type displayed during thousands of years by the Egyptians, the Negros, and the Jews. The latter supposition is inherently probable, as there are numerous instances of change of language being effected without any change of race. Language, in short, is mutable, race persistent. The question therefore arises, which of the five or six types found among the speakers of Aryan languages represents most faithfully the type of the primitive Aryans? Penka contends that the purest blood is

---

[1] Schrader, *Sprachvergleichung und Urgeschichte*. (Jena, 1883.) From the proof-sheets of the forthcoming revised edition of this book an English translation by Mr. F. O. Jevons is announced for early publication.

[2] Penka, *Die Herkunft der Arier.* (Wien, 1886.)

found in Scandinavia among the fair-haired, blue-eyed, dolichocephalic Swedes. The pure Aryans, he maintains, are represented only by the North Germans and Scandinavians, a most prolific race, of great stature, muscular strength, energy, and courage, whose splendid natural endowments enabled it to conquer the feebler races to the East, the South, and the West, and to impose its language on the subject peoples. That the nations of Central and Southern Europe exhibit hardly any traces of the fair northern blood is due, he believes, to the tendency of mixed races to revert to one of the original types. He contends that the northern race, which is prolific in cold climates, becomes sterile in southern latitudes, and ultimately dies out; while the fact that among the Southern Aryans the nobles are fairer and taller than the peasants is an indication of conquest by northerners.

To take an instance from historical times, we see how completely in Italy and Spain the blood of the fair-haired Gothic conquerors from the Baltic has died out, while in Sweden, Northern Germany, and the north of England, the fair type survives because the climatic conditions permit of its preservation. The influence of climate has exterminated the Aryan race in India, Persia, Greece, Italy, Spain, France, and Southern Germany, the Aryan speech alone being left as the permanent evidence of early Aryan conquest.

Penka has undoubtedly weakened his argument by the unnecessary contention that Scandinavia was the cradle of the whole Aryan race. It is difficult to believe that a sufficiently extensive area for the growth of such a numerous people can be found in the forest-clad valleys of Norway and Sweden, which moreover are unadapted for the habitation of a nomad pastoral people, such as the primitive Aryans must have been. Isolated valleys, moreover, tend to the rapid growth of dialects, unity of language being the result of the wanderings of nomad tribes over an extensive plain. In mountain regions like Switzerland and the Caucasus, the people of contiguous valleys speak different languages, while the same language extends over vast regions in the steppes of Central Asia. Penka would have done better to have adopted Cuno's argument, and to have placed the cradle of the Aryans in the great plain of Northern Europe, from which a later emigration to Scandinavia might easily have taken place. This would also have avoided the objection that the primitive Aryans could hardly have possessed the means of migrating across the Baltic in the vast swarms which the hypothesis demands. Sweden is almost as unsuited for the cradle of the Aryans as the Rokitno swamp suggested by Pösche.

We shall, however, hereafter see that the tall, fair Scandinavians are not the only tall, fair people which may represent the ancestral Aryan stock, and that many of the difficulties—geographical, linguistic, and anthropological—which beset Penka's theory disappear at once if we assume that the Celtic race of Central Europe, rather than the Teutonic race of Scandinavia, are the lineal descendants of the primitive Aryans.

Penka also, as we have already seen, accounts for the differentiation of the Aryan languages by a development of Spiegel's theory, which he works out with much ingenuity, that each conquered race, on acquiring the language of its conquerors, would leave upon the acquired speech the impress of the language that was lost.

Of higher quality in every respect is the book of Dr. Schrader, which must long remain the standard work on the subject, as Dr. Schrader reviews, in a judicial spirit, the arguments of preceding writers, and collects in a convenient form the philological and archæological materials on which the solution of the question must be based. The chief defect of Dr. Schrader's work is that, being chiefly a philologist, he leaves out of account those anthropological considerations which are no less important than the archæological and linguistic arguments.

The materials accumulated by Dr. Schrader will however be so freely drawn upon in the ensuing pages that it will not now be necessary to do more than briefly to state the final conclusions at which he has arrived, and which, it may be added, are substantially those of the present writer.

In discussing the question of the origin of the Aryans, Dr. Schrader thinks there are two fixed points which may be regarded as settled. At the earliest period to which the evidence of history, tradition, or linguistic archæology extends, we find the European Aryans in Northern Europe, and the Asiatic Aryans on the Jaxartes.

As for the European Aryans, he considers that not a particle of evidence has been adduced in favour of any migration from the East. At the earliest time to which the evidence reaches they seem rather to have been extending themselves towards the South and the South-East, and it would appear that the region occupied by them before the linguistic separation must be sought north of the Alps. The precise region can, he thinks, be approximately indicated. The beech does not now grow east of a line drawn from Königsberg to the Crimea, and its northern limit must formerly have been still more restricted. Hence the cradle of the Latin, Hellenic, and Teutonic races, which had the same name for this tree,[1] must have been to the west of the ancient beech-line. But since the Slavo-Lithuanian name is a Teutonic loan-word (old Slavonic *buky*, Russian *buk*, Lithuanian *bukas*), we must place the cradle of the Lithuanians and the Slaves to the east of this line. But since there are philological reasons for believing in the unbroken geographical continuity of the European Aryans previous to the linguistic separation, they must be placed in Northern Europe astride of the beech-line; the Slavo-Lithuanians in European Russia; and the Celts, Latins, Hellenes, and Teutons farther to the West.

As for the Indo-Iranians, there can be no doubt, Dr. Schrader thinks, that the Sanskrit-speaking race entered India from the North-West. In the Vedic period they lived on the banks of the Indus, and had only an indirect knowledge of the Ganges. But the Indians and Iranians must previously have formed a united people somewhere to the north of the Himalaya. Both branches retained traditions of the Jaxartes, the greatest river of this region, and on the banks of this stream we must place their earlier seat.

Hence, in our investigations as to the origin of the undivided Aryans, we have these two fixed points—the earliest known seat of the European Aryans was in Northern Europe, and that of the Asiatic Aryans on the Jaxartes.

[1] See p. 27, *supra*.

The only question which remains is whether the European Aryans came from Asia, or the Asiatic Aryans from Europe?

For the solution of this question Dr. Schrader submits six points for consideration—

(1) The old assumption, that because the Indo-Iranian speech is more archaic than the European, therefore the cradle of the Aryans was towards the East, must be given up, because our knowledge of Zend and Sanskrit dates from an earlier period than our knowledge of the European languages. He thinks, moreover, that the greater rudeness of the European languages is itself the sign of a more primitive condition than the literary culture exhibited by Zend and Sanskrit.

(2) The results yielded by Linguistic Palæontology are not, he thinks, decisive. We can only conclude that the cradle of the undivided Aryans was in the North, because the words for snow and ice are common to all Aryan languages, and because only two, or at most three, seasons of the year were originally distinguished. To this it may be added that the primitive type of the Aryan race was probably that of one of the energetic Northern races.

(3) We have a right to conclude that the primitive Aryan race, at the time of its geographical continuity, extended over a very large region. A semi-nomadic pastoral people, such as the primitive Aryans doubtless were, must have required a vast space to nurture the cattle necessary for their support. A Tartar family in Central Asia requires three hundred head of cattle, and occupies rather more than two thousand acres. Hence a tribe consisting of 10,000 people would occupy from 4000 to 6000 square miles. The whole of

France would support about 50,000 people as pastoral nomads, and the whole pastoral zone of Northern Europe not more than a million. Before the Aryans had emerged out of the hunting into the pastoral stage, the population must have been still more sparse.

That practically the same language, with dialectic differences, might prevail over a vast region occupied by nomad herdsmen, is proved by the case of the Turko-Tartar race, which, at the time of its greatest extension, occupied a region not far inferior in extent to the hypothetical extension of the primitive Aryans, from the Jaxartes to the Atlantic—about 3000 linear miles. In the sixteenth century the Turkic races extended from the mouth of the Lena as far as the Adriatic, and all these tribes were mutually intelligible, speaking merely dialects of the same language. At the present time a Turcoman from Anatolia is able to understand a Yakut from the shores of the Arctic Ocean.

(4) No sharp line of division can be drawn between the European and the Asiatic branches of the Aryan family. Certain races and languages of Europe are more closely connected with those of Asia than the rest. More especially to be noted are the close relations between the Indo-Iranians and the Greeks, as evidenced by the names of weapons, and of words referring to agriculture and religion.

(5) The grade of civilisation attained by the undivided Aryans, as exhibited by the conclusions of linguistic palæontology, agrees very closely with that disclosed in the oldest Swiss pile dwellings of the stone age. This would indicate the existence of Aryans in Europe at an early epoch, little if at all later than the linguistic separation.

(6) The movements of the Aryan races, according to the earliest historical notices and traditions, were in a southward and to some extent in an eastward direction. If we may credit early tradition, a portion of Western Asia must have received from Europe its Aryan population of Phrygians and Armenians. This tradition is supported by the near relationship of Armenian to the European languages. On the other hand, no indisputable evidence exists of any migration of Aryans from the East to the West.

Such are the materials, according to Dr. Schrader's investigations, on which the solution of the problem depends. The question as to whether the earliest home of the Aryan race was in Europe or in Asia does not, he thinks, admit of any positive answer. But he concludes by withdrawing the opinion which he had formerly expressed that the Aryans had originated in Asia, and says that he is now unable to conceal his conviction that the European hypothesis—that is, the view that the origin of the Aryan race must be sought in the West rather than in the East—appears to be far more (*weitaus*) in accordance with the facts.

The simultaneous publication in 1883 of Penka's and Schrader's books, one treating the question mainly from the side of anthropology, the other from that of philology, drew renewed attention to the Aryan controversy.

The first result was the abandonment of the Asiatic hypothesis by several scholars, who, like Dr. Schrader himself, had supported it in former years. The first to announce his conversion to the new view was Professor Sayce,[1] a man honourably

[1] In *The Academy*, December 8th, 1883; and in his *Introduction to the Science of Language*, third edition, 1885.

distinguished by the fact that he has never hesitated to confess that he has seen reason, on the production of fresh evidence, to change opinions which he had formerly advocated. The European hypothesis has also obtained the published adhesion of Professor Rhys, who has ably expounded the new doctrine in the *Princeton Review*. On the Continent it has been espoused by Tomaschek, who declares for Eastern Europe; by Von Löher, who prefers Germany; by Wilsce, who in the main follows Penka; and by Friedrich Müller, who agrees with Cuno's selection of Central Europe. Ujfalvy, Hommel, Fessl, Professor Max Müller, and two American writers, Messrs. Hole and Morris, still advocate various forms of the Asiatic hypothesis.

Professor Max Müller, the only surviving scholar of the old school, has recently given a final pronouncement on the subject. He thus writes in 1887:[1] "If an answer must be given as to the place where our Aryan ancestors dwelt before their separation I should still say, as I said forty years ago, 'Somewhere in Asia,' and no more." At all events, "somewhere in Asia" is more vague, and therefore more probable, than Bactria, which was his earlier and more definite selection. But though he says that he retains his old opinion, he does not appear to have made any new additions to his old argument, which was merely Grimm's theory of the "irresistible impulse," and Pott's assumption that migration has always followed the sun's course, westward from the East.

[1] *Good Words*, August 1887, reprinted in "Biographies of Words."

CHAPTER II.

THE PREHISTORIC RACES OF EUROPE.

§ 1. *The Neolithic Age.*

THE startling revelations as to the antiquity of man in Europe which succeeded each other with such rapidity in 1860 and the following years were, as we have seen, a chief cause of the revulsion of opinion as to the origin of the Aryans. The conclusions of the philologists, which had hitherto been accepted without question, had to be revised in the light of the discoveries of geology, archæology, and anthropology. The credit of recognising the changed conditions of the problem is due to Theodor Benfey, himself a philologist. As early as 1868 Benfey ventured to declare that "since it has been established that from immemorial times Europe has been the abode of man, the whole of the arguments which have been adduced in favour of the migration of the Aryans from Asia fall to the ground."[1]

These investigations as to the primitive inhabitants of Europe have so materially affected the whole question that it will be needful to devote a chapter to a summary of the results which have been attained.

It is no longer possible to confine the existence of

[1] See p. 26, *supra*.

man upon the earth to a period of six thousand years. It has been demonstrated that man was a contemporary of the mammoth and the woolly rhinoceros, and followed the retreating ice sheet which had covered Northern Europe during the last glacial epoch.

From astronomical data Dr. Croll has calculated that in the northern hemisphere the last glacial epoch began some 240,000 years ago, that it lasted with alternations of a milder and even tropical temperature for nearly 160,000 years, and finally terminated about 80,000 years ago. With these calculations Professor Geikie essentially agrees:[1] He believes that palæolithic man must have occupied parts of Western Europe shortly after the disappearance of the great ice sheet, and that there are reasons for supposing that he was interglacial,[2] like the mammoth and the reindeer, whose remains exist below the till, which was the product of the last extension of the glaciers.[3]

With this remote period we are not concerned. The flint flakes which constitute the earliest evidences of the existence of man in Europe afford no criteria of language or even of race. Nor can we affirm that the men by whom they were produced were endowed with articulate speech. The men of the quaternary period, the contemporaries of the mammoth, may or may not have been the ancestors of existing races. But coming down to the later or neolithic period, when the geological and climatal conditions were essentially the same as they are now, we find that

---
[1] Geikie, *The Great Ice Age*, p. 114.
[2] *Ibid.*, pp. 552-565.
[3] *Ibid.*, p. 160.

three, if not four, of the existing European types occupied approximately their present seats.

Archæologists have established the chronological sequence of the ages of stone, bronze, and iron. These are not necessarily synchronous in different countries. Greece had advanced to the iron age while Italy was still in the bronze period, and the rest of Europe in the age of stone. Bronze was used in the Mediterranean lands long before it reached the shores of the Baltic; and the Guanches were still in the stone age when, in the fifteenth century, the Canary Islands were re-discovered by the Spaniards.

The iron and bronze ages may be excluded from the present inquiry. We need only concern ourselves with the period of polished stone implements, since it has been proved that the ethnology of Europe is now essentially the same as it was before bronze had superseded stone. Bronze weapons were not introduced, as was formerly supposed, by any new conquering race. Their use gradually spread by the peaceful processes of commerce, and largely through the enterprise of Phœnician traders. The pile dwellings of Central Europe, beginning in the stone age, extend over the whole of the bronze age to the age of iron, and prove that in these regions there were no displacements of population by conquest or immigration, but that the same race, inhabiting the same sites, gradually abandoned stone weapons for weapons of bronze, and bronze swords for swords of iron. The same conclusion is established elsewhere by the fact that the oldest types of copper or bronze implements are modelled on the patterns of the earlier implements of stone or bone.

The age of stone has been divided into two epochs

THE PREHISTORIC RACES OF EUROPE. 57

—the palæolithic period, or age of chipped flints; and the neolithic period, when the implements were ground or polished. In the palæolithic period man was the contemporary of the cave bear, the mammoth, the woolly rhinoceros, and other extinct carnivora and pachyderms. The climate was severe; the distribution of land and water was different from that which now prevails; pottery, even of the rudest type, was unknown; the people were nomad hunters, living in caves or rock shelters: whereas in the neolithic period the distribution of land and water was essentially the same as it is now; caves were used for burial rather than for habitation; animals had been domesticated; pottery was fabricated; and the European fauna differed little from that which is found at the commencement of the historic period.

Some anthropologists have asserted that Europe was inhabited by the ancestors of existing races in the palæolithic period. With their arguments we need not concern ourselves, since philologists will probably admit that within the limits of the neolithic age it would be possible to find sufficient time for the evolution and differentiation of the Aryan languages. If it can be shown that the races who inhabited Europe at the beginning of the neolithic period were the ancestors of the races who now inhabit the same regions, we may leave undetermined the question whether they originated in Europe, or whether they emigrated from Asia or from Africa.

It is possible that the palæolithic period may have begun, as M. de Mortillet believes, in the quaternary period of the geologists, some 240,000 years ago; but the neolithic period is comparatively recent. Even M. de Mortillet does not claim for its commencement an antiquity of more than from 10,000 to 20,000 years.

The calculations on which these estimates are based can only be regarded as affording rough approximations to the truth, and they must be taken only for what they are worth.

Some of the best of these natural chronometers are found in Switzerland. But even the earliest Swiss lake dwellings exhibit a state of civilisation considerably more advanced than the civilisation which linguistic palæontology demands for the primitive Aryans. Consequently we obtain from them only a minimum and not a maximum limit of time for Aryan settlement.

At Pont de la Thièle, between the Lakes of Bienne and Neufchâtel, there is a pile dwelling of neolithic age which is now 3000 feet inland from the present shore of the lake. A calculation made by Professor Gilliéron of the rate at which the lake is being filled up with sediment would give for the foundation of this settlement a minimum antiquity of 6750 years, or about 4900 B.C.[1] At this time, therefore, the neolithic people had abandoned the nomad life of the undivided Aryans, and had acquired the skill requisite to build their habitations on piles driven into the bed of the lake; but how much earlier the neolithic period may have begun we have no means of ascertaining.

At the neighbouring settlement of Chamblon, on the Lake of Neufchâtel, there is a later pile dwelling, founded towards the close of the neolithic period.

[1] See Keller, *Lake Dwellings*, p. 462; Lyell, *Antiquity of Man*, p. 29; Lubbock, *Prehistoric Times*, p. 401; De Mortillet, *Le Préhistorique*, p. 621.

A calculation of the rate at which the lake is being filled up with sediment shows that this settlement must have begun before 1500 B.C.[1]

M. Morlot considers that the age of the oldest neolithic lake dwellings in Switzerland may be from 6000 to 7000 years. Dr. Keller thinks this is too much, and prefers 3000 to 4000 years as a safer estimate.[2] But these structures belong to a comparatively late part of the neolithic period. Some of the pile dwellings in Southern Germany belong to an earlier period in which there were no domestic animals, and when even the rudiments of agriculture were unknown.

From the growth of the cone of the delta of the Tinière, a small stream which falls into the Lake of Geneva near Chillon, a calculation has been made by M. Morlot, which, making every probable deduction, would show that about 6400 years ago Switzerland was inhabited by people who used implements of polished stone, while for the stratum in which bronze implements were found we have a probable antiquity of about 3800 years. Hence in Switzerland the epoch of bronze must almost certainly be as old as 1000 B.C., and may possibly be older by another thousand years.

This estimate agrees essentially with that obtained from the pile dwellings in the valley of the Po, which began in the neolithic age, but, as Helbig has shown,[3] had reached the bronze age when they were destroyed by the invasion of the Etruscans, which must have been earlier—how much earlier we do not know— than the middle of the eleventh century B.C. The

---

[1] G. de Mortillet, *Le Préhistorique*, p. 618.
[2] Keller, *Lake Dwellings*, pp. 526-528.
[3] Helbig, *Die Italiker in der Poebene*, p. 100.

bronze period must therefore have commenced considerably before this date.

The burnt city at Hissarlik, and the tombs at Mycenæ, excavated by Dr. Schliemann, also belong to the age of bronze. They are generally assigned to the twelfth or thirteenth century B.C.

Localities which were further removed from the influences of Semitic civilisation were more backward, and hence the foregoing calculations are not irreconcilable with those of M. Arcelin, who from the rate of deposition of the alluvium of the Saône has come to the conclusion that as late as 1150 B.C. stone implements were still exclusively used in Central Gaul, and that about 400 B.C. bronze had not yet been replaced by iron.

The Victoria Cave, near Settle, in Yorkshire, was inhabited by neolithic people who had made considerable advances in civilisation, having apparently domesticated the ox, and possibly the horse. From the accumulation of *débris*, due to the slow weathering of the limestone rock, Professor Boyd Dawkins has calculated that the neolithic occupation of this cave ceased between 4800 and 5000 years ago, or before 3000 B.C.[1]

The stone implements found in the kitchen middens or shell mounds of Denmark are more archaic in character than those from the Swiss lake dwellings; indeed they are considered by some authorities to be mesolithic, forming a transition between the palæolithic and neolithic periods. The people had not yet reached the agricultural or even the pastoral stage—they were solely fishermen and hunters, the

---

[1] Dawkins, *Cave Hunting*, p. 115.

only domesticated animal they possessed being the dog, whereas even in the oldest of the Swiss lake dwellings the people, though still subsisting largely on the products of the chase, had domesticated the ox, if not also the sheep and the goat. The shell mounds belong therefore to a very early stage of the neolithic period, the civilisation which they disclose being ruder than that of the undivided Aryans.

The accumulation of these mounds must have occupied an enormous period. They are very numerous, and some of them are more than 900 feet long, and from 100 to 200 feet broad. They are usually from three to five feet, but occasionally as much as ten feet, in thickness. They are composed of the shells of oysters and mussels, of the bones of animals and fish, with occasional fragments of rude pottery, and numerous implements of flint or bone, and similar refuse of human habitation.[1]

The flint tools are so abundant that in an hour and a half two visitors collected from one of the mounds 380 specimens. As the population subsisted solely on fishing and the chase, it must have been extremely sparse, probably as thinly scattered as are the Eskimos and the Fuegians, who are in a similar stage of civilisation. If the population was as dense as that of the former territories of the Hudson Bay Company the neolithic population of Denmark would not have exceeded 1500, if it was as dense as in Patagonia it must have been under 1000, and if as sparse as in Australia before the settlement of Europeans, not half as much.[2]

Making every allowance, it is manifest that such

[1] Lubbock, *Prehistoric Times*, pp. 230-233.
[2] *Ibid.*, pp. 607, 608.

enormous heaps of refuse, and such a vast quantity of implements could only have been accumulated during long periods of time, many centuries at least, more probably several milleniums.

But the time when the kitchen midden period came to a close must be itself remote, as is proved by the alteration of the coast-line, and by the change of climatic conditions which have taken place.

Some of these mounds are now at a considerable distance from the sea, which can only be due to the slow secular elevation of the land, which is still in progress at the rate of a few inches in a century. In other places the mounds are wanting, evidently owing to the encroachment of the sea.

We have in Denmark three successive periods of vegetation—first the age of fir, second the age of oak, and third the age of beech. In the Roman period the country was covered, as it now is, by vast forests of beech, the fir and the oak having then disappeared. These changes in the vegetation are attributed to slow secular changes of climate. Now the stone age agrees mainly with that of the fir, and partly with that of the oak; the bronze age agrees mainly with the period of the oak, and the iron age with that of the beech. The shell mounds, which belong to the early neolithic period, are proved to belong to the age of the fir, since the bones of the capercailzie, a bird which feeds on the young shoots of the fir, have been found in the kitchen middens, while stone implements of the kitchen midden type have been discovered in the peat bogs among the stumps of the firs. Taking these considerations into account, Professor Steenstrup, the highest authority on the subject, is of opinion that a period of from

10,000 to 12,000 years must be allowed for the accumulation of the vast mounds of refuse, and for the successive changes of the forest trees from fir to oak, and from oak to beech, which can only be due to considerable changes of climate—changes, moreover, which had already been effected at the commencement of the iron age.[1]

Another chronometer is afforded by the peat, in which, at various depths, neolithic implements are buried. Professor Steenstrup has calculated that from 4000 to 16,000 years would be required for the formation of certain of these peat bogs. The presence of pottery proves that the shell mounds belong to the neolithic age, the commencement of which can hardly therefore be placed later than 10,000 years ago.

§ 2. *The Methods of Anthropology.*

Broca has laid down the axiom that the ethnic characteristics of the first order of importance are not linguistic but physical. As to the nature of the speech of the neolithic peoples of Europe we have inferences rather than any positive facts to guide us. As to their physical characteristics the evidence is abundant and conclusive. This evidence consists partly of the statements of Greek and Roman writers, but is derived mainly from the measurements of skulls. The shape of the skull is one of the least variable characteristics of race, so much so that the skulls from prehistoric tombs make it possible to prove that the neolithic inhabitants of Europe were the direct ancestors of the existing races. The skull

---

[1] Penka, *Herkunft der Arier*, p. 62.

form is expressed by the numerical ratios of certain measurements, which are called indices. Of these the most important are the latitudinal, or, as it is commonly called, the cephalic index, which gives the proportion of the extreme breadth to the extreme length of the cranium; the altitudinal, or vertical index, which gives the proportion of the height of the skull to the length; the orbital index, which gives the proportion of the height of the eye orbit to the breadth; the facial angle; the nasal index; and the index of prognathism, by which we estimate the shape of the face. These indices, taken in conjunction with the shape of certain bones, especially the femur and the tibia, enable us to determine with considerable certainty the ethnic relationship of prehistoric to existing races.

The latitudinal or "cephalic" index is thus determined. Divide the extreme breadth of the skull by the length from front to back, and multiply by 100. Thus, if the breadth is three-fourths of the length, the index is said to be 75. Cephalic indices vary from 58 to 98.

The term dolicho-cephalic, or long-headed, is applied to skulls with low indices; brachy-cephalic, or broad-headed, to those with high indices; and ortho-cephalic, or meso-cephalic, to the intermediate class. The black races are dolicho-cephalic, the white races incline to ortho-cephalism, and the yellow races to brachy-cephalism. Anthropologists are not entirely agreed as to the precise limits of index to which these terms should be restricted, but we shall not be far wrong if we call skulls with indices below 75 dolicho-cephalic, from 75 to 78 sub-dolicho-cephalic, from 78 to 80 ortho-cephalic, below 83 sub-brachycephalic, and of 83 and over brachycephalic. The Swedes are the most dolicho-cephalic race in Europe, the Lapps the most brachy-cephalic, the English the most ortho-cephalic. North Germany is sub-dolicho-cephalic, South Germany sub-brachycephalic.

The orbital index, which gives the proportion of the height to the breadth of the orbit is believed by Broca to be of especial value as a test of race, since it is not liable to be affected by causes connected with the struggle for existence. Among the black races it is lowest, varying, in Africa, from 79.3 to 85.4, and descending to 61 among the Tasmanians; among the yellow races it is high, varying from 82.2 to 95.4; among the Europeans it is usually between 83 and 85. A similar test applies to the section of the hair. In the Mongolian or yellow race it is circular; in the black or African race it is flat or ribbon-shaped; in the white or European race it is oval. The hair of the Mongolian is straight, that of the African frizzled or woolly, that of the European is inclined to curl.

All these tests agree in exhibiting two extreme types—the African, with long heads, long orbits, and flat hair; and the Mongolian, with round heads, round orbits, and round hair. The European type is intermediate—the head, the orbit, and the hair are oval. In the east of Europe we find an approximation to the Asiatic type; in the south of Europe to the African. The neolithic tombs of Europe exhibit notable approximations both to the African and to the Asiatic types.

The position of the European races between the African and the Asiatic may be exhibited graphically by the diagram on the following page.

5

Where, it has been asked, did the human race originate? Darwin inclines to Africa, De Quatrefages to Asia, Wagner to Europe in the miocene epoch,

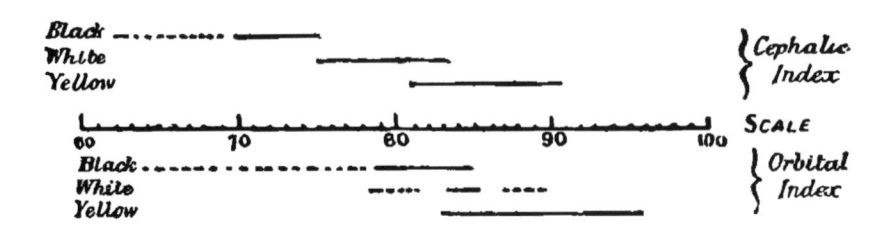

```
Black  -..-----  ——
White              ————              } Cephalic
Yellow             ————                  Index

|----|----|----|----|----|  SCALE
60   70   80   90   100
Black .----..-----  ——
White       ----  ——  ----          } Orbital
Yellow              ————              Index
```

when the climate was sub-tropical. If it originated in Europe we may suppose it was differentiated into the extreme Asiatic and African types; or, on the other hand, Europe may have been the place where the African and Asiatic types met and mingled. Those who hold the former view may believe with Penka that the Aryans represent the oldest European race; those who hold the latter opinion may maintain that while Aryan speech came originally from Asia it was subsequently acquired by men who were largely of African race.

§ 3. *The Races of Britain.*

In Cæsar's time there were in Gaul three races—the Aquitanians, the Celts, and the Belgæ; as well as a fourth race, the Germans, eastward of the Rhine. In the neolithic tombs of Europe the remains of these four races can be traced, and from them alone the Aryan-speaking peoples of Europe have descended. But it is evident that only one of these four races can represent the primitive Aryans, the others being merely Aryan in speech, but non-Aryan by descent.

On the Continent there were no insurmountable physical obstacles to impede the immigration of intrusive races; but in Britain the "silver streak" has rendered the ethnological problem less complicated. At the beginning of the bronze age we discover in British tombs the remains of two out of the four races of the Continent. One of these arrived towards the close of the neolithic age, before which time Britain seems to have been inhabited by one race only, which may possibly have descended from the people of palæolithic times, and who may even have migrated from the Continent with the great pachyderms before the formation of the channel.

The older race was of feeble build, short stature, dark complexion, and dolichocephalic skull. They buried their dead in caves, and when caves were no longer available, in long barrows provided with interior chambers and passages. Some of these long barrows are 400 feet in length and fifty feet in breadth, and resemble artificial caves—imitations or survivals, as it were, of the earlier sepulchral caverns. The long barrows are plainly of later date than the cave sepulchres. Thus in a sepulchral cave at Cefn, near St. Asaph, the skulls are of precisely the same type as those in a long barrow at the same place, but their relative antiquity is shown by the fact that the remains of wild animals are rare in the barrow but common in the cave. Plainly the people had reached the pastoral stage when the cave was abandoned for the barrow[1] The long barrows all belong to the stone age. Canon Greenwell asserts that "no trace of metal has been found . . . in any

---

[1] Dawkins, *Cave Hunting*, pp. 164, 165.

undisturbed part of a long barrow," while "pottery of any kind is very unfrequent."[1] In barrows of this description, from Caithness to Wiltshire, the skulls are all of one type, and archæologists are agreed that in the long barrow period Britain was inhabited by one race only.

This race is identified by ethnologists with the British tribe of the Silures, who at the time of the Roman Conquest inhabited the counties of Hereford, Radnor, Brecon, Monmouth, and Glamorgan. From their physical characteristics Tacitus concluded that they belonged to the Iberian race. His words are, "Silurum colorati vultus torti plerumque crines, et posita contra Hispania, Iberos veteres trajecisse, casque sedes occupasse, fidem faciunt."[2]

No importance must be attached to the conjecture that the Silures had emigrated from Spain. It was a guess, based on a valuable observation as to the physical resemblance of this swarthy British tribe to the Iberians.

Modern ethnologists have made the same observation, and have more especially noted the resemblance of the Spanish Basques to the small dark Welshmen of Denbighshire. The same type is found in some of the Hebrides, especially in Barra. It is found in Kerry, and also west of the Shannon, in Donegal and Galway, notably in the Isle of Aran in Galway Bay, where in an old graveyard Dr. Beddoe found four dolichocephalic skulls, with a mean index 74.25, the lowest in the British Isles.[3] Dr. Beddoe also found an approach to this index in the region occupied by the Silures,

---

[1] Greenwell, *British Barrows*, pp. 543, 508.
[2] Tacitus, *Agricola*, c. 11.
[3] Beddoe, *Races of Britain*, p. 227.

five skulls from Micheldean giving a mean index of 74.8. In a more or less modified form this type prevails throughout the Silurian region of Wales and the west of England, where we find an oval-featured race, of short stature and feeble muscular development, with dolichocephalic skull, dark hair, and black eyes.[1]

The Continental extension of this type will be discussed hereafter.[2] Suffice it to say that skulls resembling those of the British long barrows have been found in sepulchral caves in Belgium, France, Spain, Algeria, and Teneriffe. It is believed that descendants of this race may be recognised among the Basques, the Corsicans, the Berbers, and the Guanches of the Canary Islands.

For this short, dark dolichocephalic type we may adopt the usual and convenient name " Iberian." Professor Rolleston prefers the term " Silurian," and it has been variously designated by other writers as the Euskarian, Basque, Berber, or Mediterranean race. By some French writers it is called the " Cro-Magnon " type, from a skull, possibly of palæolithic age, found in a sepulchral cavern at Cro-Magnon in Périgord.

Towards the close of the neolithic age, or possibly at the beginning of the bronze age, the southern and eastern portions of Britain were invaded and occupied by a wholly different race—tall, muscular, brachycephalic, and almost certainly with xanthous or rufous hair and florid complexion. They are known as the people who buried in round barrows, and to

---

[1] Greenwell, *British Barrows*, p. 630; Elton, *Origins of English History*, pp. 137, 141; Dawkins, *Early Man in Britain*, p. 330; Penka, *Origines Ariacæ*, p. 90.

[2] See p. 92, *infra*.

them in all probability we may ascribe the erection of Avebury and Stonehenge,[1] and also the first introduction into Britain of Aryan speech and of implements of bronze. This race Dr. Thurnam identifies with the Celts, and he calls the type the "Turanian" type, believing it to be an offshoot, through the Belgic Gauls, from the great brachycephalic stock of Central and North-Eastern Europe and Asia. It is also the prevailing type among the Slavonic races. This "Turanian" type of Dr. Thurnam is the "type Mongoloide" of Prüner-Bey. By Professor Rolleston it is called the "Cimbric" type, on the ground that it resembles that of the broad-headed neolithic people of Denmark, the old Cimbric Chersonese. Dr. Thurnam identifies the round barrow people of Britain with the broad-headed neolithic race of Belgium and North-Eastern France, who undoubtedly spoke a Celtic language, and who are designated by Broca as the Kymry, to distinguish them from the short, dark, brachycephalic race of Central France, to whom he maintains the name Celts properly belongs. But as there can be little doubt that the people of the round barrows introduced into Britain what is usually called "Celtic" speech, it will be convenient, though perhaps incorrect, to designate the people of the round barrows as the Celtic race.

The interments of these two races, the "Iberians" of the long barrows and the "Celts" of the round barrows, can be readily distinguished. The skulls, as Canon Greenwell observes, are "as markedly different as any two series of crania can be."[2] The difference is well exhibited in the skulls figured below, both

[1] Elton, *Origins*, p. 146.
[2] Greenwell, *British Barrows*, p 482.

THE PREHISTORIC RACES OF EUROPE. 71

from the wolds of the East Riding of Yorkshire, and here reproduced by Canon Greenwell's kind permission. The first is the skull of a middle-aged man of the "Iberian" race, found at Rudstone,[1] in a long barrow,

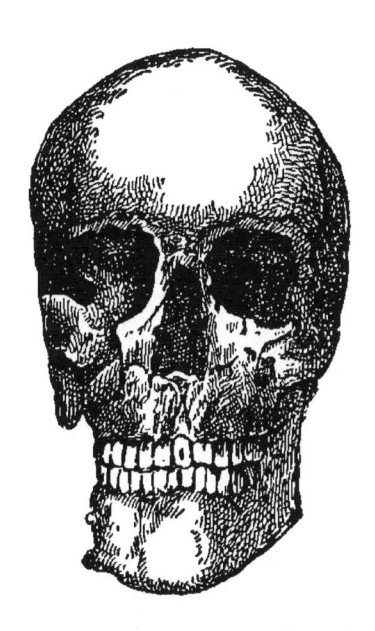

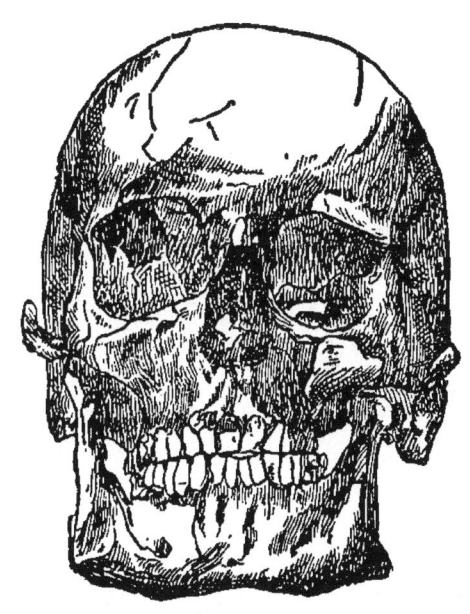

LONG BARROW SKULL (MALE), FROM RUBSTONE, E.R.

ROUND BARROW SKULL (MALE), FROM COWLAM, E.R.

210 feet long, and varying in breadth from 75 to 45 feet. It is of a pronounced dolichocephalic type, the index being as low as 72. The second is the skull of a man, also in the middle period of life, of the other, or "Celtic" race, which was found in a round barrow, 70 feet in diameter, in the neighbouring parish of Cowlam.[2] This skull is decisively brachycephalic, the index being as high as 84. Flint implements accompanied both of these interments, but no articles of metal.

[1] Greenwell, *British Barrows*, pp. 501, 613.
[2] *Ibid.*, pp. 226, 587.

The two races are distinguished not only by the difference in the shape of the skull, but by the whole

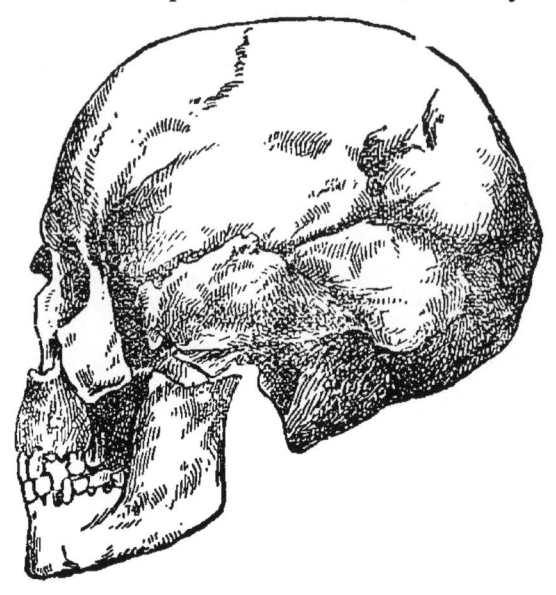

RUBSTONE SKULL (SIDE VIEW).

character of the face. In the Celtic skull, of which that from Cowlam is a favourable specimen, the head

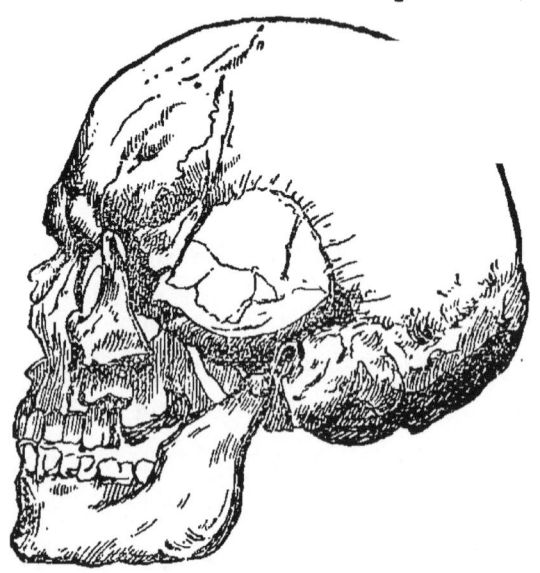

COWLAM SKULL (SIDE VIEW).

is massive and powerful, the face angular and prognathous, with a projecting mouth and powerful square jaws. The broad, capacious forehead and the short, square chin indicate mental power and determination of character. The cheek bones are high and broad, the orbits of the eyes nearly circular, with supraciliary ridges well developed, which must have given a fierce and beetling aspect to the face. The nose must have projected forwards, and the sockets of the front teeth are oblique. The skulls of this race are usually distinguished by their capacity and vertical height, which is actually greater than the breadth.[1]

To this type the skulls of the Iberian race present the greatest possible contrast. The face is oval, feeble, and orthognathous; the forehead narrow; the chin weak, pointed, and elongated. The nose is usually not so broad as in the other race, but longer by a quarter of an inch, the space between the nostrils and the mouth considerable, giving a weak upper lip, and the sockets of the front teeth are vertical. Neither the cheek bones nor the supraciliary ridges are developed, and the orbits of the eyes are somewhat elongated. The aspect of the face must have been mild and gentle. The vertical views of these two skulls show that the greater length of the one, and the greater breadth of the other, are mainly due to occipital developments. The difference in the skulls extends also to the other bones of the skeleton. The Iberian race was short, with slender bones, and feeble muscular attachments, while the Celtic race was tall, powerful, and muscular.

In both races the distinctive characters are less highly accentuated in the skulls of the women, as will be

[1] Greenwell, *British Barrows*, p. 645.

seen from the representations of two female skulls from the Yorkshire wolds—one a long skull of the Iberian type, orthognathous, with an index of 68, from a barrow on Sherburn wold;[1] the other a broad

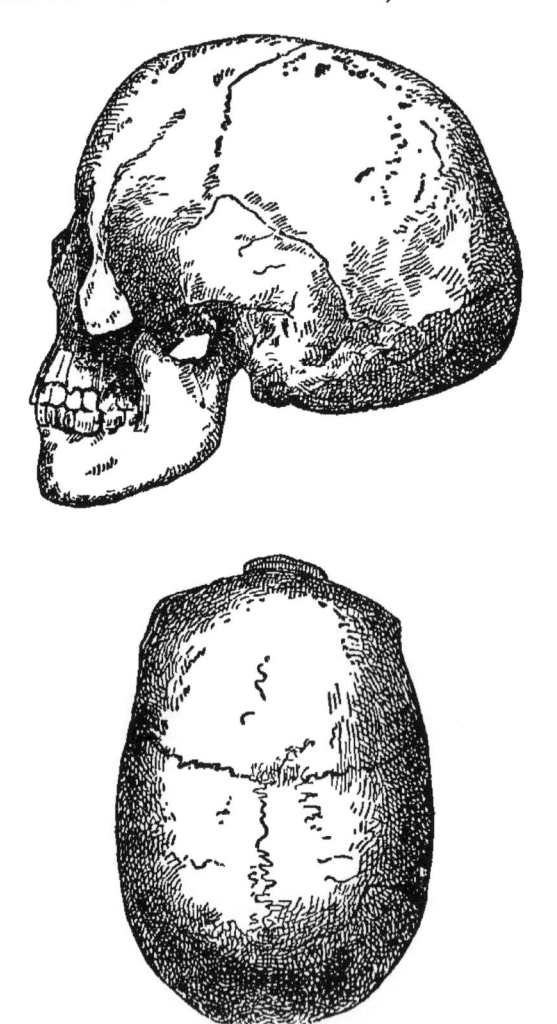

LONG BARROW SKULL (FEMALE), FROM SHERBURN WOLD, E.R.

skull of the Celtic type, from a neighbouring barrow at Flixton,[2] strongly prognathous, and with an index of 82.

[1] Greenwell, *British Barrows*, p. 608.   [2] *Ibid.*, p. 575.

From ninety-five round barrow skulls we obtain a mean cephalic index of 81, and a mean altitudinal index of 77; while sixty-seven long barrow skulls give a mean cephalic index of 71.25, and a mean altitudinal index of 73.

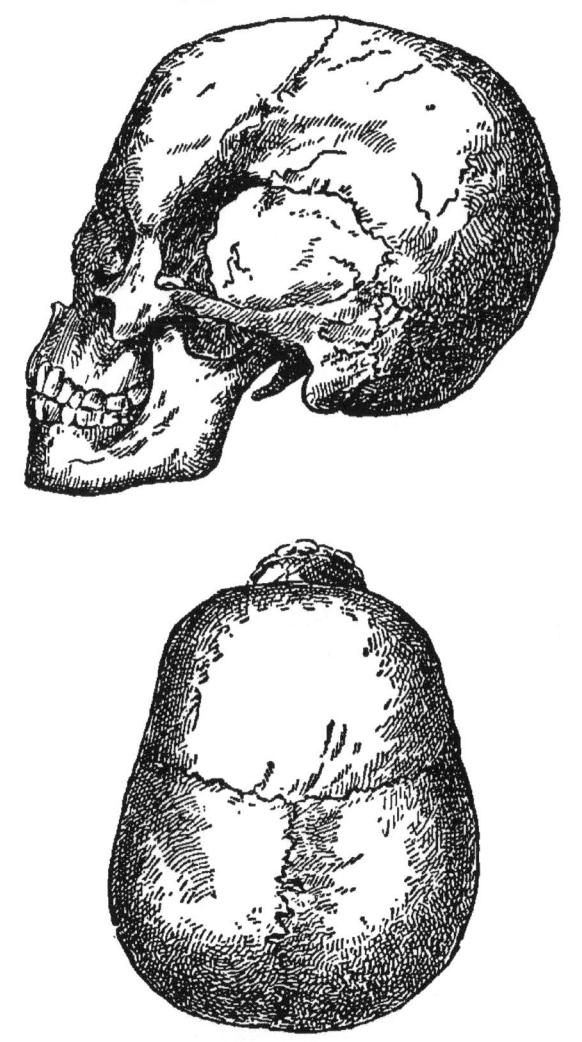

ROUND BARROW SKULL (FEMALE), FROM FLIXTON WOLD, E.R.

The difference of stature between the two races is considerable. In the Iberian race the average height for both sexes was 5 feet 4½ inches (or 5 feet

5½ inches for the men), the tallest of the men measuring 5 feet 6 inches, and the shortest of the women 4 feet 8 inches. In the Celtic race the height, calculated from the length of the thigh bones, ordinarily varied from 5 feet 7 inches to 5 feet 9 inches, the average height being 5 feet 8½ inches.

The stature of the Celts struck the Romans with astonishment. Cæsar speaks of their *mirifica corpora*, and contrasts the short stature of the Romans with the *magnitudo corporum* of the Gauls. Strabo also, speaking of the Coritavi, a British tribe in Lincolnshire, after mentioning their yellow hair, says, " to show how tall they are, I saw myself some of their young men at Rome, and they were taller by six inches than any one else in the city."[1] This might seem an exaggeration, but is borne out by the bones found in some round barrows. For instance, at Gristhorpe, in the East Riding, a round barrow was opened containing the skeleton of a man whose stature must have been 6 feet 2 inches.

There can be little doubt that the Iberian race was dark in complexion, with black hair and eyes. As to the Celtic race, it is almost certain that they were fair, with red or yellow hair, and blue or blue-grey eyes. The most conclusive statement comes from Dio Cassius, who has left us a description of Boadicea, who almost certainly belonged to this race. He describes her as of great bodily proportions, ἦν δὲ καὶ τὸ σῶμα μεγίστη. The fierceness of her appearance struck beholders with awe, and the expression of her countenance was exceedingly severe and piercing. Her voice was harsh, and she had a profusion of tawny hair, τήν τε κόμην πλείστην τε καὶ ξανθοτάτην,

[1] Elton, *Origins*, p. 240.

which reached down to her hips. The word ξανθός is used for various tawny shades of colour, either golden, or auburn, or with a tinge of red.

We have other testimonies to the same effect. Lucan says the Britons were *flavi;* Silius Italicus describes their hair as golden; and Vitruvius, referring seemingly to the same race, speaks of their huge limbs, their grey eyes, and their long straight red hair.

The Coritavi, the Celtic tribe which occupied part of Lincolnshire and the valley of the Trent, are described by Strabo as having yellow hair, but not so yellow as that of the Gauls; and Tacitus mentions the red hair and huge limbs—*rutilæ comæ et magni artus*—of the Caledonians, who, in this respect, he compares with the Germans.

The Belgic Gauls, who, as we shall presently see, were probably of the same race as the round barrow people of Britain, are uniformly described by ancient writers as tall, large-limbed, and with red or yellow hair. Pösche, Diefenbach, and De Belloguet have collected numerous testimonies to this effect.[1] Thus, according to Diodorus Siculus, the Galatians were xanthous, ταῖς δὲ κόμαις . . . ξανθόι. Livy describes the *promissæ et rutilatæ comæ* of the Gauls. Claudian says, *flava repexo Gallia crine ferox.* Ammianus Marcellinus describes the great stature, the white skin, and the red hair of the Gauls. Silius Italicus speaks of the huge limbs and golden locks of the Boii; and Strabo says the Germans resembled the Gauls, but were taller, more savage, and more xanthous. Manilius, speaking of the tall Germans

[1] Pösche, *Die Arier*, p. 25; Diefenbach, *Origines Europææ*, p. 161; De Belloguet, *Ethnogenie Gauloise*, ii. pp. 63, *seq.*

with their yellow hair, says that the Gauls were not so red.

The old Celtic type, tall, powerful, red-haired, with a florid complexion, and inclined to freckle, may be recognised in some of the Scotch clans, such as the MacGregors and the Camerons, who are altogether different from the Frasers, or the dark clans of the Western Isles.

In Ireland there were the same two races, which are graphically described by McFirbis in his *Book of Genealogies*. One race, which he calls the Fir-Bolg, had dark hair and eyes, small stature and slender limbs, and constituted the despised servile class of the Irish people. They belong, says Mr. Skene, "to the same class with the Silures, and may be held to represent the Iberian race which preceded the Celtic." The other race, called the Tuatha Dè Danann by McFirbis, was tall, with golden or red hair, fair skin, and blue or blue-grey eyes. They "correspond in character with Tacitus's large-limbed and red-haired Caledonians."[1]

As to the relative priority of the Iberian and Celtic races in Britain there can be no question. The Iberians were plainly the primitive inhabitants of the island, and the Celts were later invaders who were not only a more powerful race, but possessed a higher civilisation. This is indicated by the form of the barrows in which they buried. The abodes of the dead represent the abodes of the living. The Iberians must at one time have been troglodytes, as the long barrow is plainly a survival of the cave. The Celts must have lived in huts or pit dwellings, on the model of which the round barrows are

[1] Skene, *Celtic Scotland*, vol. i. p. 178; cf. Elton, *Origins*, p. 159.

THE PREHISTORIC RACES OF EUROPE.

constructed. In the long barrows metal is absent, and pottery is rare, while the presence of pottery is a distinctive feature of the round barrows,[1] and bronze is not unknown.

As bronze has been found in round barrows, it is frequently asserted that the Celts were armed with bronze weapons when they invaded Britain. This conclusion is not borne out by the evidence, which indicates that the Celts arrived in the neolithic period, and obtained bronze by commerce from Gaul at a later time. Canon Greenwell tabulates 485 interments in round barrows; in 201 cases these were associated with pottery, in 150 cases with implements of stone, bone, or horn, and in only twenty-three with bronze. Of these twenty-three cases only five were primary interments, fifteen were secondary interments, and the rest doubtful.

Mr. Mortimer, who has opened 241 round barrows in the East Riding, containing 629 bodies, found pottery in 203 cases, stone implements in 150, and bronze in twenty-six. These facts make it probable that when the round barrows were first erected bronze was either unknown or extremely rare, but that it had, to some extent, come into use when secondary interments took place in barrows which had been raised at an earlier period.

Moreover, no brachycephalic skull has been found in any primary interment in a long barrow, though they occur in secondary or later interments; while in the round barrows the skulls are usually brachycephalic, though dolichocephalic skulls are occasionally found in them, especially on the Yorkshire wolds.[2]

[1] Greenwell, *British Barrows*, pp. 508, 458-478.
[2] *Ibid.*, pp. 543, 549.

From these facts we may confidently draw the conclusion that during the greater part of the neolithic age Britain was inhabited solely by a short, dark, dolichocephalic race, originally troglodytes, and that towards the conclusion of the stone age it was invaded by a tall, fair, brachycephalic hut-building race, which either brought with them, or before long acquired, implements of metal.

We may also accept Dr. Thurnam's conclusion that the older dolichocephalic race was pre-Aryan, belonging to the same stock as the Spanish Basques, and that the later brachycephalic invaders spoke an Aryan language, which there can be little doubt was Celtic.

If these conclusions, now very generally accepted, can be maintained, we have reached a fixed point in the discussion as to who the Aryans were. The first Aryan-speaking race which appeared in Britain was brachycephalic, tall, and red-haired, of the type characterised by Professor Rolleston as "Turanian," and by Prüner-Bey as "Mongoloide."

It is not improbable, as Professor Rhys has suggested, that there may have been two successive Celtic invasions of Britain. The first, he thinks, was that of the Goidels, who spread to Ireland and Scotland, amalgamating with the Iberian aborigines, and imposing on them their language. The second invasion was that of the Brittones, who seized the more fertile portions of the island, driving the Goidels before them to the West and North.[1] This theory helps to explain some linguistic facts, and is not without support from craniological indications.

The mean index of Dr. Thurnam's long barrow skulls is, as we have seen, 71.25, and that of the round

[1] Rhys, *Celtic Britain*, p. 213.

barrow skulls of Yorkshire 81. But in North Wales, and in Professor Huxley's skulls from the tumulus at Keiss in Caithness—districts where we might expect to find an amalgamation of the two races—the mean index is 75.5, which may represent the mixed "Goidelic" type of Professor Rhys.

§ 4. *The Celts.*

We have now to trace the two neolithic British races on the Continent—the Celtic type eastward to the confines of Asia; the Iberian type southward through France and Spain to Northern Africa.

The Celts appear to have crossed to Britain from Belgic Gaul. In the neolithic age a race indistinguishable from that of the British round barrows occupied Belgium. A sepulchral cave at Sclaigneaux, fourteen miles from Namur, contained numerous skeletons of the round barrow type, with indices of 81.1 and 81.6. Implements of bone and flint, of late neolithic forms, were found, but no bronze. Bones of the dog, the ox, and the goat indicate that these people had reached the pastoral stage.[1]

The skull figured on the next page resembles some of the ruder skulls from the British round barrows.

In the early neolithic age the southern frontier of the Belgic Gauls seems to have been the line of the Meuse. They held the modern province of Hainault; while another race, as will presently be shown, occupied the province of Namur.[2] At a later time

---

[1] Dawkins, *Cave Hunting*, pp. 219, 199.
[2] See p. 118, *infra.*

they advanced southward, imposing their Celtic speech on the earlier races of Central France. In the artificial sepulchral grottoes on the Marne and the Oise skulls of this race are found, together with those of the earlier population.

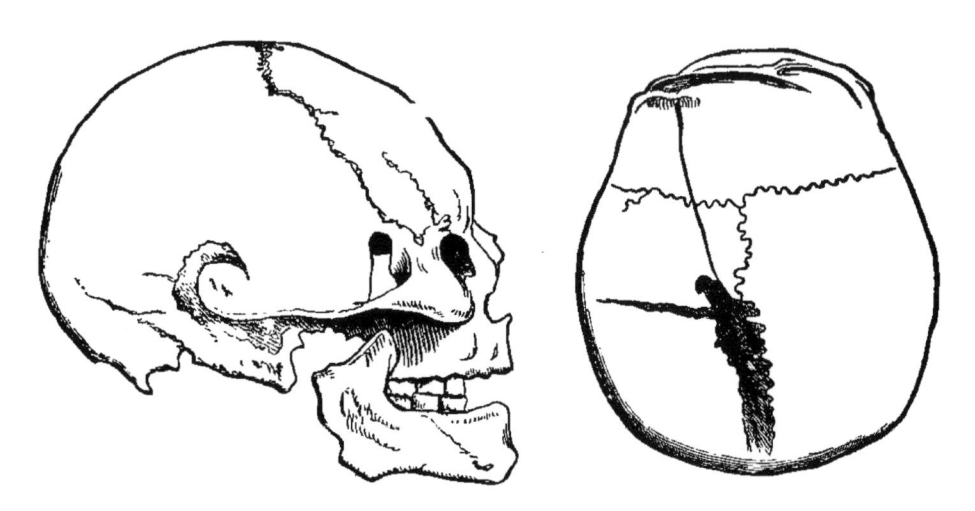

SKULL FROM SCLAIGNEAUX, BELGIUM.

This race may also be traced eastward to Denmark. Dr. Rolleston observes that "the bronze period Briton very closely resembles in his osteological remains the brachycephalous Dane of the neolithic period; and the likeness between these and some of the modern Danes has been noticed by Virchow."[1] From a neolithic tumulus at Borreby, in the Danish island of Falster, four skulls of the round barrow type were obtained, whose indices were 80, 81, 82, and 83. One of these Borreby skulls is figured below,[2] and bears a striking similarity to the ruder skulls from the British round barrows.

[1] Greenwell, *British Barrows*, p. 680.
[2] Hamy, *Précis de Paléontologie Humaine*, p. 368.

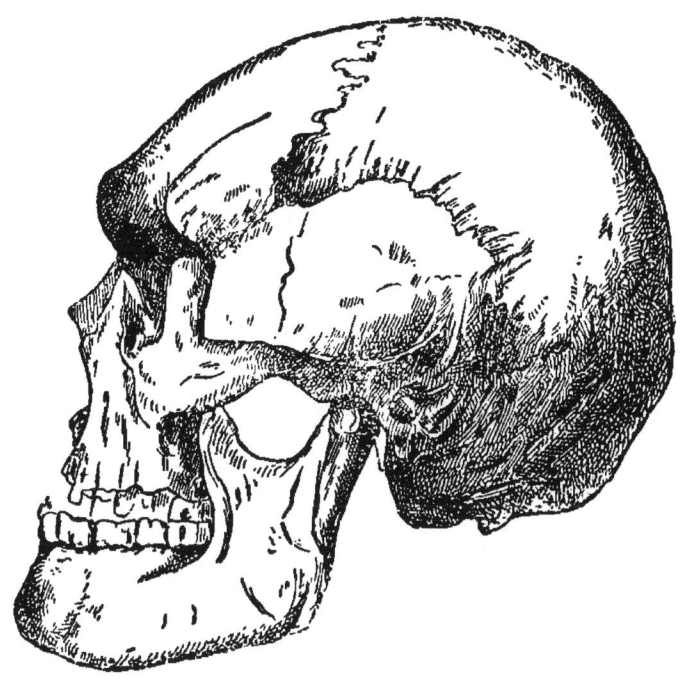

MALE SKULL FROM BORREBY, DENMARK.

This resemblance will be seen by superimposing the outline of the Borreby skull on that of a Celtic skull

——— BORREBY.
······ ILDERTON.
SKULLS FROM BORREBY AND FROM ILDERTON, NORTHUMBERLAND,
SUPERIMPOSED.

from Ilderton in Northumberland,[1] the index of which is 82.

In Denmark this brachycephalic type has been singularly persistent. To judge by the skulls of Flambard, and other Danish ecclesiastics buried at Durham, the Danes 800 years ago were brachycephalic. According to Dr. Beddoe the modern Danes are of the same type as the round barrow people. The mean cephalic index of the Danes is 80.5, and their average height nearly 5 feet 7 inches; the mean index of the round barrow people being 81, and their mean stature 5 feet 8½ inches. The hair of the Danes, according to Dr. Beddoe, is either pale yellow or light brown, and their eyes are almost invariably light in colour, usually either blue or bluish-grey. Some of the Danes, however, seem to have been dark. Dr. Beddoe found a black-haired race in the island of Moen, where brachycephalic skulls have been found in ancient graves. These black-haired Danes may be the Dubhgaill, or "black strangers," who are contrasted by Irish chroniclers, who describe the Viking inroads, with the Finngaill, or "fair strangers," who are supposed to have been Norwegians.[2] Possibly we may thus account for the tall, dark brachycephalic people who are met with in some of the Danish districts in England.

At the beginning of the historic period the valleys of the Main and the Upper Danube were occupied by Celtic tribes. In this region Celtic names abound. The Boii, a Celtic people, gave their name to Bavaria (Boio-varia), and to Bohemia (Boio-hemum).

The ethnic frontier between Celts and Teutons

---
[1] Greenwell, *British Barrows*, p. 583.
[2] Skene, *Celtic Scotland*, vol. i. p. 304.

was the continuous mountain barrier formed by the Teutoberger Wald, the Thuringer Wald, and the Riesen Gebirge. North of this line the population is now dolichocephalic, the index in the neighbourhood of Hanover, for instance, being 76.7, and at Jena 76.9, while to the south of this line the people are more brachycephalic, the mean index being 79.2 in Hesse, 79.3 in Swabia, 79.8 in Bavaria, 80 in Lower Franconia, and 80.1 in the Breisgau.[1]

The people of the modern kingdom of Würtemberg are also brachycephalous. Hölder, the chief authority on the anthropology of Würtemberg, now considers the type to be "Turanian," or "Sarmatian," and not, as he had formerly supposed, "Ligurian."

German ethnologists believe that a Celtic people worked the salt mines in the neighbourhood of Halle, a name which, like that of Hallstadt, also a Celtic settlement, is more easily explained from Celtic than from Teutonic speech. The present inhabitants of this district differ from the North German type; they are brachycephalic, with a mean index of 80.5, which is the same as that of the Danes, and differs little from that of the round barrow skulls of Britain, which is 81.

Halle seems to have been the most northern outpost of the Celts in Germany, since beyond the Teutoberger Wald, a few miles to the north of Halle, the type changes, and the mean cephalic index drops from 80.5 to 76.7.

Southern Germany is now Teutonic in speech, the local names and the persistent ethnic type alone bearing witness to the primitive Celtic occupation. We know, however, that in the early centuries of our era

[1] Peschel, *Völkerkunde*, p. 59.

Southern Germany was Teutonised in speech by German invaders, whose tombs, known as the Row Graves, contain dolichocephalic skulls with a mean index of 71.3. The older Celtic sepulchres of this region are known as the Grave-Mounds, and contain orthocephalic or brachycephalic skulls, with a mean index of 78.8, rising to a maximum of 82.9.

In Würtemberg and Bavaria a number of pile dwellings of the neolithic age have been discovered which seem to be prototypes of those which are so numerous in the Swiss lakes. These people must gradually have spread southwards from Germany, since the older pile dwellings on the Lake of Constance belong to an earlier period than those on the lakes of Neufchâtel and Bienne.

The Swiss craniologists, His and Rütimeyer, attribute the erection of the lake dwellings in Switzerland to "our Celtic ancestors," the Helvetii.[1] The mean index of eight skulls[2] found in the pile dwellings is 80.95. The index of the round barrow skulls of Britain is 81. One of these Helvetian skulls, called the "Sion type" in the *Crania Helvetica*, is figured on the next page. It resembles the round barrow skulls, such as those from Cowlam and Gristhorpe, and the Borreby skull from Denmark.[3] But, as we might expect from the comparatively high civilisation attained by the people of the Swiss pile dwellings, their skulls are somewhat larger, loftier, and better formed than the ruder skulls of the British round barrows.

[1] His and Rütimeyer, *Crania Helvetica*, pp. 34, 35.

[2] The indices are—Auvernier skulls, 77.2 and 78.5; Nidau, 78 and 78.4; Möringen, 83; Meilen, 83.2; Pfiedwald, 83.8; Robenhausen, 85.5. If Robenhausen be excluded, as possibly Rhætian, the mean index will be reduced to 80.03.

[3] See pp. 72, 83, *supra*.

Towards the close of the neolithic age the same Aryan-speaking race which constructed the Swiss pile dwellings seems to have crossed the Alps, erecting their pile dwellings in the Italian lakes and in the marshes of the valley of the Po. Helbig has proved that these people must be identified with those whom we call the Umbrians.[1] This conclusion, established solely on archæological grounds, is confirmed by the close connection between Celtic and Italic speech,

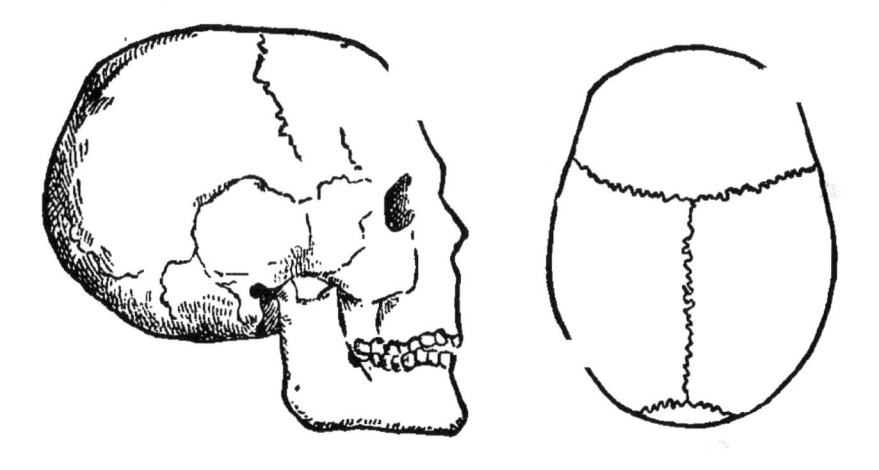

HELVETIAN SKULL [SION TYPE].

and also by the almost identical civilisation disclosed by the pile dwellings of Italy and those of Switzerland.

Further, the craniologists have proved that while the people of Southern Italy are dolichocephalic, belonging apparently to the Iberian race, they become more and more brachycephalic as we go northward, especially in the district between the Apennines and the Alps. In Venetia, Lombardy, and the Emilia, the region occupied by the Umbrians, Professor Calori has measured 1106 modern skulls, of which

[1] Helbig, *Die Italiker in der Poebene*, pp. 29-41.

963, or 87 per cent., were brachycephalic, with indices above 80. In Lombardy and the Emilia dolichocephalic skulls, with indices under 74, amounted to less than 1 per cent. In the Neapolitan provinces, on the other hand, 17 per cent. of the skulls had an index below 74, and 64 per cent. below 80.[1] The mean index of the Umbrian skulls found in a pre-Etruscan cemetery at Bologna is 79.35, and the index of a typical ancient Umbrian skull, which is figured by Professor Calori, is 81.79.

Latin and Umbrian were merely dialects of the same language, but in Rome there was a large admixture of Etruscan and Campanian blood. Skulls of the pure Latin race are rare, owing to the prevalent practice of cremation, while skulls ostensibly Roman often prove on investigation to be those of freedmen or provincials. The best accredited genuine skull of the old Latin race comes from a sarcophagus discovered in the Roman cemetery at York. We learn from the inscription that this sarcophagus contained the body of Theodorianus of Nomentum, a town in Latium. This skull, figured on the following page, is of the brachycephalic Celtic type, the cephalic index being 80.

There is a very marked resemblance in the outlines of the Latin and Helvetian skulls, and those of the better class from the British round barrows. They exhibit no greater differences than the refinement of type due to the progress from neolithic barbarism to the high civilisation of Rome.

The oldest Umbrian settlements—such as the pile-dwellings in the Lake of Fimon, near Vicenza—prove

---

[1] Peschel, *Völkerkunde*, p. 60.

that the Umbrians, when they arrived in Italy, were in much the same stage of civilisation as the undivided Aryans. They lived chiefly by the chase, but had

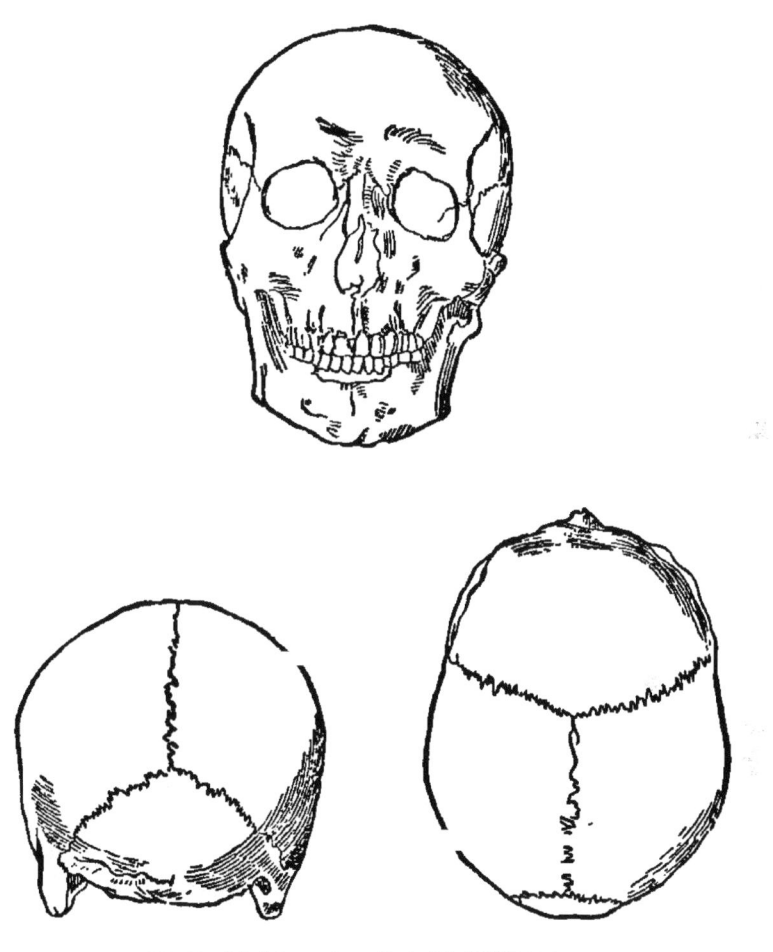

SKULL OF THEODORIANUS OF NOMENTUM.

domesticated the ox and the sheep. Agriculture, even of the rudest description, seems to have been unknown, since no cereals were found; but there were considerable stores of hazel nuts, of water-chestnuts, and of acorns, some of which had been already roasted for food.[1]

[1] Keller, *Lake Dwellings*, vol. i. p. 375.

Before the arrival of the Umbro-Latin race, Italy was inhabited by Iberian and Ligurian tribes. In the neolithic cave at Monte Tignoso, near Leghorn, two skulls were found—one of them dolichocephalic, with an index of 71, doubtless Iberian; the other highly brachycephalic, with an index of 92, probably Ligurian. Another neolithic cave, the Caverna della Matta, contained an Iberian skull, index 68, and a Ligurian skull, index 84. The Olmo and Isola del Liri skulls, believed to be of palæolithic date, are dolichocephalic.

The round barrow race, which we have now traced from the Tyne to the Tiber, extended eastward down the Danube, and across the great plain of Russia. All the nations of Slavic speech are brachycephalic, and their hair and eyes are mostly light in colour.

The Great Russians, who occupy the territory east of a line from the Sea of Azov to the Gulf of Finland, have chestnut hair, brown eyes, and a mean index of 80.2. The White Russians, who occupy the old Lithuanian territory, have flaxen hair, and grey or light blue eyes. Black hair and eyes are only found among the Little Russians, near Kiev, who are probably largely of Tartar race.

The index of the Ruthenians in Galicia is 80.4; of the Slovaks, 81; of the Croats, 82; of the Czechs, 82.1; of the Roumanians, who are to a great extent of Slavic blood, 80; of the Poles, 79.4; of the Serbs, 78.8.[1]

The same light-haired brachycephalic type prevails

---

[1] Peschel, *Völkerkunde*, p. 59 Weisbach's measurements are somewhat higher. He gives for the Ruthenians 82.3; Poles, 82.9; Czechs, 83 1. Broca gives 82.8 for the Roumanians, and 84 83 for the Croats.

also when we pass beyond the frontier of Aryan speech into Finno-Ugric territory.

The Finno-Ugric tribes are all brachycephalic, and most of them have light eyes and fair or rufous hair. Of the Wotiaks 50 per cent. have blue eyes; the rest are grey, green, or brown eyed, black eyes being unknown. In only 2 per cent. the hair is black. It is usually brown or red, and occasionally flaxen. The Zyrianians of the Petschora have also fair hair and blue eyes.[1] Many of the eastern Finns, especially the Tscheremis, the Tschuvash, the Woguls, and the Ostiaks of the Obi, have red hair, and the eyes are blue, grey, green, or chestnut. The cephalic index varies from 80.4 to 83.7, and the index of their kinsmen the Magyars is 82.3. The Tavastian Finns have flaxen hair and blue or grey eyes; the Karelians chestnut hair and greyish-blue eyes. Both races are brachycephalic, the Karelians less so than the Tavastians, the index varying from 81.48 to 83.7. The Esthonians are fair, with yellow or flaxen hair and blue eyes. They are brachycephalic, with a mean index of 80.48.

Vambéry describes the Turcomans as ordinarily blonde. The mean cephalic index of the Mongols is 81, which is precisely that of the round barrow people, whom they resemble in their prognathism, their high cheek bones, and the squareness of the face. In all these particulars the Cowlam skull figured on page 71 agrees very closely with the Mongol type.[2]

The foregoing investigation has brought us to the

---

[1] Pösche, *Die Arier*, p. 136.

[2] The Gristhorpe skull figured in the *Crania Ethnica*, Fig. 104, is strikingly Mongolian.

conclusion at which Dr. Thurnam arrived many years ago. He says that to him it appears to be proved that the type of the Celtic skull, at least that of the dominant race in the bronze period in Britain, was of the brachycephalic "Turanian type." How the Celtic became the language of a people with this Turanian skull-form, and how this Turanian skull-form became the skull-form of a Celtic and so-called Indo-European people, are questions which he thinks are yet to be determined. Meanwhile, he continues, the idea of a connection between the ancient Celtic brachycephalic type, and that of the modern Mongolian or Turanian peoples of Asia, cannot be overlooked, and remains for explanation.

In the following pages an attempt will be made to find an answer to the enigma which Dr. Thurnam has so lucidly propounded.

§ 5. *The Iberians.*

It has been shown in the preceding section that some of the chief European races—the Celts, the Danes, the Umbrians, the Romans, and the Slaves—belong to the brachycephalic type found in the neolithic round barrows of Britain. We have seen that they stretch in a broad, continuous zone across Central Europe into Asia. We have now to trace the dolichocephalic long barrow race through Belgium, France, and Spain, and to identify them with their existing representatives.

The Iberians, as they may be conveniently called, were an Atlantic and Mediterranean race. They do not seem to have reached Germany or North-Eastern Europe. Their furthest extension in this direction is marked by a sepulchral cave at Chauvaux on the Meuse, not far from Namur, which contained skulls of the long barrow type, with a cephalic index of 71.8, together with pottery of the neolithic age.[1]

Before the arrival of the brachycephalic Ligurian race, the Iberians ranged over the greater part of France. We trace them in the valleys of the Seine, the Oise, and the Marne,[2] frequently in association with the remains of the Ligurian invaders.

If, as seems probable, we may identify them with the Aquitani, one of the three races which occupied Gaul in the time of Cæsar, they must have retreated to the neighbourhood of the Pyrenees before the beginning of the historic period. It is in this region, mainly in the valley of the Garonne, that their sepulchral caves are the most numerous.

Some of these caves, such as those at Bruniquel, Laugerie Basse, Aurignac, and Cro-Magnon, have been assigned to palæolithic times; but as this early date is now disputed,[3] and as the remains in these older caverns differ to some extent from those of the long barrows, it will be safer to begin by leaving all doubtful interments out of account, and confine ourselves to caves whose neolithic age is undisputed. For the determination of the characteristics of this Iberian or Aquitanian race no more typical sepulchre can be selected than the celebrated Caverne de l'Homme Mort in the Department of the Lozère. It lies in an inaccessible and desolate ravine which traverses a barren limestone plateau. Here the feeble Iberian race seems to have maintained itself for a

---

[1] Dawkins, *Cave Hunting*, p. 217.
[2] De Baye, *L'Archéologie Préhistorique*, p. 129.
[3] *Ibid.*, p. 20.

time, after the more fertile surrounding lands had been seized by the brachycephalic intruders, whose descendants now occupy the region. In this cave some fifty persons must have been interred, and in fifteen cases the skeletons have been so well preserved as to admit of accurate measurement, and even of the determination of the sex.

No such extensive series of neolithic skeletons, all belonging to the same type and to the same period, has been found elsewhere. The skulls have been described by Paul Broca, the most eminent of French anthropologists,[1] whose careful measurements establish the identity of this race with the long barrow people of Britain. Like them, they were orthognathous and dolichocephalic, with oval faces, mild features, weak and slender forms, and short stature. They agree both in the shape of the skull and in the peculiar formation of the bones of the leg. The tallest of those buried in this cave slightly exceeded 5 feet 5 inches, the mean stature being 5 feet 3¾ inches. The mean stature of the skeletons in the Perthi-Chwareu cave in Denbighshire was 5 feet 4 inches, that of the long barrow people 5 feet 4½ inches.

The long barrow people of Britain were, as we have seen, extremely orthognathous. This is the most characteristic feature of the skulls in the Caverne de l'Homme Mort. The Guanches and the Corsicans are the most orthognathous of existing races, and next to them come the Spanish Basques. The men of the Caverne de l'Homme Mort plainly belong to the same racial group, being more orthognathous even than the Guanches.

---

[1] Broca, *Revue d'Anthropologie*, vol. ii. pp. 1-53.

These races agree also in constituting a great leptorhinic group, distinguished by an extremely low nasal index. This index is for the Guanches, 44.25; for the Berbers, 44.28; for the Spanish Basques, 44.71; and for the Caverne de l'Homme Mort, 45.46. They agree also in cranial capacity. The mean for male skulls is, for the Corsicans 1552 cubic centimetres; for the Guanches, 1557; and for the Spanish Basques, 1574. In the Caverne de l'Homme Mort, it rises to 1606.

The orbital index constitutes, in Broca's opinion, one of the surest tests of race. The orbital index of the Guanche mummies and of the skulls in the Caverne de l'Homme Mort is lower than that of the Spanish Basques, which is the lowest of any existing European race.

It would be tedious and needless to discuss in detail the characteristics of the skulls in the neighbouring sepulchral caves of this region. It may suffice to say that some of the most eminent of the French anthropologists—Broca, Mortillet, and De Quatrefages—consider that the people of the Caverne de l'Homme Mort were the survivors of an earlier race which inhabited the same region in the reindeer period, whose remains have been found in caves at La Madeleine, Laugerie Haute, Aurignac, Laugerie Basse, and Cro-Magnon. This earlier race was tall, athletic, and prognathous. In spite of these differences the general osteological characters are the same, the cephalic index is the same, the mean index at Cro-Magnon being 73.34, and in the Caverne de l'Homme Mort, 73.22. Broca moreover affirms that of all the skulls with which he is acquainted, the nearest approach to the unique and exceptional skull of the old man interred in the

Cro-Magnon cavern is to be found in two Guanche skulls in the Museum at Paris.

Certain characteristic peculiarities in the forms of the bones of the leg and the arm which distinguish the Cro-Magnon skeletons are seen in an attenuated form in several of the skeletons in the Caverne de l'Homme Mort,[1] as well as in some of the Welsh caves, notably in the Cefn Cave near St. Asaph and the Perthi-Chwareu Cave in Denbighshire, where we find interments which may be ascribed to remote ancestors of the people of the long barrows.[2]

The chief importance of the skeletons of the Cro-Magnon type is that in stature, prognathism, and the shape of the orbits they exhibit a greater approximation to the negro type than any others which have been found in Europe.

The Iberian race seems to have extended over the whole Spanish peninsula as well as the coasts and islands of the Mediterranean. In the Genista Cave at Gibraltar two skeletons were discovered with orthognathous and dolichocephalic skulls, which, according to Busk, resemble those found in the Perthi-Chwareu Cave in Denbighshire, and those of the Spanish Basques. One of the Genista skulls had a cephalic index of 74.8 and an

SKULL FROM GENISTA CAVE.

---

[1] Mortillet, *Le Préhistorique*, p. 610.
[2] Dawkins, *Cave Hunting*, pp. 155-159.

altitudinal index of 71.4, and one of the Denbighshire skulls had a cephalic index of 75 and an altitudinal index of 71. The agreement could hardly be more exact.[1]

In the Canaries we find an interesting survival of the customs of these French and Spanish troglodytes. The Guanches of Teneriffe must be regarded as an isolated branch of the Berber race, preserving in great purity the primitive type and mode of life. In Pliny's time the Canaries were uninhabited. When occupied by the Spaniards at the beginning of the fifteenth century the natives were still in the stone age, using caves both for habitation and sepulture. Mummied bodies from the Teneriffe caves are in most of the museums of Europe. The mean cephalic index of these mummies is 75.53; in the Genista Cave at Gibraltar it is 75.5; in the Denbighshire caves, 76.5; in the Caverne de l'Homme Mort, 73.22. The mean index of the Berbers is 74.63; of the Corsicans, 75.35; of the Spanish Basques, 76; of the ancient Egyptians, 75.58.

The same race inhabited Corsica, Sardinia, Sicily, and Southern Italy. In prehistoric caves of Italy and Sicily dolichocephalic skulls of the long barrow type have been found.[2] Seneca informs us that Corsica was peopled by Ligurians and Iberians. Pausanias says that the Sardinians were Libyans, a people whose existing representatives are the Berbers. We learn from Thucydides, and also from a passage of Ephoros preserved by Strabo, that the oldest inhabitants of Sicily were Iberians.

[1] Dawkins, *Cave Hunting*, p. 171. See also the figures on p. 123, *infra*.
[2] See p. 90, *supra*.

These statements are confirmed by modern craniological measurements. It is found that the dolichocephalic type maintains itself in Southern Italy; while Northern Italy is overwhelmingly brachycephalic. In the former States of the Church Professor Calori found 24 per cent. of the inhabitants were dolichocephalic, with indices below 74, and only .04 per cent. in Lombardy.

The ethnology of Greece is obscure, but it is probable that the pre-Hellenic Autochthones belonged to the Iberian race, and that the Hellenic invaders were of the same type as the Umbrians and Romans. Some light is thrown on this question by Dr. Schliemann's excavations at Hissarlik. He discovered four

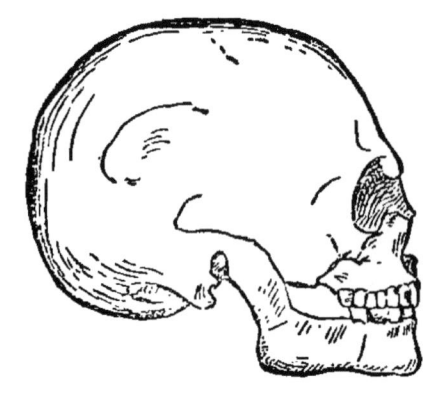

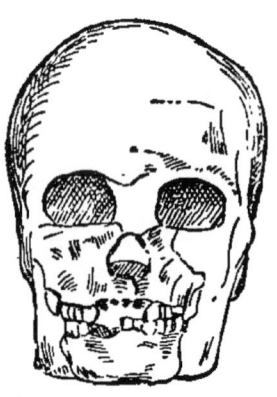

SKULL OF A MAN FROM HISSARLIK [BRONZE AGE].

skulls, which have been put together and described by Professor Virchow. One skull, decidedly brachycephalic, with an index of 82.5, was found in the second or neolithic stratum.[1] This may perhaps be referred to the Ligurian race, which it resembles in some striking features. The other three skulls,[2] found in the burnt city, which is of the bronze age, have indices respectively of 68.6, 71.3, and 73.8, giving a

[1] See p. 114, *infra;* Schliemann, *Ilios*, p. 271.
[2] *Ibid.*, pp. 508, 511.

mean index of 71.23, which agrees with that of the long barrow skulls. They are orthognathous, and in their outline bear some resemblance to those from the Genista cave at Gibraltar, though the cephalic index is lower.

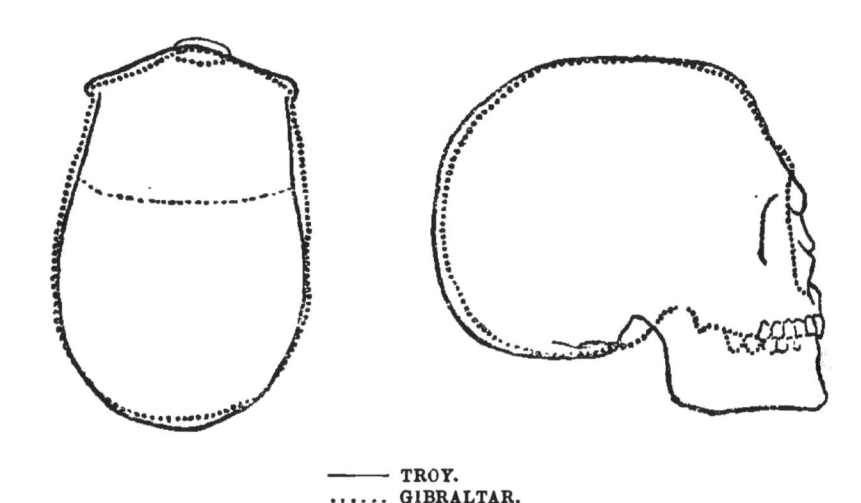

——— TROY.
...... GIBRALTAR.
SKULLS FROM TROY AND GIBRALTAR SUPERIMPOSED.

Unfortunately all the skulls from Hissarlik were so fragile and imperfect as to make it unsafe to draw from them any positive conclusions. Virchow doubtfully refers them to the old Hellenic type, and it is possible that he may be right.

The Iberian race was probably of dark complexion, with black hair and eyes. Their presumed descendants, the Welshmen of Denbighshire, the Irish of Donegal and Kerry, the Corsicans, the Spanish Basques, and the Berbers are swarthy. On the other hand, the Kabyles are of lighter tint, and blue eyes are not uncommon among them, while some of the Guanche mummies appear to have been fair-haired. The Tuariks of the Sahara are fair-haired and blue-eyed.

But the complexion and the colour of the hair and eyes is of less value as an anthropological characteristic than the shape of the skull and of the orbits of the eyes. It is believed that under certain circumstances fair races may become dark, and dark races light, the cuticle, however, being affected sooner than the hair or the iris of the eyes. In the southern, as in the northern hemisphere, we find a zone of lighter coloured people running through the temperate regions. The Caffres of South Africa are not so black as the negroes of the tropics, and in South America the Patagonians and the Fuegians are lighter in tint and taller in stature than the races nearer the Equator. Some of the Araucanians of Chili are almost white. The physical strength and great stature which distinguish the northern Europeans are reproduced under similar conditions of climate among the Patagonians.

The Cro-Magnon people were exclusively hunters and fishers; they had no domestic animals and no cereals. They were acquainted with fire, and were clad in skins, which they stitched together with bone needles. They wore collars and bracelets of shells strung together, and painted or tattooed themselves with metallic oxides. They were not destitute of religious ideas, since they believed in a future life; the care bestowed on the interments and the objects deposited with the deceased proving that they thought the spirits of the dead had wants beyond the tomb, and were able to make use of ornaments and weapons.[1]

From distant parts of Europe where the remains of the Iberian race are found there is evidence that

[1] De Quatrefages, *Hommes Fossiles*, p. 68.

they were occasionally addicted to cannibalism. Such evidence is supplied by human bones which have been broken in order to extract the marrow. The best authenticated cases come from a cave in the island of Palmaria in the Gulf of Spezzia,[1] from Keiss in Caithness,[2] and from the Césareda Caves in the valley of the Tagus.[3]

If, as is contended by Broca and De Quatrefages, the Cro-Magnon people exhibit a remote ancestral type of the Iberian race, the question of the ultimate origin of the Iberians would be greatly simplified. Broca considers that their resemblance to the Berbers shows that they immigrated into Europe from Africa, while the resemblance of the Guanche and Berber skulls to those of the ancient Egyptians allies them to the great Hamitic stock, the Cro-Magnon skeletons forming a link between the Berbers and the negroes.

On the ground that the Iberian type is found as far north as Caithness, Professor Boyd Dawkins believes in its Asiatic origin. The difficulty in the way of this view is that while the Iberian type of skull stretched continuously in neolithic times from Britain through France and Spain to Africa, it has not been found in Northern Europe east of Namur.

If, however, the abnormal Neanderthal skull may be regarded as a remote prototype of the typical Scandinavian skull, and if the equally abnormal Cro-Magnon skull may be regarded as an archaic form of the Iberian type, the difficulty would not be so great, as these two abnormal types agree more closely than the less savage types which prevailed in more recent periods.

[1] Dawkins, *Cave Hunting*, p. 259. [2] *Ibid.* p. 197. [3] *Ibid.* p. 146.

§ 6. *The Scandinavians.*

In Britain three cranial types characterise the three ages of stone, bronze, and iron. The "Iberian" type is distinctively neolithic, the "Celtic" type prevailed in the bronze period, while in graves of the iron age a new type appears, which we may call the "Scandinavian" or "Teutonic."

The skulls from these Anglo-Saxon graves, although dolichocephalic, like those from the long barrows, are unmistakably dissimilar. The forehead is more retreating, the cranial vault lower, and the mean cranial capacity much less, in the one case amounting to 1524 cubic centimetres, or 93 cubic inches, in the other only to 1412 cubic centimetres, or 86 cubic inches.

The bony structure of the face is also different. The Iberians were highly orthognathous, the Anglo-Saxons somewhat prognathous. The Anglo-Saxon jaw was powerful, the Iberian weak. The Iberian face, during life, would appear feeble, owing to its narrowness, and especially to the long weak chin, whereas the facial bones of the Anglo-Saxons were massive. Moreover, one race was tall, often over six feet, the other exceptionally short.

An earlier and more typical form of the Teutonic skull, which is known as Ecker's "Row Grave" type, with a mean index of 71.3, has been found in numerous graves of the iron age in the south-west of Germany. These are assigned to Frankish and Alemannic warriors of the fourth and following centuries. This Row Grave type differs hardly at all from a type with a mean index of 70.7 found in graves of the post-Roman period in Western Switzerland, which is called the Hohberg type by the authors of the *Crania Helvetica*. That the Hohberg type is that of the Burgundians has been established by the recent discovery at Bassecourt, some eighteen miles south-west of Basel, of a Burgundian cemetery containing five skulls of the Hohberg type, with indices varying from 70.1 to 73.9, giving a mean index of 72.3.[1]

The Row Grave men were tall, often upwards of six feet in height, in which they resemble the Swedes who are the tallest existing race in Europe. The forehead is narrow, the brow low and retreating, the cranial vault low, the nose narrow but prominent, the orbital ridges are well marked, and the back of the skull greatly developed.

This Row Grave type of skull having been found over the whole region of Gothic, Frankish, Burgundian, and Saxon conquest, as well in England as in France, Spain, Italy, and Eastern Europe, it must be taken to represent the type of the old Teutonic race. It still survives in Sweden, as Ecker has shown by a comparison of his Row Grave skulls, whose mean index is 71.3, with two modern Swedish skulls, having indices of 69.5 and 72.2.

Owing probably to the infusion of Slavonic or Celtic blood this type is practically extinct in other Teutonic lands, with the exception of certain Frisian districts, notably the islands of Urk and Marken in the Zuider Zee, where Virchow claims to have discovered pure descendants of the old Frisian race. These islanders are more platycephalic even than the

[1] Kollman, *Craniologische Gräberfunde in der Schweiz*, p. 360. (Verhandlungen der Natürforschenden Gesellschaft in Basel, vol. vii, 1882.)

Hottentots, the mean altitudinal index being as low as 69.8, while in a characteristic skull from Marken, which Virchow has figured, it is only 67. Nowhere else are skulls of the Neanderthal type so numerous as here.[1]

In the neolithic age this platycephalic type extended from the mouths of the Rhine to the Neva, and as far south as Galicia. It has been found by Schaffhausen in Westphalia and by Virchow east of St. Petersburg. In prehistoric Pomeranian graves Dr. Lissauer has found platycephalic skulls with an index of 70, and a cranial capacity of less than 80 cubic inches, lower than that of the Bosjemen, and not far above that of the Neanderthal skull, which is estimated at 75 cubic inches. Nilsson and Von Düben affirm that in the neolithic period, and throughout the bronze and iron ages, down to the present time, the same type has continuously prevailed in Sweden.

The lands vacated by the Goths, Vandals, and Burgundians in Northern Germany were re-occupied by brachycephalic Slaves, who have since been Teutonised.

Denmark, though Scandinavian in speech, is no longer purely Scandinavian in blood. The modern Danes belong rather to the brachycephalic Slavo-Celtic type; but whether by blood they are Celts or Slaves is doubtful.

At all events the change of type began early, as is proved by the neolithic tumulus at Borreby, in the island of Falster,[2] where we find dolichocephalic skulls of the Row Grave type, with indices as low as 71.8,

[1] Virchow, " Anthropologie der Deutschen," in *Transactions of the Berlin Academy* for 1871, p. 52.
[2] See p. 82, *supra*.

but mostly between 72 and 73, together with brachycephalic skulls resembling those of the British round barrows, with indices usually between 80 and 83, but in one case as high as 85.7. No craniologist would admit that they can belong to the same race.

The interments in the Borreby tumulus seem to indicate that the dolichocephalic aborigines were conquered, and probably Aryanised, by brachycephalic invaders of the same Slavo-Celtic race which buried in the round barrows of Britain, while the dolichocephalic skulls from Borreby must be assigned to the people of the shell mounds.

The most undoubted representative skull of this kitchen midden race comes from Stængenæs in Sweden, where in 1844 Nilsson discovered in an undisturbed portion of a kitchen midden, at a depth of 3 feet, the skeleton of a man whose stature exceeded 5 feet 10 inches, and whose skull was of a marked dolichocephalic type, with an index between 72 and 73.[1]

The kitchen middens belong to the early part of the neolithic age, if indeed they are not mesolithic, bridging over the supposed hiatus between neolithic and palæolithic times. The French anthropologists are inclined to believe that the ancestors of the Scandinavian race may be traced still further back, and be identified with the savages who peopled Northern Europe in the palæolithic age. But as some doubt attaches to this conclusion, we may provisionally designate them as the Canstadt race —a name given to them by De Quatrefages and Hamy from a skull found in 1700 at Canstadt, near

[1] Nilsson, *Les Habitants primitifs de la Scandinavie*, quoted by De Quatrefages, *Hommes Fossiles*, p. 19; cf. Hamy, *Précis*, p. 129.

Stuttgart, associated, it is said, with bones of the mammoth. A similar skull was discovered in 1867, together with remains of the mammoth, at Eguisheim, near Colmar, in Alsace.

The celebrated Neanderthal skull (index, 72), found near Dusseldorf in 1857, is less human and more simian in character than any other known skull, but is nevertheless classed by Hamy and De Quatrefages as belonging to their Canstadt type. Its precise age is doubtful, and it would be unsafe to regard it as the type of a special race, since its characteristics, as we shall presently see, have been occasionally reproduced in modern times.

A more favourable specimen of this type is the celebrated skull (index, 70.52) which was found seventy miles south-west of the Neanderthal in a cavern at Engis, on the left bank of the Meuse, eight miles south-west of Liège. It was embedded in a breccia with remains of the mammoth, the rhinoceros, and the reindeer. It has usually been referred to the quaternary period, but as a fragment of pottery was found in the same deposit it is possible that the contents of the cave may have been swept in by water, so that the skull may be only of neolithic age.

Of this Engis skull Virchow writes, " It is so absolutely dolichocephalic that if we were justified in constituting our ethnic groups solely with reference to the shape of the skull, the Engis skull would without hesitation be classed as belonging to the primitive Teutonic race, and we should arrive at the conclusion that a Germanic population dwelt on the banks of the Meuse prior to the earliest irruption of a Mongolic race."

In the oldest skulls of the Canstadt race the ridges

over the eyes are greatly developed, the cranial vault is low, the forehead retreating, the eye orbits enormous, the nose prominent, but the upper jaw is not so prognathous as the lower. This primitive savage, the earliest inhabitant of Europe, was muscular and athletic, and of great stature. He had implements of flint, but not of bone, and was vain of his personal appearance, as is proved by his bracelets and necklaces of shells. He was a nomad hunter, who sheltered himself in caves, but was without fixed abodes, or even any sepulchres.

The chief interest that attaches to these repulsive savages is that French anthropologists consider them to be the direct ancestors of their hereditary enemies the Germans, while German anthropologists assert that the Teutons are the only lineal representatives of the noble Aryan race. How far this contention can be maintained we shall hereafter see.

That the earliest inhabitants of Europe belonged to the Canstadt race may, however, probably be granted, since skulls of this type have been found underlying those of the Iberian and Ligurian races in the very oldest deposits at Grenelle;[1] while in many cases there are indications, more or less trustworthy, of the Canstadt race having been contemporary with the extinct pachyderms.

Its chief habitat seems to have been the valley of the Rhine, but it extended to the south as far as Würtemberg, and to the east as far as Brüx in Bohemia. Only at a later time, when the reindeer had retreated to the north, it reached the shores of the Baltic.

Though this type has now become extinct in Germany, owing to the prepotence of the Celtic or

[1] See p. 116, *infra.*

Turanian race, and though it has been favourably modified by civilisation in Scandinavia, yet even in modern times we find curious instances of atavism or reversion to an earlier type. These cases are found chiefly among men of Norman or Scandinavian ancestry. Such may occasionally be noticed in the Scandinavian districts of England. The skull of Robert Bruce, who was of pure Norman blood, exhibits a case of such reversion. Another case is that of the skull of St. Mansuy, or Mansuel, the Apostle of Belgic Gaul, who in the fourth century became Bishop of Toul in Lorraine. A still more remarkable case is that of Kai-Likke, a Danish gentleman who lived in the seventeenth century, whose skull is of the Neanderthaloid or Canstadt type, with receding forehead, and an enormous development of the supraciliary ridges.[1]

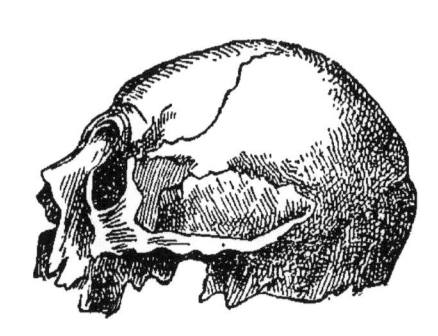

SKULL OF ST. MANSUY, BISHOP OF TOUL.

Zeuss, Pösche, Penka, and other writers[2] have collected a large number of passages from ancient authors which show that the Germans had the tall stature, yellow hair, and blue eyes of the modern Scandinavians. Ausonius describes the blue eyes and yellow hair of a Suevic maiden. Lucan mentions the *flavi Suevi*, Claudian the *flavi Sicambri*, Martial the *flavorum genus Usipiorum*.

---

[1] De Quatrefages, *Hommes Fossiles*, pp. 61-64.
[2] Zeuss, *Die Deutschen*, p. 50, seq.; Pösche, *Die Arier*, p. 25, seq.; Penka, *Or. Ar.*, p. 122; Diefenbach, *Or. Eur.*, p. 161, seq.; De Belloguet, *Eth. Gaul.*, ii. p. 64, seq.

Tacitus speaks of the *truces et caerulei oculi, rutilæ comæ, magna corpora* of the Germans, and according to Calpurnius Flaccus, *Rutili sunt Germanorum vultus et flavi proceritas*, and Procopius describes the Goths as tall and handsome, with white skins and fair hair.

There is a superficial resemblance between the Teutons and the Celts, but they are radically distinguished by the form of the skull. No anthropologist would admit that the Row Grave skulls and the round barrow skulls could belong to the same race. Both races, however, were tall, large limbed, and fair-haired. But the pink and white complexion of the Teuton is different from the more florid complexion of the Celt, who is inclined to freckle. The eyes of the pure Teutons are blue, those of the Celts green, grey, or greyish-blue. The hair of the Teutons is golden, that of the Celts is often fiery red. In the Roman period the Gauls are described as resembling the Germans, but not so tall, so fair, or so savage.

De Quatrefages has conjectured that this race may have roamed farther to the East. He thinks the type may be recognised in the Ainos of Japan and Kamtshatka, and in the Todas of the Neilgherries, who bear no resemblance to any of the contiguous tribes. Both the Ainos and the Todas are fully dolichocephalic, differing in this respect from the Japanese and Dravidians, who are brachycephalic. The profile is of the European type, and instead of the scanty beard of the Mongolians and Dravidians, they are as amply bearded as the Scandinavians, and, like many North Europeans, they have much hair on the chest and other parts of the body.

§ 7. *The Ligurians.*

Cæsar found three races in Gaul, differing in language, laws, and customs. The Aquitani in the South-West have been identified with the long barrow "Iberian" race of Britain; the Belgæ in the North-East were probably of the same race as our own round barrow people; while the Celtæ occupied the central region between the Garonne to the South-West, and the Seine and the Marne to the North-East. Who these Celtæ were is one of the problems of ethnology.

A few years ago they were unhesitatingly identified with the speakers of what we call the "Celtic" languages, the Irish and the Welsh. But in two very ingenious papers, whose arguments have convinced many of the French anthropologists, Broca[1] has maintained that there never have been any Celts in Great Britain or Ireland, that no British people ever called themselves Celts, or were so called by ancient writers, and that they do not possess the physical characters of the Celts of history. The real Celts, he considers, are the people of Central France, who are the descendants of the Celts of Cæsar; so that the term Celt is an ethnological misnomer, if applied to either of the two British races by whom what is commonly called "Celtic speech" is spoken, either the tall, red-haired brachycephalic Irishman and Scot, or the short, dark, dolichocephalic race of Donegal, Galway, Kerry, and South Wales.

A small portion of the Bretons, he says, are the

---

[1] Broca, "La Race Celtique Ancienne et Moderne (*Revue d'anthropologie*, vol. ii. pp. 577-628); and "Qu'est ce que les Celtes?" (*Memoires*, vol. i. p. 370).

only Celts by race who speak a "Celtic" language, and in this case their Celtic speech was acquired from the fugitives who fled to Brittany at the time of the Saxon Conquest of Wessex.

The hilly region of Central France, which was occupied by the Celts of Cæsar, has been continuously inhabited, as Broca maintains, by their lineal descendants, a short, dark, brachycephalic race, who are the true Celts of history and ethnology, as distinguished from the so-called Celts of philology and popular archæology. This type, which cannot with any certainty be traced among the existing population of Great Britain, or in the British barrows, is found in its greatest purity in Auvergne, Dauphiny, Savoy, the Grisons, and the Maritime Alps.

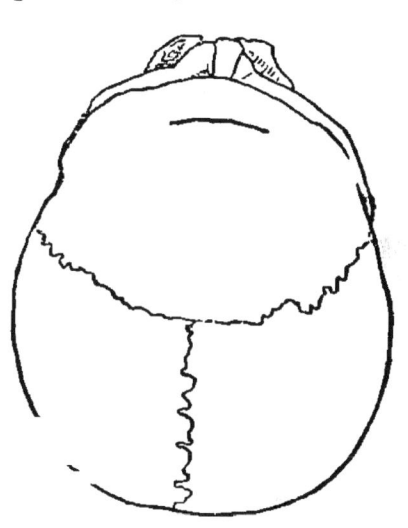

SKULL OF AUVERGNAT.

There can be no doubt, however, that at the time of the Roman Conquest, Cæsar's Celts, the people of Central Gaul, spoke what we call a "Celtic" language; but, as will hereafter be shown, there are reasons for believing that this may have been only an acquired tongue, imposed on them by the Belgic Gauls, and not their primitive non-Aryan form of speech. This acquired tongue was, however, the Aryan language of the so-called "Celtic" people of Britain, and hence modern philologists have assumed an identity of race when there was merely an identity of language.

The true "Celts" of Central France are of short

stature, black-haired, and extremely brachycephalous, having a mean index of 84. The so-called Celts of the British round barrows were, as we have seen, tall, with hair probably rufous or flavous, and only moderately brachycephalous, with a mean index of 81. Many English writers, ignoring Broca's arguments, identify the two races; and they contend that the shorter stature and the darker hair of the race of Central France arose from a union of the short, dark dolichocephalic Iberians with the tall, fair brachycephalic people of the round barrows. But in such case the resulting type would be intermediate between the two parent types; and it is difficult to understand how a race with an index of 72 uniting with another having an index of 81 should have resulted in a race with an index of 84, or how the cross of a tall, fair race with a short, dark race should have produced a hybrid race shorter and darker than either of the parent races.

These difficulties will have to be explained before we are entitled to identify the two brachycephalic "Celtic" races—that of Auvergne, and that of the round barrows.

In any case it must be admitted that the popular usage of the word "Celtic" is unfortunate; the Celts of history and ethnology having probably only an indirect linguistic relation to the Celts of philology. The blunder, if it is a blunder, cannot now be remedied; to use the word Celtic in its strict historical and ethnological sense would be to introduce endless confusion. The word Celtic is too firmly established as a linguistic term to be now displaced, and it has therefore not been discarded in these pages. But if for convenience it has to be employed in its ordinary philological signification, it becomes all the more needful to find some other name for the short, dark, brachycephalic race who are claimed as the true Celts of ethnology and history.

From their physical resemblance to the Lapps the term "Lappanoïde" has been proposed by Prüner-Bey. But as this involves the assumption of a genealogical relationship, which, though not improbable, is only an ethnological hypothesis, it will be better to select some other name. Rhætian, Savoyard, Breton, and Auvergnat have been suggested. Breton is objectionable, as, though the people of the southern part of Brittany are of this race, those of the northern coast were fugitives from the Saxon invasion of Wessex, and belong mainly, as Broca has shown, to the Silurian race. Auvergnat is better than either Rhætian or Savoyard, as Auvergne is in the heart of Cæsar's "Celtic" region. The term Ligurian is, however, very generally used on the ground that the modern Ligurians, who were never Celticised in speech, may claim to be the purest descendants of this race, having an index of 86, higher even than that of the Auvergnats.

The resemblance of this type to the Lapps cannot be overlooked. The mean cephalic index of the Auvergnats is 84 according to Broca, and 84.6 according to Durand. That of the Lapps is 84 by Prüner-Bey's measurements, and 85 by those of Broca. The Auvergnats also resemble the Lapps in their swarthy complexion, and their black hair and eyes. But the chief reason for identification is that the Lapps and Auvergnats agree in having the smallest parietal angle of any existing races—that is, the head is abnormally narrow across the cheek bones, and wide at the temples. The mean parietal angle of the Lapps is 5° 30', with a minimum angle of −3°; the mean angle of the Auvergnats is 2° 30', with minimum of −5°. This peculiarity is seen in the front view of the skull of a girl found by Dr. Schliemann in the second or neolithic stratum at Hissarlik.

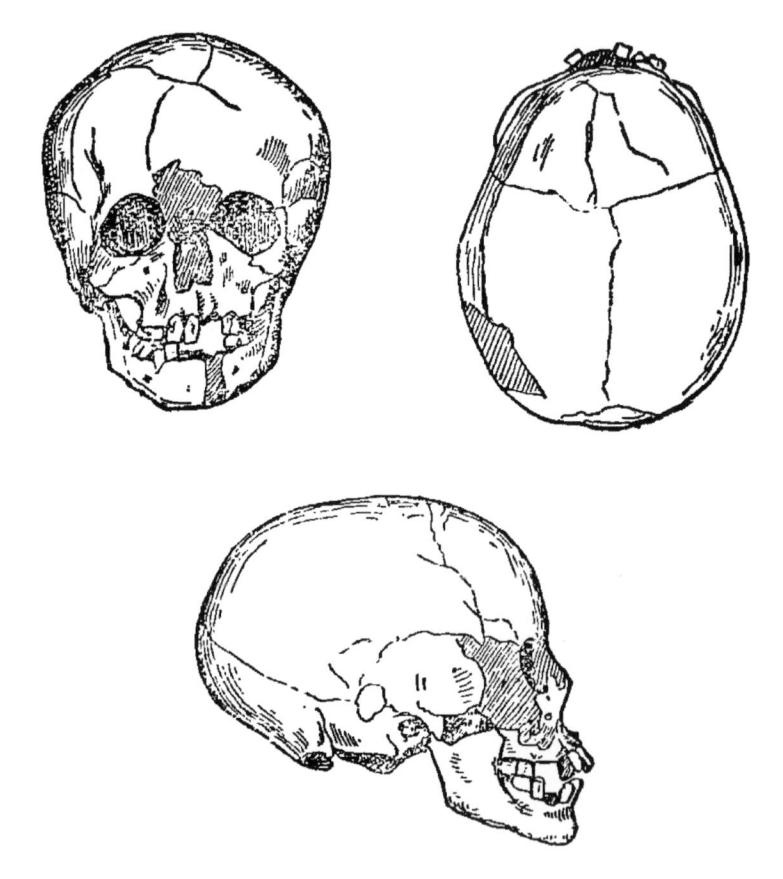

SKULL OF A YOUNG WOMAN FROM HISSARLIK [STONE AGE].

Among the Eskimo, whose heads are pyramidal, the mean parietal angle is as high as 15°, and it is 10° among the Guanches. All the Turanian races, with their broad cheek bones, have a high parietal angle.

Significant also, but less decisive, is the agreement in stature. The Lapps are the shortest race in

Europe, their average stature being 5 feet 2 inches. The Auvergnats are not only the shortest race in France,[1] but the shortest race who now speak any Aryan language.

Attempts have been made to connect the Ligurians with the Finns rather than with the Lapps. The difficulty, or rather the facility, of such contentions arises from the fact that the Finns are not of homogeneous race. The stature, the colour of the hair and eyes, and the cephalic indices differ. Some of them resemble the Slaves, others approach the Swedes, and some share the characteristics of the Lapps, whose language is an archaic form of Finnic speech. The Lapps, however, are orthognathous, and the Finns mostly slightly prognathous. Broca gives 80.39 as the mean index of the Esthonian Finns, and 83.69 as that of the Finns of Finland. The mean stature of the Finns of Finland is given as 5 feet 3 inches.

There is less difficulty in determining the neolithic ancestors of the Ligurians. We must search the dolmens and sepulchral caves of Western Europe for a race combining short stature with a very high cephalic index.

The earliest vestiges of any people who answer to this description have been discovered at Grenelle near Paris.[2] Here, in the alluvium and the underlying

---

[1] French conscripts who measure less than 5 feet 1½ inches are exempted from serving. In the Department of the Puy de Dôme and the two adjacent departments, the Haute Vienne and the Corrèze, which are the home of the Auvergnat race, the exemptions are from 15 to 19 per cent., while in Belgic Gaul they are under 5 per cent. In the Auvergnat Departments the number of conscripts above 5 feet 8 inches is only 3 per cent.

[2] De Quatrefages, *Hommes Fossiles*, p. 72; Penka, *Origines Ariacæ*, p. 91; Hamy, *Précis de Paléontologie Humaine*, p. 252.

gravels, deposited in a bend of the ancient bed of the Seine, skulls of three successive races have been found. The lowest, and therefore the oldest, beds of gravel contain skulls of the Canstadt or Scandinavian type, dolichocephalic and platycephalic, resembling the Stængenæs skull. In the alluvium which overlies the gravel, and at a depth of from 9 to 12 feet from the surface, there are dolichocephalic skulls of the Cro-Magnon or Iberian type. Above these, at a depth of from 4 to 7 feet, are the remains of a short brachycephalic race, quite different from the other two, with a mean stature of 5 feet 3½ inches, and a mean cephalic index of 83.6, measurements which accord very closely with those of the Auvergnats.

Farther to the north, certain limestone caves near Furfooz, in the valley of the Lesse—a small river which joins the Meuse near Dinant in Belgium—have yielded remains of one or possibly two short brachycephalic races. A cave called the Trou-Rosette[1] was inhabited by a race with the high index of 86.1. In a neighbouring cave called the Trou de Frontal skulls were found with indices varying between 79.8 to 81.4. The mean index is 80.35, the mean index of five Esthonian skulls at Paris being 80.35.

The stature of both of the Furfooz races was short. The tallest skeleton measured 5 feet 4 inches, the shortest 4 feet 11 inches. The mean stature of one race was 5 feet 2 inches, that of the other was just over 5 feet. The Trou-Rosette skulls bear a resemblance to those of the Lapps; the Trou de Frontal type, which may still be recognised among the

[1] Hamy, *Précis*, p. 354.

inhabitants of the valley of the Lesse, and among the peasants who frequent the markets of Antwerp, is more prognathous and nearer to the Finns.

Of the stage of civilisation attained by the Grenelle race we know nothing; but the Furfooz races have left many traces of their industries in the caves which they inhabited, and in which they also buried their dead. They seem to have been a peaceful people, possessing no bows and arrows, or weapons for combat, but merely javelins tipped with flint or reindeer horn, with which they killed wild horses, reindeer, wild oxen, boars, goats, chamois, and ibex, as well as squirrels, lemmings, and birds, especially the ptarmigan.

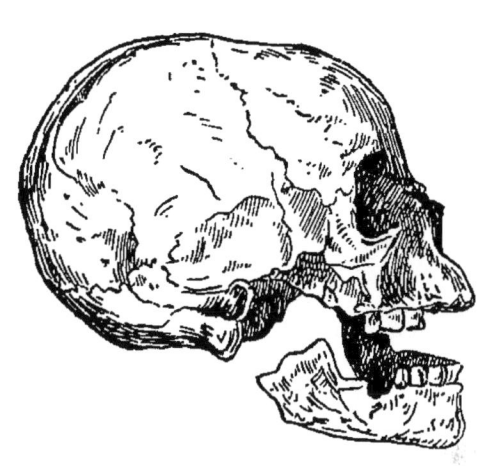

SKULL FROM THE TROU DE FRONTAL.

Some of these animals, especially the reindeer, the ibex, the chamois, and the ptarmigan, prove that the climate was then subarctic. As the climatal conditions grew less severe some of these people may have followed the reindeer and the ptarmigan to more northern latitudes, while others accompanied the ibex and the chamois to the Alps, or conformed themselves, in the hilly regions of Central France, to new conditions of existence.

Their clothing consisted of skins, sewn together with bone needles. They tattooed or painted themselves with red oxide of iron, and wore as ornaments, shells, plaques of ivory and jet, and bits of fluorspar. But the most noticeable fact is that the materials for their ornaments and weapons were brought from distant regions far to the south and south-west, which are now inhabited by a similar short brachycephalic race, while they seem to have been unable to avail themselves of the natural resources of the contiguous districts to the north and the north-east, where the ethnic type is different. The flints for their implements were not obtained from the chalk formation of Hainault, a few miles to the north, but must have been brought from Champagne, and even from Touraine, more than 250 miles distant in a direct line. The jet came from Lorraine, and the shells from Grignon. Manifestly these people of the valley of the Lesse—some fifteen miles south of Namur—could range upwards of 300 miles to the south-west, but not more than twenty-five miles to the north, or they would have got their shells from Liège instead of from the Loire, and their flints from Hainault instead of from Champagne. Here, therefore, we recognise an ancient ethnic frontier. The people of the Lesse were unable to pass the line of the Sambre and the Meuse; the hills of Hainault must have been held by a hostile and more powerful race.[1]

That this was the case is also indicated by the fact that near Mons, forty miles north-west of the Lesse, deposits of flint instruments have been discovered, differing in type as well as in material from those found in the valley of the Lesse. The latter agree in type with those of the Dordogne in central France, while the implements from Mons agree with those found in the valley of the Somme and other

[1] De Quatrefages, *Hommes Fossiles*, p. 74.

districts of Belgic Gaul. At a later time these distinctions disappear, the weapons are made of Hainault flint, and the types are the same as in the Hainault district.[1]

It would appear, therefore, that in the early neolithic age the Auvergnat race was pressed back in Southern Belgium by a more powerful northern people who, we may conjecture, were the ancestors of the Belgic Gauls.

But while the Auvergnat race was in retreat on their northern frontier they were themselves encroaching on the territory of the feebler Iberian people to the south.

The artificial sepulchral grottoes of the Marne, excavated in the soft chalk of this region, form the transition between the natural caves used for sepulture on the Lesse, and the later dolmens of Central France. In these grottoes we find evidence that the brachycephalic people of the Lesse lived in peaceable association with the dolichocephalic Iberian race. They contain skulls with cephalic indices varying from 71.65, which agrees with that of the Iberians, up to 85.71, which is that of the Furfooz people.

Three hundred miles farther south is the Department of the Lozère, now inhabited by the brachycephalic Auvergnat race. The Caverne de l'Homme Mort and other early sepulchral caves of this district contain only dolichocephalic skulls of the Iberian type.[2] But in the dolmens, which are of later date, M. Prunière has found numerous skulls of a pronounced brachycephalic type, mingled with a few decidedly dolichocephalic, and others of mixed type.

[1] De Quatrefages, *Hommes Fossiles*, p. 104.
[2] See p. 93, *supra*.

Hence we conclude that the cave men were invaded by the dolmen builders. That the invaders met with resistance is proved by the fact that in some of the cave interments arrow-heads, of types believed to have been used only by the dolmen builders, are found embedded in the bones.[1] Hence De Quatrefages concludes that early in the neolithic age the dolichocephalic autochthones of this region were attacked by an intrusive brachycephalic race in a higher state of civilisation; that the two races ultimately amalgamated; and that finally the dolichocephalic race was either absorbed, or retired to the south-west, where, in the district between the Lozère and the Aveyron, there are dolmens containing only dolichocephalic skulls.[2] It is believed that the Spanish Basques represent the earlier race, the Auvergnats the invaders, and the French Basques the mixed race.

The chief importance of these researches consists, as we shall hereafter see, in their bearing on the moot question of the linguistic affinities of the Basque speech.

The Auvergnats are separated from the Savoyards, who belong to the same type, by the valley of the Rhone, which is inhabited by a later intrusive race of much higher stature.

We are informed by Zosimus that there were "Celts" in Rhætia.[3] Here, consequently, if Broca's theory as to the Celts is correct, we ought to find traces of a people of the Auvergnat type. In the prehistoric graves of Eastern Switzerland, the ancient

---

[1] De Quatrefages, *Hommes Fossiles*, p. 99.
[2] *Ibid.*, p. 105.
[3] Zeuss, *Die Deutschen*, p 229.

Rhætia, we find brachycephalic skulls which constitute what is called the Disentis type by the authors of the *Crania Helvetica*.[1] The mean cephalic index is 86.5, higher than that of any existing race. The nearest approach to it is 86, which Broca gives as the mean index of the modern Ligurians, and 85, which is that of the Lapps. A skull of the Disentis type was found in the neolithic stratum of the cone of the Tinière, to which an antiquity of from 6000 to 7000 years has been assigned by M. Morlot.[2]

The pile dwellings in the lakes of Northern and Western Switzerland were, as we have seen,[3] probably erected by the Helvetians, a people akin to the Umbrians and the Belgic Gauls.

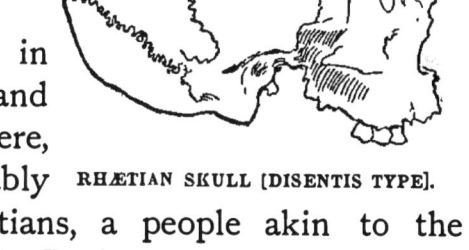

RHÆTIAN SKULL [DISENTIS TYPE].

The Helvetic and Rhætian skulls, though both brachycephalic, are very different. The first agree with those of the round barrow people of Britain, the second with those of the Ligurians, and to some extent with those of the Lapps.

The mean index of ninety-five skulls from British round barrows is 81, that of seven skulls from the lake-dwellings is 80.3. The index of the Disentis type varies from 81.8 to 97.5, the mean being 86.5. The index of the modern Lapps is 84 or 85, and it seems formerly to have been even higher, skulls from an ancient Lapp cemetery giving an index of 90.28. The mean cranial capacity of the round barrow

---

[1] His and Rütimeyer, *Crania Helvetica*, passim.
[2] See p. 59, *supra*.
[3] See p. 86, *supra*.

people was 98 cubic inches, of the Helvetii 97, of the Rhætians 83. The Rhætians, like the Lapps, are orthognathous, while the round barrow people were prognathous.

The authors of the *Crania Helvetica* are of opinion that the Rhætian type is quite distinct from that of the British round barrows and of the Danish tumuli. On the other hand, Dr. Thurnam maintained that the brachycephalic races of Britain, France, and Denmark are cognate with the modern Finns. Professor Huxley goes further, and considers that the Disentis type, the South Germans, the Slaves, and the Finns all belong to one great race of fair-haired, broadheaded Xanthochroi, "who have extended across Europe from Britain to Sarmatia, and we know not how much further to the east and south."

Professor Boyd Dawkins, in spite of the difference of stature, thinks the short Furfooz type is the same as that of the tall people of the round barrows of England, and of the neolithic tombs at Borreby and Moen.[1] With all deference to the opinions of these high authorities, it seems more in accordance with the evidence to class the tall people of the round barrows, who were almost certainly xanthous in hair and complexion, with the tall, red-haired Ugric race, and to class the short, brachycephalic race of France, Belgium, and Switzerland, who were almost certainly dark, with the Lapps, or possibly with some of the Finns. But as stature, prognathism, and the colour of the hair and eyes are more variable characteristics than the shape of the skull and of the orbits, it is possible that the two brachycephalic types, the Celts of ethnology and the Celts of philology, may be remote branches of the

[1] Dawkins, *Cave Hunting*, p. 238.

THE PREHISTORIC RACES OF EUROPE. 123

same race, which, with Dr. Thurnam, we may call "Turanian." But for the purposes of the present inquiry it has seemed safer to consider them provisionally as distinct, more especially as the short, dark Ligurian race appear in Europe at a much earlier period than the tall, fair Celto-Slavic people. Certain linguistic theories bearing on the possible ultimate relationship of the two brachycephalic races will be discussed in a subsequent chapter.

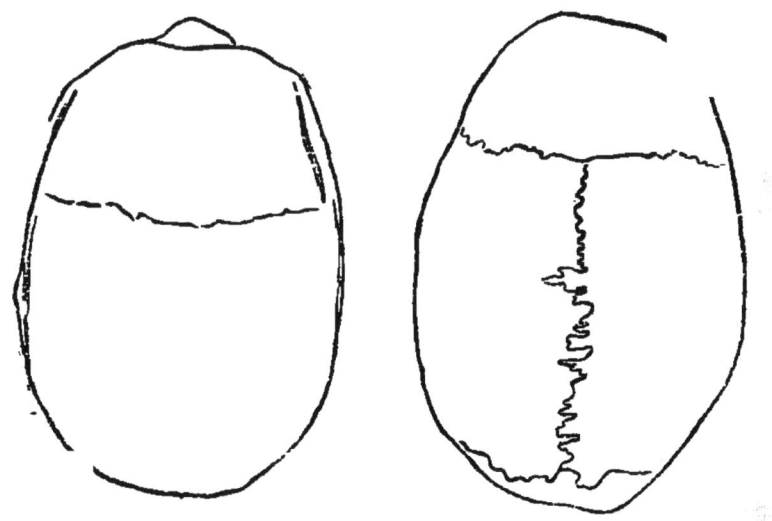

SKULL FROM GENISTA CAVE, GIBRALTAR.

DOLICHOCEPHALIC SILURIAN SKULL FROM RODMARTON, GLOUCESTERSHIRE.

It has been already observed[1] that it is not impossible that the two dolichocephalic races may have descended, at some very remote period, from common ancestors. If, as De Quatrefages and Broca maintain, we may take the Cro-Magnon race as the ancestral type of the Iberians, and the Canstadt race as that of the Scandinavians, we find in the very oldest skulls a certain approximation of type. There was a time when the only inhabitants of Europe

[1] See p. 101, *supra.*

were dolichocephalic, and it is not impossible that the Neanderthal and Cro-Magnon people may have been descended from a common palæolithic stock, and both of the brachycephalic races from another. We should thus have only two primitive races to deal with, instead of the four which we recognise in tombs of the later neolithic age.

CHAPTER III.

THE NEOLITHIC CULTURE.

§ 1. *The Continuity of Development.*

THIRTY years ago, when the science of prehistoric archæology was in its infancy, the so-called "Finnic theory" was very generally accepted. The philologists having determined, to their own satisfaction, that the Aryans had migrated from Central Asia, the archæologists proceeded to identify them with the introducers of metal into Europe. They affirmed that prior to the Aryan migration neolithic Europe was occupied by Finnic races, who were encountered and exterminated by Aryan invaders armed with the bronze weapons which they brought with them from the East. It was also asserted that these Aryan invaders introduced most of our domesticated animals and cultivated plants, and were also in possession of an elaborate mythology, consisting chiefly of storm gods, dawn maidens, and solar heroes.

The evidence in support of these theories has now to be investigated, and we have to frame from the evidence of linguistic palæontology an account of the civilisation attained by the undivided Aryans, and to compare it with the picture of neolithic culture as disclosed by the science of prehistoric archæology.

The theory that bronze weapons were introduced into Europe by a conquering people coming from the East has been overthrown, despite the arguments of M. Troyon,[1] by the evidence afforded by the Swiss lake dwellings, which establish the fact that bronze implements were gradually introduced among a neolithic population by the peaceful processes of barter. The successive "relic beds" superimposed one upon another prove that many of the lake settlements were founded in the age of stone, and passed through the age of bronze to the age of iron. No traces of any such hiatus as the Finnic theory demands have been discovered. The fact that with very few exceptions these lake settlements are exactly opposite to some modern town or village built upon the shore[2] shows that habitation has been usually continuous down to our own days. Evidently, as population increased and life became more secure, the limits of the settlement were extended from the water to the land, and the pile dwellings, being no longer needed, gradually fell into disuse.

From an examination of the pile dwellings in the valley of the Po, Helbig has proved that the same gradual transition from stone to bronze took place among the Umbrians, an Aryan people. Here, however, at some time in the bronze age, the Umbrian civilisation was suddenly overthrown by the invasion of the Etruscans, none of these Italian settlements reaching into the age of iron.

Thus the pile dwelling opposite Peschiera, on the

---

[1] Troyon, *Habitations Lacustres des temps anciens et modernes.* M. Troyon's conclusions are completely refuted by Keller, *Lake Dwellings*, p. 667.
[2] Keller, *Lake Dwellings*, p. 671.

Lago di Garda, was founded in the stone age, and was in continuous occupation through the age of copper to the age of bronze.[1] The remains of the settlement in the Lake of Fimon are specially instructive, as it must have been founded very soon after the Umbrians arrived in Italy, and was destroyed before they had passed from the pastoral to the agricultural stage. There are two successive relic beds, the oldest belonging entirely to the neolithic age. The inhabitants did not yet cultivate the soil, but subsisted chiefly by the chase. The bones of the stag and of the wild boar are extremely plentiful, while those of the ox and the sheep are rare. There are no remains of cereals of any kind, but great stores of hazel nuts were found, together with acorns, some of them adhering to the inside of the pipkins in which they had been roasted for food. The settlement seems to have been burnt, and then after a time rebuilt, the newer relic bed containing numerous flint chips and a solitary bronze axe. Cereals are still absent, although acorns, hazel nuts, and cornel cherries are found. But the pastoral stage had plainly been reached, since the bones of the stag and the wild boar become rare, while those of the ox and the sheep are common.[2]

These Italian settlements are of especial importance in our inquiry, as Helbig has satisfactorily proved that they were inhabited by the Umbrians, who spoke an Aryan language. We learn therefore that when the Aryans first reached Italy they were in the early pastoral stage, and were ignorant of agriculture and of metals.

We gather also that the knowledge of metals came from the South and not from the East. Settlements

---

[1] Keller, *Lake Dwellings*, p. 363.   [2] *Ibid.*, p. 368.

exclusively of the stone age are found chiefly north of the Po, while those which contain bronze are mostly farther south. It is the same in Switzerland. Settlements of the stone age are most numerous on the Lake of Constance; those of the bronze age on the lakes of Geneva, Bienne, and Neufchâtel.

Our own island formed the last refuge of the theory that Aryan invaders first introduced metal among a neolithic people. As late as 1880 Professor Boyd Dawkins maintained[1] that the round barrow invaders established themselves among the Silurian aborigines of Britain by the aid of the bronze weapons which they brought with them. But even in this, by far the strongest case, further investigation has shown the probability of the overlapping of the ages of bronze and stone. It has already been shown[2] that bronze is very rarely found in the primary interments of the round barrows, which, at all events in Yorkshire, belong more often to the age of stone than to the age of bronze. Moreover in Britain, as elsewhere, the oldest bronze weapons are plainly modelled on the type of earlier implements of stone, forms which, being unsuitable for bronze, were soon abandoned.[3] The tombs which contain bronze weapons of these archaic forms not infrequently contain stone weapons as well. Thus in a tumulus at Butterwick, in the East Riding of Yorkshire, a bronze celt of the very simplest form, modelled on the pattern of a stone axe, was found, accompanied by a flint knife.[4] In Derbyshire a skeleton was found buried in a hide, with the hair turned inwards, together with an implement of flint

---

[1] Dawkins, *Early Man in Britain*, p. 342.
[2] See p. 79, *supra*. [3] See the engraving on p. 141, *infra*.
[4] Greenwell, *British Barrows*, p. 187, Fig. 38.

and a bronze celt of the plainest stone pattern. No fewer than twenty-seven bronze celts, modelled on the type of stone celts, have been found in England alone,[1] and it is possible to trace the gradual development of the forms more suited to the new material from the forms suited to the old.

Hence it seems most probable that the Aryan invasion of Britain took place in the neolithic age.

These conclusions, which are now generally accepted by archæologists, are fatal to the old theory that the Aryans were a comparatively civilised people, who invaded Europe from the East, bringing with them bronze weapons, which enabled them to subdue the aboriginal inhabitants of Europe who were of Basque or Finnish race. The knowledge of metals proceeded from the Mediterranean northwards, being mainly attributable to the gradual extension of Phœnician commerce.

In no part of Europe has it been proved that there was any interruption of continuity between the ages of stone and metal, and there is no evidence whatever to show that the present inhabitants of Europe are not descended from the people of the neolithic age, whose civilisation was of a very rudimentary character. Hence the grounds on which a comparatively high degree of culture was assigned to the primitive Aryans will have to be reconsidered. The old conclusions were based on philology; but scholars are now inclined to rank the archæological evidence as of chiefest value, and to assign to philology only a subordinate importance.

A good instance of the way in which the conclusions of philology as to early culture have been

[1] Evans, *Bronze Implements*, p. 42.

corrected by the more trustworthy evidence of archæology is supplied by the parallel cases of the horse and the dog. The names of the horse (Sanskrit *açva*, the swift one) and of the dog (Sanskrit *çvan*) are found in almost every Aryan language, and it was formerly supposed that the horse, a native of the steppes of Central Asia, was tamed by the primitive Aryans, and brought with them on their migration to the West.

Now in many of the very early stations, supposed to be palæolithic, such as those at Solutré and Thäyngen, the remains of the horse, associated with those of the reindeer, are extremely abundant, and the animal evidently formed a chief portion of the food of the people; but the horse was manifestly wild. In the oldest of the neolithic Swiss lake dwellings the remains of the horse are absent, or very rare; afterwards they become more common, and in the late bronze age the discovery of bits proves that horses had at last been tamed. Hence it is evident that the common Aryan name for the horse must have referred to the animal as an object of the chase, and has no more significance than the existence of the common names for the wolf and the fox.

With the dog, however, it is different. That the bones of dogs are found in the Danish kitchen middens by itself proves nothing; they may have been eaten like the wolf and the fox, whose bones occur also in the refuse heaps; but we conclude the dog had been domesticated, since those bones of birds and quadrupeds which are eaten by dogs are uniformly absent.[1] Hence it is evident that

[1] Lubbock, *Prehistoric Times*, p. 240; Lyell, *Antiquity of Man*, p. 15.

the conclusions of philology must be received with hesitation, unless they can be checked by evidence supplied by archæology.

The archæological discoveries of the last thirty years have placed the whole question of early Aryan civilisation on a new footing.

In the kitchen middens of Denmark we find the refuse of the feasts of the rudest savages, ignorant of agriculture, subsisting mainly upon shell-fish, and possessing no domesticated animal except the dog.

In the oldest lake dwellings of Germany and Switzerland we find the remains of a people, believed to have been the ancestors of the Celtic race, usually in possession of cattle, but living mainly on the products of the chase. We trace them, during a period which must cover many centuries, at first clad only in skins, then learning to weave mats from the bark of trees, and finally from flax. We find them at first in possession only of the ox, and successively domesticating the goat, the sheep, the pig, and, last of all, the horse. We then see them acquiring by degrees considerable proficiency in agriculture, and passing gradually from the age of stone to the age of bronze, and from the age of bronze to that of iron. In the pile dwellings of Northern Italy we can in like manner trace the same gradual development of civilisation, and the passage from the hunting stage through the pastoral to the agricultural stage, and from the stone to the bronze age, of a people who are believed to have been the ancestors of the Umbrians, and closely related to the Latin race.

Dr. Schliemann's excavations at Mycenæ and Hissarlik belong to a later period of culture, and disclose the remains of nations unacquainted with iron, but possessed of a civilisation splendid in its way, familiar with the uses of bronze, copper, and even of lead, and fabricating in great profusion highly artistic ornaments of gold, ivory, and silver.

It is plain that the civilisation which we find in Europe at the beginning of the historic period was gradually evolved during a vast period of time, and was not introduced, cataclysmically, by the immigration of a new race. Just as in geological speculation great diluvial catastrophes have been eliminated and replaced by the action of existing forces operating during enormous periods of time, so the prehistoric archæologists are increasingly disposed to substitute slow progress in culture for the older theories which cut every knot by theories of conquest and invasion.

The most recent results of philological research, limited and corrected as they have now been by archæological discovery, may be briefly summarised. It is believed that the speakers of the primitive Aryan tongue were nomad herdsmen, who had domesticated the dog, who wandered over the plains of Europe in waggons drawn by oxen, who fashioned canoes out of the trunks of trees, but were ignorant of any metal, with the possible exception of native copper. In the summer they lived in huts, built of branches of trees, and thatched with reeds; in winter they dwelt in circular pits dug in the earth, and roofed over with poles, covered with sods of turf, or plastered with the dung of cattle. They were clad in skins sewn together with bone needles; they were acquainted with fire, which they kindled by means of fire-sticks or pyrites; and they were able to count up to a hundred. If they practised agriculture, which is doubtful, it must have been of a very primitive kind; but they probably collected and pounded in stone mortars the seeds of some wild cereal, either spelt or barley. The only social institution was marriage; but they were polygamists, and practised human sacrifice. Whether they ate the bodies of enemies slain in war is doubtful. There were no enclosures, and property consisted in cattle and not in land. They believed in a future life; their religion was shamanistic; they had no idols, and probably no gods properly so-called, but reverenced in some vague way the powers of nature.

This general picture of primitive Aryan culture has now to be substantiated in detail, and the gradual progress in civilisation and the arts of life has to be traced from the scanty materials which we possess.

§ 2. *Metals.*

That the Aryans, before the linguistic separation, were still in the stone age may be inferred from the fact that no Aryan etymology has been found for the word " metal " ($\mu\acute{\epsilon}\tau\alpha\lambda\lambda ov$), which is regarded by Oppert and Renan as a Semitic loan-word obtained from the Phœnicians. There is no common word in Aryan speech to denote the art of the smith,[1] and many of the words relating to his trade refer primarily to stone. Each of the Aryan families of speech has an independent name for the smith, a sufficient proof that the arts of smelting and forging metal were later than the linguistic separation. More especially the old theory that the Celts were the vanguard of the Aryan race, who brought with them into Europe the knowledge of metals, falls to the ground, in face of

[1] Schrader, *Urgeschichte*, pp. 221-225.

the fact that the Celts have for the smith their own peculiar designation, *goba*, which bears no resemblance to the corresponding words in other Aryan languages, such, for instance, as the Latin *faber*, the Greek χαλκεύς, the Teutonic *smid*, or the Slavonic *vutri*.

The Ural-Altaic races must also have been in the stone age when they came into contact with the Aryans, since the name for the smith was borrowed by the Finns from the Lithuanians, by the Lapps from the Scandinavians, and by the Magyars from the Slaves.

It is a very suggestive fact that the Greek words for the apparatus of the smith—the names for the anvil, the bellows, the tongs, and the furnace—are not related to the corresponding terms in Latin.[1] Even among the Indians and Iranians, whose linguistic separation was so much later than that of the other Aryan races, these words also differ, with the single exception of the name for the furnace, which may primarily have denoted an oven used for other purposes. Not only are there no common Aryan words for the smith and his tools, but there is no common word for iron, or even for tin, a necessary constituent of bronze. Two metals only, gold and copper, are, as a rule, found in the metallic state. They were known both in Egypt and in Babylonia at the earliest period of which we have any historical cognisance, and in all probability they were the first metals with which the Aryans became acquainted. Native gold is very generally distributed, and native copper is found in Saxony, Hungary, Sweden, Norway, Spain, and Cornwall.

The glittering particles of gold found in the sands

---

[1] Helbig, *Die Italiker in der Poebene*, p. 115.

THE NEOLITHIC CULTURE. 135

of so many rivers must have attracted attention at a very early period. But it is clear that gold was unknown to the undivided Aryans. The Greek χρυσός (Hebrew *chārutz*) being a Semitic loan-word, gold must have been first brought to Hellas by the Phœnicians, not earlier than the thirteenth century B.C. We know that the Phœnicians mined for gold at Thasos. The tombs at Spata on Mount Hymettus in Attica, at Thera, at Mycenæ, and at Ialysos in Rhodes, contain objects exhibiting the influence of Phœnician art, and in all of them gold is more or less abundant. These tombs cannot in any case be older than the fourteenth or fifteenth century B.C., as at Ialysos, where the ornament is of the most archaic type, a scarab was found with the cartouche of Amenhotep III.[1] The probable date of the earliest of these tombs is the thirteenth century B.C. But gold was not known in Italy before the eleventh century B.C., since in the latest pile dwellings of the Emilia, which belong to the bronze age, and which even contain amber obtained by commerce from the Baltic,[2] neither gold nor silver has been found. In two or three of the Swiss pile dwellings of the bronze age, which survived to a later time than the pile dwellings of Italy, gold has very sparingly been found; in one instance only has a gold ornament been found in a settlement of the neolithic age.[3]

That gold was unknown to the Aryans when they entered Italy may also be concluded from the fact that its name, *aurum* in Latin, and *ausum* in Sabine,

---

[1] Duncker, *History of Greece*, p. 53; *History of Antiquity*, vol. ii., pp. 63, 72, 73; Newton, *Essays on Archæology*, p. 294.
[2] Helbig, *Die Italiker in der Poebene*, p. 21.
[3] Keller, *Lake Dwellings*, p. 459.

is a word of Italic origin, denoting the "shining" metal, and related to the word *aurora*, the "shining" dawn.

The story of Brennus casting his sword into the scale to be weighed against Roman gold proves that gold must have been known to the Gauls not later than their invasion of Italy in 390 B.C. It is probable that it was not known to them at any earlier time, since the Celtic name (old Irish *ór*, Cymric *awr*) was borrowed from the Latin; and since the primitive *s* could not have changed to *r* in the Celtic speech, the word must have been borrowed after *ausum* had become *aurum* in Latin, a change which could not have been effected much earlier than the invasion of the Gauls.[1]

Gold must, however, have reached the Lithuanians, probably in exchange for amber, before it became known to the Celts, since the old Prussian name *ausis* (Lithuanian *auksas*) exhibits the earlier form of the Italic word. The Albanian *âri* proves that the Illyrians obtained their knowledge of gold at a somewhat later time, and also that they obtained it from Italy and not from Greece.

Gold was known to the Indians before they entered India, and before their separation from the Iranians, since the Sanskrit name, *híranya*, is identical with the Zend *zaranya*, the word being also found in the other branches of the Iranian family—Afghan, Baluchi, and Ossetic. It must have been from the Iranians, probably from Scythic tribes belonging to the Iranian stock, that it penetrated to the Eastern Finns; the Mordwin, Wogul, Ostiak, Wotiak, Zyrianian, and Magyar names, *sarni*, *sorni*, or *sirna*, being loan

[1] Schrader, *Urgeschichte*, p. 251.

words from the Iranian. The Teutonic name *gulth* means the "glowing" or "yellow" metal, and the form of the old Slavonic name *zlato* proves that the Slaves must have borrowed the word from the Teutons at an early period. The Western Finns, however, must have obtained it from the Germans, as is shown by the Esthonian name *kuld*, and the Lapp *golle*.[1]

Hence it appears that gold was not in the possession of the undivided Aryans, but was known to the Indians and Iranians before their separation, and possibly also to the undivided Slaves and Teutons.

Its introduction was later than the separation of the Greeks from the Latins, of the Latins from the Celts, and of the Eastern from the Western Finns. The Greeks obtained it from the Phœnicians, and the Celts, Illyrians, and Lithuanians from the people of Italy.

It was unknown to the Greeks before the thirteenth century, when the Phœnicians reached the coasts of Hellas; it was unknown in Italy in the eleventh century, when the Etruscan invaders destroyed the Umbrian settlements; but it had probably reached Italy as early as the ninth century, when the Greeks and Phœnicians had established themselves at Cumæ and Cære. It reached the Baltic before the fifth century, and Gaul and Illyria in the fourth. In Switzerland bronze was plentiful while gold was still unknown.

The discovery of copper must have preceded that of gold by many centuries. Not only the lake dwellings of Switzerland and Italy, but the Babylonian

[1] See Schrader, *Urgeschichte*, pp. 243-254.

and Egyptian monuments prove that copper was the earliest metal to be discovered.

There is one Aryan word whose wide diffusion has to be explained, and which has been confidently adduced to prove that the undivided Aryans were acquainted with either bronze or copper.[1] This is the Sanskrit *ayas*, which corresponds with the Latin *æs*, the Gothic *aiz*, the German *erz*, and the English *ore*. The Latin *æs* denoted copper as well as bronze, the Gothic *aiz* meant brass or bronze, while the Sanskrit *ayas* is believed to have originally denoted copper, then metal in general, and afterwards iron. If copper was, as seems probable, the first metal to be discovered, it is easy to see that the name might have been generalised to denote metal, and then specialised to denote either iron, brass, or bronze. In any case the original meaning could not have been iron, since, for the linguistic and archæological reasons already stated, it is certain that the primitive Aryans had not reached the iron age.

That the metal designated by *ayas* or *æs* was copper and not bronze is also indicated by the fact that there is no common Aryan name for tin, which is a necessary constituent of bronze. The Greek name κασσίτερος is borrowed from the Semitic (Assyrian *kasazitirra*), which again is derived from the Accadian *id-kasduru*. Two small bars of tin have been found in Swiss pile dwellings of the bronze age, and also at Hallstadt, but tin has not been found at Hissarlik.

Lenormant has drawn attention to a curious fact, very difficult to explain. The oldest known word for copper is the Accadian *urud* or *urudu*. Copper is

---

[1] Schrader, *Urgeschichte*, p. 267.

urraida in Basque, *rauta* denotes iron in Finnic, and *ruda* means metal in old Slavonic, while *rôd* is brass in Beluchi, and *eru* is copper in the Semitic Babylonian. It is difficult to suppose that these resemblances can be merely accidental, and yet there are the strongest reasons for believing that both the Finns and the Basques were in the stone age when they came into contact with the Aryans, since the Basque word for knife primarily means a stone, and the Finnic names for smith are Aryan loan-words.

If the word *ayas*, *æs*, or *aiz* is primitive, and if it meant copper, it is difficult to explain the entire absence of metal from the early Aryan settlements.

Three solutions are possible. It may have been a commercial loan-word, which is improbable. It may originally have denoted not smelted metal but ore, probably the lumps of iron pyrites found not uncommonly in neolithic tombs,[1] and which seem to have been used for procuring fire by striking them with flint, and may afterwards have come to denote the metal smelted out of such heavy stones. A third explanation finds favour with Dr. Schrader. He is inclined to consider the Latin *monile*, a word which reappears in the Indo-Iranian, Greek, Teutonic, and Slavonic languages, as an indication that copper rings, rudely beaten out with stone hammers from lumps of native copper, or obtained by barter from the East, may have been used as ornaments by the undivided Aryans.

The archæological evidence from the Swiss lake dwellings and elsewhere lends as yet no support to this theory, more especially as the earliest bronze celts, all those, for instance, found in the pile dwellings

[1] Greenwell, *British Barrows*, p. 266.

of Northern Italy, are cast and not hammered.[1] It is, however, possible that such copper rings were so rare and precious, being obtained only by barter from the distant East, that they do not happen to have been found.

At all events the Greeks, who were the most advanced in culture of the Aryan nations, seem to have been unacquainted with copper when they were first visited by Phœnician mariners. The Greek name for copper, χαλκός, is isolated in the Aryan languages. It has been supposed either to be a Semitic loan word,[2] or, just as the Latin *æs cuprium*, the source of our word *copper*, was derived from the name of the island of Cyprus, so the Greek word χαλκός, copper, may have been derived from the Eubœan city of Chalcis, which itself may have taken its name from the κάλχη, or purple murex, in quest of which the Phœnicians first resorted to the coast.[3] In either case, the Greeks seem to have been ignorant of copper when the Phœnicians first reached their coasts.

That a copper age preceded the bronze age, and that *ayas* or *æs* originally denoted copper rather than bronze, is also indicated by the fact that some of the oldest metal celts, which are imitations of the earlier stone celts, are of copper, not of bronze. In the museum at Berlin there is a copper celt, found in an Etruscan tomb, which is of the precise shape of an ordinary stone celt,[4] and even appears to have been cast in a mould formed by means of a stone implement of the same type. Celts of the simple flat

---

[1] Helbig, *Die Italiker in der Poebene*, p. 19.
[2] Cf. Hebrew *chălăk*, smooth. Wharton, *Etyma Graeca*, p. 132.
[3] Schrader, *Urgeschichte*, p. 278.
[4] Evans, *Ancient Bronze Implements*, p. 39.

THE NEOLITHIC CULTURE. 141

stone type, without flanges, either of pure copper or of copper with so small a percentage of bronze as to be almost indistinguishable from copper, were found by Dr. Schliemann at Hissarlik, and by General di Cesnola in very early tombs in Cyprus. Flat celts of copper, of the stone type, have also been found in India, Austria, Hungary, France, and Italy.[1]

In the pile dwelling at Maurach on the Lake of Constance, which belongs to the stone age, among fifty stone implements the only object of metal was a broken copper axe.[2] At Sipplingen, also on the Lake of Constance, no bronze implements were found, but there were 350 stone axes, and one of copper, very simple in form, resembling the stone axes.[3] And at Gerlafingen, also a settlement of the stone age, on the Lake of Bienne, were found two chisels of pure copper of the simplest stone type.[4]

The figure represents the copper celt of the stone type from the lake dwelling at Sipplingen.

The recent explorations of the MM. Siret among the prehistoric tombs in the south-east of Spain have clearly revealed the existence of a copper age, intermediate between the stone and bronze epochs. Eighty axes of polished stone, and seventy flat copper axes of the stone type, were discovered in these tombs.

Dr. Evans explains the scarcity of copper imple-

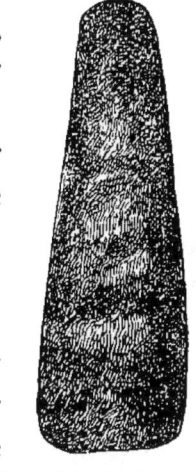

COPPER CELT FROM SIPPLINGEN.

---

[1] Evans, *Ancient Bronze Implements*, p. 40.
[2] Keller, *Lake Dwellings*, vol. i. p. 121.
[3] *Ibid.*, p. 126, plate xxix. [4] *Ibid.*, p. 452.

ments by the supposition that on the discovery of bronze the copper implements were melted down and recast in bronze. But while in many parts of the Continent there is sufficient evidence that the bronze age was preceded by a copper age, there is no such evidence in Britain. It is therefore probable that bronze, introduced by traders from Gaul, was the first metal known in our island. Even as late as Cæsar's time the Britons obtained their bronze by commerce from the Continent. The type of the British bronze weapons differs both from the Scandinavian and the Hungarian types, but agrees with the type characteristic of the north of France. The types in the Swiss lake dwellings agree with those of Northern Italy and the south of France.[1] Hence we conclude that the knowledge of metals penetrated gradually to the north from the Mediterranean lands which were visited by Phœnician ships.

Since silver rarely occurs in a native state, and is a difficult metal to reduce, we cannot be surprised to find that it was unknown to the primitive Aryans. The Celtic and Illyrian names were borrowed from the Latin, the Teutonic and Slavonic from the Semitic, while the Latin, Greek, and Sanskrit names were independent formations. It was probably unknown to the Celts before they invaded Italy, as the Celtic name (old Irish *argat*) is an Italic loan word (Latin *argentum*, Oscan *aragetud*). This word is from the Aryan root *arg*, and means the "white" or "bright" metal. In Greek, Sanskrit, and Zend the name is formed from the same obvious root, but with a different suffix, showing an

[1] Evans, *Ancient Bronze Implements*, pp. 482-484.

independent invention of the word. The two earliest sources of silver seem to have been Armenia and Spain. In the south-east of Spain, where silver occurs in a native state, ornaments of this metal have been found in tombs of the early bronze age. It seems to have become known to the Greeks, probably through Phœnician commerce, shortly before the Homeric period. Dr. Schliemann found silver in the tombs at Mycenæ, which are of the Phœnician style of architecture, and he discovered electrum, a natural alloy of gold and silver, in the second and third strata at Hissarlik. Silver has not been found in the oldest Phœnician tombs in Greece, which may date from the twelfth century B.C., nor as yet in the Italian pile dwellings of the bronze age.[1] But in some of the latest of the Swiss pile dwellings of the iron or late bronze age, probably dating from the fourth or third century B.C., three or four silver ornaments have been discovered. In the time of Herodotus silver was unknown to the nomad Aryan tribes north of the Euxine; but the northern name (Gothic *silubr*), which is common to Lithuanians, Slaves, and Teutons, is believed to be a loan-word from the Semitic (Assyrian *sarpu*), an indication that the Baltic nations first obtained it by the trade route of the Dnieper from the region of the Euxine.[2]

Hence we gather that it reached the Greeks earlier than the tenth century, and the Celts not before the fifth.

There can be no question that the age of iron was later than the age of bronze. The Greek words χαλκεύς, a smith, and χαλκεών, a smithy, are derived

---

[1] Helbig, *Die Italiker in der Poebene*, p. 21.
[2] Schrader, *Urgeschichte*, pp. 256-265.

from the name of copper, not of iron. The pile dwellings in the valley of the Po belong to the ages of stone and bronze, but afford no trace of iron. Hence we obtain an approximate limit for the introduction of iron into Italy. Helbig has shown good reasons for believing that these settlements must be assigned to the Umbrians, an Aryan people, and that they were destroyed at the time of the Etruscan conquest of Northern Italy. Now, according to a tradition preserved by Varro, the Etruscan era began in 1044 B.C., a date which agrees roughly with that assigned to the Thessalean and Dorian invasions of Greece, with which it was probably connected, while the Dorian inroad led to the Mœsian settlements of Æolian, Achæan, and Ionian tribes, dim memories of which lie at the base of the Homeric epos. These events clearly occurred towards the close of the bronze age. Iron was unknown to the Umbrians of Northern Italy at the time of the Etruscan inroad. The third or burnt city at Hissarlik, which Dr. Schliemann identifies with the Homeric Troy, was also in the bronze age, and in none of the five prehistoric cities at Hissarlik are there any vestiges of iron. Iron, however, plays a considerable part in the *Iliad*, another proof, if proof were wanted, of the comparatively late date of the Homeric poems, and also affording a rude but valuable indication of the limits of date between which iron must have become known to the Greeks. Again, the great tombs discovered by Dr. Schliemann at Mycenæ must be assigned to that earlier period of Greek civilisation which was overwhelmed and destroyed by the rude Dorian conquerors. In the excavations at Mycenæ iron knives were found, but only in certain late deposits, which are assigned by Dr. Schliemann to the fifth century B.C. Hence three concurrent lines of evidence tend to show that iron was unknown in Argos, Mœsia, and Northern Italy in the twelfth or eleventh century B.C.

In the time of Homer the age of iron was just commencing in Greece. He constantly mentions bronze weapons, while iron is still a rare and precious metal. Hesiod, *circa* 850 B.C., refers to a time when bronze had not yet been superseded by iron, which had already become commoner and cheaper than copper, as was the case in Assyria in the eighth century B.C. Homer mentions seven metals—gold, silver, lead, tin, copper, bronze, and iron. He also mentions the smith, the anvil, the hammer, and the pincers. Iron was at first chiefly used for swords, as Hesiod gives Heracles a sword of iron, but even down to the time of Pindar (*circa* 470 B.C.) bronze was still used for certain weapons, as he repeatedly mentions spear heads and axes of bronze.

Another indication of date is afforded by the Italic name of iron. The Latin word *ferrum*, which points to an earlier *fersum*, is isolated in Aryan speech, and is believed to be a loan-word from the Semitic *bar(e)zum*, an indication that the metal was first introduced into Italy by Phœnician traders. The Phœnicians must have reached Sicily about the twelfth century,[1] and soon afterwards established a trading station in Central Italy, probably at Cære.

Like the Latin *ferrum*, the Greek name of iron, σίδηρος, is isolated in the Aryan languages. Dr. Evans compares this with the Latin *sidera*, and suggests a

[1] Duncker, *History of Antiquity*, vol. ii. p. 87.

reference to meteoric iron.[1] But as Semitic and Greek tradition both point to the land of the Tibareni on the shores of the Euxine as the earliest source of iron, Dr. Schrader is of opinion that the Greek name may be a loan-word from one of the languages of Asia Minor.

In any case the knowledge of iron must have been derived from the East. It is denoted in the Semitic languages by a word borrowed from the Accadian. In Egypt it was known as early as the twelfth dynasty. But the knowledge of copper must have preceded that of iron, since the sign for copper is used as a determinative or generic sign for the word *men*, iron, while the copper mines in the Peninsula of Sinai were worked by the Egyptians as early as the second or third dynasty, and by the Babylonians probably at the time of the sixth.

Another curious indication of the relative priority of iron and copper, as well as of the locality where iron was first smelted in Northern Europe, is afforded by the history of our own word " iron." In Gothic, as we have seen, *aiz* meant brass or bronze, while iron is denoted by the derived word *eisarn*. But the suffix *arn* is distinctively Celtic, and hence the Teutons must have derived their knowledge of iron from their Celtic neighbours. Out of *ais* "bronze" the Celts must have constructed the derivative *aisarn*, and then, in accordance with a well-known euphonic law of the Celtic languages, the *s* fell out between two vowels, leaving for iron the name *iarn* in old Irish, and *haiarn* in old Welsh. But before this loss of the sibilant, the Celtic word must have found its way into Teutonic speech, iron being denoted by *eisarn* in Gothic, *isern*

[1] Evans, *Ancient Stone Implements*, p. 6.

THE NEOLITHIC CULTURE. 147

in Anglo-Saxon, *isarn* in old Norse, *eisen* in German, and *iron* in English.[1]

The evolution of the Teutonic and Celtic names for iron must have taken place in some region where iron ores were abundant, and where Celts and Teutons were in approximate contact, and also not far from the primitive seat of the Goths on the southern shores of the Baltic. Hallstadt, where iron has been found in the prehistoric salt-workings of a Celtic people, is probably too far to the South; but all the conditions of the problem are found united in the region of the Erzgebirge, which divide Bohemia from Saxony. As the name implies, these mountains are rich in metallic wealth, while down to the first century B.C. they formed the ethnic frontier between Celts and Teutons. Here most probably we may locate the earliest iron manufacture in Northern and Western Europe. This must, however, have been as early as the fifth century B.C., as the Gauls possessed iron swords when they invaded Italy.

The Slavonic and Lithuanian name for iron is also derived from a word denoting copper. The Slavo-Lithuanian name for iron is *gelezis*, and the probable source of this word is the Greek χαλκός, copper or bronze. The knowledge of metals must have reached them from the Greek trading colonies of the Euxine, probably about the sixth century B.C. In the time of Herodotus the Scythians had no bronze, but the Massagetæ had gold and copper, but neither iron nor silver.[2]

There is no common Aryan name for lead. The knowledge of lead must, however, have preceded that

---
[1] Schrader, *Urgeschichte*, p. 293.
[2] Evans, *Ancient Bronze Implements*, p. 17.

of iron, since lead was abundant at Mycenæ, which was in the bronze period, and lead occurs in all the five prehistoric strata at Hissarlik, in none of which any iron has been found.

As for salt, Benfey, Schleicher, and Max Müller have asserted, on linguistic grounds, that it was known to the undivided Aryans. The name runs through the European languages, but its existence in Indo-Iranian is disputed. The word *sara* means "water" in Sanskrit, but Hehn maintained that this is no sufficient proof that the Indians were acquainted with salt. Curtius and Benfey observed that the Sanskrit word is employed in the sense of "briny," to which Bohtlingk replied that this signification does not appear at any earlier date than in a Sanskrit dictionary of the twelfth century A.D., and therefore proves nothing.[1]

As for any absolute dates for the introduction of the various metals, the calculations that have been made can be regarded as only approximate. Besides, while one nation was in the stone age, another may have been acquainted with bronze, and a third with iron. Besides, the introduction of each metal was very gradual. Arrows continued to be tipped with flint or bone long after bronze was used for other weapons. Arrows are more liable to be lost, and therefore flint was preferred when metal was costly. Flint arrowheads are frequently found in barrows, together with bronze celts.[2]

From the gradual improvement in the types of the bronze implements, Dr. Evans thinks that the bronze age must have lasted for many centuries, eight or

---

[1] Schrader, *Urgeschichte*, p. 56.
[2] Evans, *Ancient Stone Implements*, 328, 353.

THE NEOLITHIC CULTURE. 149

even ten, but this estimate would have to be extended if M. Morlot is right in assigning certain bronze implements found in the cone of the Tinière, near the head of the Lake of Geneva, to about the year 1900 B.C.

It is thought that gold and copper may have been known to the Indo-Iranians as early as 2000 B.C.[1] The Greeks were probably acquainted with bronze before the thirteenth century B.C., with gold as early as the twelfth, with silver not before the eleventh, and with iron before the ninth century.

In Italy bronze had certainly been known for a considerable period before the eleventh century, possibly as early as the ninth. Gold was not known in the eleventh century, and iron not before the tenth.

Dr. Evans places the beginning of the bronze period in Britain between 1400 and 1200 B.C., and Sir John Lubbock between 1500 and 1200 B.C.—estimates which give us a minimum date[2] for the appearance of the round barrow Aryan-speaking people in our island. Dr. Evans thinks iron swords were used in Gaul in the fourth or fifth century B.C., and in the south of Britain a little later. He considers that in the third or second century B.C., bronze had practically fallen into disuse for cutting implements.[3]

Iron probably became known to the Slaves and Teutons in the sixth or fifth century B.C., and to the Celtic peoples of Central Europe somewhat earlier. In the time of Pausanias, 174 A.D., we are told that iron was unknown to the Sarmatians.

---

[1] Duncker, *History of Antiquity*, vol. iv. p. 30; Evans, *Ancient Bronze Implements*, pp. 471, 472.

[2] See p. 128, *supra*.

[3] Evans, *Ancient Bronze Implements*, pp. 471, 472.

§ 3. *Weapons.*

The names of weapons, though they differ as a rule in the Aryan languages, occasionally afford proof of a descent from the stone period. Thus the old Norse *sax*, the old High German *sahs*, the Anglo-Saxon *seax*, a sword, is plainly related to the Latin *saxum*, a stone, and the Iranian *asti*, arrows, is related to the Latin *os*, a bone, and proves that the primitive arrows were tipped with bone and not with bronze or iron. Even during the late bronze period in Europe, the arrow heads were of flint or bone, bronze being too valuable a metal to be shot away and lost.

It is noteworthy that while the European words connected with pastoral and agricultural pursuits agree to a considerable extent, those for weapons are mostly different. The Greek and Latin designations for bow, arrow, sword, spear, shield, helmet, and armour, are unconnected, while on the other hand the Greek words for bow-string, arrow, spear, sling-stone, battle-axe, and shield can be traced in Sanskrit. One Italic word, *ensis*, which originally denoted a knife —doubtless of stone—rather than a sword, is the only Latin name for a weapon which can be traced in the Indo-Iranian tongues. The *ensis* was a stabbing weapon, the cutting sword being designated in Latin by the word *gladius*, which is believed to be a loan-word from the Celtic (old Irish, *claideb;* Cornish, *cledyf*). The legend of Brennus makes it probable that the *gladius* became known in Italy after the invasion of the Gauls. It was much the same in Greece. No trace of a sword has been found in any of the prehistoric strata at Hissarlik, which is itself a proof of the late date of the *Iliad.* The Homeric name ξίφος being a Semitic loan-word (cf. the Arabic *seifun*) is an indication that the Greek sword was obtained from the Phœnicians, as the Roman sword was from the Gauls. The Roman *lorica* was made of leathern thongs, and the shield, *scutum*, was, as the name implies, originally an oxhide. The Greek names prove that the primitive shields were made of hides or wickerwork, and that the helmet was at first merely a cap of dogskin. The names of weapons common to Zend and Sanskrit prove that the Indo-Iranians, before their separation, must have been acquainted with the bow, the spear, the javelin, the sword, the knife, the battle-axe, and the club, but only with one defensive weapon, the shield. The terms for defensive armour, mail and helmet, are later than the separation of Indians and Iranians.

The bow, a favourite weapon with the Southern and Eastern Aryans, seems to have been of late introduction in the North, the German *pfeil*, arrow, being a loan-word from the Latin *pilum*, while the old Irish *saiget*, arrow, is a loan-word from the Latin *sagitta*.

The chief northern weapon seems to have been the stone axe or hammer. So late as the thirteenth century Sir William Wallace went into battle against the English armed with a celt or stone axe; and weapons of stone seem to have been used by Harold's armed peasants at the battle of Hastings.[1]

§ 4. *Cattle.*

The sepulchral caverns and dolmens of France and Belgium prove that at the beginning of the neolithic

---

[1] Helbig, *Die Italiker in der Poebene*, p. 42. See, however, Evans, *Ancient Stone Implements*, p. 132.

age the inhabitants of Europe were nomad hunters, sheltering themselves in caves, subsisting on the products of the chase, and possessed of no domesticated animal. In the kitchen middens of Denmark we find that the first onward step in progress had been made, and the dog had been trained as an assistant in the chase. The oldest lake dwellings of Southern Germany exhibit a further stage in culture. The people had fixed dwellings constructed with considerable skill, and we can trace their gradual progress from the life of the hunter to that of the herdman.

The wild horse, which roamed in immense herds over the plains of Europe, and had formed the chief food of the people who sheltered themselves in the caverns at Solutré, Auvernier, Salève, and Thäyngen, had become scarce;[1] but the wisent, or bison, and the huge wild ox which had been a contemporary of the mammoth and the rhinoceros, were still abundant; gradually disappearing, however, with the introduction of improved weapons. In the earliest lake settlements the bones of the urus, the marsh cow, and the marsh hog abound.[2] In Austria and Bavaria the stag and the wild boar seem at first to have constituted the chief food of the people.[3] But as the population increased, and the wild animals became scarce or more difficult of approach, we can trace the neolithic hunters gradually passing into the pastoral stage, and finally acquiring no inconsiderable skill in agriculture.

One of the oldest lake dwellings is that at Schussenried, on the Feder See in Würtemberg,

---

[1] Keller, *Lake Dwellings*, p. 552.
[2] *Ibid.*, p. 538.   [3] *Ibid.*, pp. 587, 592, 615.

which, from the character of the flint implements, has been thought to be coeval with the Danish kitchen middens.[1] Here we find the earliest trace of any pastoral people, though the chase still constituted the chief means of support. This is shown by the fact that of the bones found in the refuse heaps those of the stag amount to about three-fifths of the whole, and those of the marsh hog are very abundant, while those of domesticated animals are extremely scarce, only just sufficient to make it possible to determine their existence. All that have been found are the remains of one sheep, of two dogs, and of three oxen of the kind called the Celtic shorthorn— a species whose bones have also been discovered in dolmens of the neolithic age.

The Celto-Latin race, to which the lake settlements in Southern Germany must be assigned, seems then to have advanced southward and occupied the fertile plains of Western Switzerland. In the oldest of the Swiss lake dwellings, such as that at Wauwyl, in the Canton of Lucerne, though the bones of wild animals still predominate, the ox has become common; but the sheep is still extremely scarce, the remains of only one specimen having been discovered. As we come down to the later neolithic pile dwellings the remains of wild animals become scarce, the sheep becomes more common, the goat makes its appearance, and finally, at the close of the stone age, the pig has to be added to the list of domesticated animals. At Nidau, which belongs to the bronze age, the pig becomes abundant. At the settlement of Möringen, which is of the late bronze or early iron age, we have evidence that the horse had been tamed. In the pile

[1] Keller, *Lake Dwellings*, p. 589.

dwellings of Northern Italy, which come down to the bronze age, the horse and pig appear, but the ass and the domestic fowl are still unknown.

The conclusions of the science of linguistic palæontology agree substantially with those of prehistoric archæology. The evidence of language proves that before the linguistic separation had become complete, the Aryan-speaking peoples had entered on the pastoral stage, and had domesticated the dog, the cow, and the sheep. The names of these animals may be traced to Aryan roots, an indication that the Aryans developed the pastoral life without the influence of any alien civilisation. That the undivided Aryans were a neolithic people, in the pastoral rather than the agricultural stage, and were herdsmen rather than shepherds, is shown by the fact that so large a number of the words common to every branch of Aryan speech refer to the cow, the terms relating to agriculture, weapons, metals, and religion having, as a rule, a more limited range.

The wealth of these primitive people consisted almost wholly of their herds. This is indicated by the fact that the collective name for cattle, which appears in Latin, Sanskrit, Zend, Lithuanian, and German, denoting originally that which has been tied up,[1] has been the source of numerous words denoting property and money, such as *peculium* and *pecunia* in Latin, and our *fee*, which is the Anglo-Saxon *feoh*, meaning both property and cattle, and identical with the German *vieh*, a cow. The ox, which is figured on early Roman coins, may be a

---

[1] Latin, *pecus;* Sanskrit, *paçu;* Zend, *pasu;* Lithuanian, *pekus;* Gothic, *faihu;* German, *vieh;* all from the root *pak*, to take, bind fast, or tie up.

survival from the time when the ox was the standard of value and the medium of exchange, and the coin may probably have at first represented the value of the animal. This is supported by the fact that in the Homeric age the measure of value was the ox. The arms of Diomed are worth nine oxen, those of Glaucus are worth an hundred. The tripod, which was the first prize for the wrestlers, was worth twelve oxen. One female slave is valued at twenty oxen, another at four.[1]

Professor Max Müller[2] has brought together some curious linguistic evidence as to the supreme importance of cattle among the Vedic Indians. The Sanskrit word *gopa*, a king, must have meant originally only a cow-herd; it then came to mean the head of a cowpen, and lastly the chief of a tribe. The word *goshtha*, which denoted primarily the cowpen, came to mean an assembly; *gotra* passed through the successive meanings of the enclosure for the cows, then the herd itself, and lastly a family, tribe, or race. The word *goshu-yúdh*, used in the Veda to denote a warrior, means etymologically "fighting for the cows," and *gávishti*, "strife," is literally a "striving for cows," which recalls the source of the quarrel between the herdsmen of Lot and Abraham.

It is also curious to note as a further indication that the primitive Aryans were a pastoral people, that the only colours whose names belong to this primitive period are the usual colours of cows. Thus the word for red runs through all the Aryan languages—Sanskrit, Greek, Latin, Slavonic, Celtic, and Teutonic; but

---

[1] Ridgeway, "Metrological Notes," in *Journal of Hellenic Studies*; Gladstone, *Juventus Mundi*, p. 534.
[2] Max Müller, *Essays*, vol. i., pp. 326-328.

common words for blue and green are wanting, the terms we possess for these colours being of later origin. This fact has given rise to much futile discussion, and even to the singular theory that the primitive Aryans were colour-blind to the hues of the grass and of the sky. It is simpler to suppose that they had not advanced beyond the pastoral stage, and at first only required, and consequently only possessed, the words required to distinguish the colours of their cows. This explanation is supported by the fact that the only words for colours among some African races are those which designate the colours of cattle and game—black, grey, white, yellow, and red. The same fact confronts us in the Finnic languages. The word for colour is *karva*, which etymologically means "hair," and loan words are employed to denote green and blue. That there is no common Aryan word for the season of harvest[1] is another indication that the undivided Aryans had not reached the agricultural stage.

The dog, the friend and servant of the hunter as well as of the herdsman, was the first animal to be tamed, his remains, as we have seen, being found in the Danish kitchen middens, from which all other domesticated animals are absent. His name probably means "the prolific one," and is found in every branch of Aryan speech.[2]

The name of the "cow" is also common to all the Aryan languages—Sanskrit, Zend, Armenian, Greek, Latin, Celtic, Teutonic, and Slavonic. The name of the "steer" is almost as widely diffused; that of the "ox" occurs in Sanskrit, Celtic, and Teutonic. The

---

[1] See p. 163, *infra*.
[2] Sanskrit, *çvan*; Zend, *spâ*; Lithuanian, *szu*; old Irish, *cu*; Greek, κύων; Latin, *canis*; German, *hun-d*.

Latin *vacca* may be traced in Sanskrit, and *vitulus* in Sanskrit and Greek.

As for the sheep, the Latin name, *ovis*, re-appears in the Greek, Sanskrit, Teutonic, Lithuanian, Slavonic, and Celtic languages. The goat, which is not found in the earliest lake dwellings, was tamed at a later period. The Greek name, αἴξ, extends only to Sanskrit, Armenian, and Lithuanian, while the Latin *caper* is also found in Celtic and Teutonic. The evidence of the Swiss pile dwellings is conclusive that the "jumper" received its name while it was still only an animal of the chase.[1]

The name of the sow is less widely extended, the Sanskrit word denoting only the wild boar. In the oldest Swiss lake dwellings the bones of the wild marsh hog are found abundantly, but the animal seems to have been domesticated at a later time than the dog, the cow, the sheep, and the goat. The linguistic evidence also indicates that the domestication of the pig took place after the separation of the Aryan peoples. The pig belongs essentially to the fixed agricultural stage. The cow and the sheep would more readily share the life of nomad herdsmen than the pig, whose winter food would be difficult to provide, and who is not so easily herded or driven from place to place as the cow. In some of the Swiss pile dwellings of the bronze age, where the domesticated pig first becomes common, stores of acorns have been found, which were doubtless collected in the autumn as winter provender for the swine.

The comparatively late date of the domestication of the pig is also indicated by the fact that tame swine were unknown to the Accadians or to the

---

[1] Hehn, *Wanderings of Plants and Animals*, p. 462.

proto-Semites. In literature they first appear in Homer, not being mentioned either in the Veda or the Avesta.

The case of the horse is of great interest. The Latin name, *equus*, is common to all the Aryan languages; and it was formerly supposed that the Aryan immigrants brought the animal with them into Europe from its Asiatic home. But recent archæological discoveries have overthrown these conclusions, and have shown that the common name must refer to the wild horse which roamed in immense herds over Europe, and formed the chief food of the palæolithic hunters. In some of the caverns in France the

HORSES FROM LA MADELAINE.

remains of the horse are more abundant than those of any other animal, more even than those of the wild ox. Thus at Solutré, near Macon, the bones of horses, which had formed the food of the inhabitants of this station, form a deposit nearly 10 feet in depth and more than 300 feet in length, the number of skeletons represented being estimated at from 20,000 to 40,000. This primitive horse was a diminutive animal, not much larger than an ass, standing about 13 hands high, the largest specimens not exceeding 14 hands. But the head was of disproportionate size, and the teeth were very powerful. He resembles the tarpan or wild horse of the Caspian steppes. A spirited representation of two of these wild horses is engraved on an antler found at the station of La Madelaine in the Department of the Dordogne.

The deposits in the caves at the foot of Monte Pellegrino, near Palermo, also afford evidence that the wild horse formed the chief sustenance of the early inhabitants of Sicily. Herds of wild horses were probably chased along the narrow valleys into pit-falls, or over the cliffs, and so destroyed. With the introduction of improved weapons of bone and horn the wild horse became less abundant, but he had a wide range over France, Belgium, Germany, Switzerland, and England.

In the neolithic age the wild horse ranged over the plains in the west of Switzerland, and formed an element in the food of the inhabitants of the earlier lake dwellings. He appears at first to have been only semi-domesticated. For the sake of their flesh and milk, herds of half-wild horses may have been driven along by the Aryan herdsmen migrating in search of pasture, as is now done by the Tartars of the Asiatic steppes.

The horse as a domesticated animal was not known to the Accadians before the Semitic conquest of Babylonia, or to the Semites before the linguistic separation of the Semitic family, and it does not appear on the Egyptian monuments till the time of the New Empire. This was after the conquest of Egypt by the Hyksos, by whom the horse was doubtless introduced from Central Asia. It was well known to the Hittites (Kheta) and to the undivided Turko-Tartaric race, an indication that it was first tamed in Central Asia. In the Swiss lake dwellings of the stone and early bronze ages, bones and teeth of horses, which were doubtless used for food, have been scantily found; but it is only at Möringen and Auvernier, which belong to the latest bronze age, that we find horses' bits of stag's horn and bronze. These bits are only $3\frac{1}{2}$ inches[1] wide, and could now hardly be used for a child's pony. I have made some measurements for the purpose of ascertaining the size of the horses for which the bits of the bronze age would be suitable. A cob of $13\frac{1}{4}$ hands required a bit $4\frac{1}{4}$ inches in width, and a Shetland pony of $11\frac{3}{4}$ hands required a bit $3\frac{3}{4}$ inches in width, and shoes 3 inches wide. Modern bits for horses vary in width from $4\frac{1}{2}$ to 7 inches, and I am informed that bits of the size of those found in the Swiss lake dwellings are now only used for donkeys.

The earliest horse-shoes come from the lake settlement at Paladru, in Dauphiné, which belongs to the late iron age, and is probably post-Roman. The shoes are from $3\frac{1}{2}$ to 4 inches in width, a proof that the horses must have been very small. The late bronze settlements of Northern Italy, which may date from the eleventh century B.C., prove that the horse had then been tamed.

For a long period after the horse was tamed the more manageable ox still continued to be used as the beast of burden and the beast of draught, the horse being reserved for chariots of war, as was the case among the Egyptians, the Assyrians, and the Hittites, and also for chariot races and triumphal processions, as among the Etruscans and the Greeks. It is curious to notice at how late a period men first ventured to mount the "swift one." In ancient Egypt, as now, the ass was exclusively used for riding. There is nothing in the Veda to show that the art of riding

[1] Keller, *Lake Dwellings*, pp. 173, 243.

was practised. We first meet with a notice of it in the Avesta, an indication that the art was first acquired by the Iranian Aryans from the contiguous Tatar tribes. The words relating to equitation are different in the Zend, Greek, Latin, and Teutonic languages. Among the Greeks of the Homeric age horses were harnessed to chariots for war or races, and a bare-backed horse might occasionally be mounted, but there was no riding in our sense of the word.[1]

The cut, taken from a terra-cotta figure found by General di Cesnola in Cyprus, is probably the earliest representation we possess of a man on horseback. Some later figures show that the horse was first ridden with a halter rather than with a bit.

The remains of the ass have not been found in the Swiss lake dwellings, or even in the Italic settlements of the bronze age. It must have been introduced into Europe from the East at a comparatively late period. The Celtic, Teutonic, and Slavonic names are obviously loan-words from the Latin, and the Latin name is a Semitic loan-word from the Phœnician. The European and Asiatic Aryan names for the ass are wholly different, but it was known to the Indo-Iranians before their separation. As the native home of the wild ass is in Central Asia, and more especially in the steppes of the Aral-Caspian plain, the fact that the primitive Aryans were not acquainted with this useful beast of burden seems as conclusive an argument against the Asiatic origin of the Aryans as the fact that they were acquainted with the beech, a tree confined to Europe.

[1] Hehn, *Wanderings of Plants and Animals*, p. 51.

The case of the camel is quite as strong. There is not the faintest indication that it was known to the undivided Aryans; but if they had migrated from Central Asia they must have been acquainted with this animal, which was known to the undivided Semites, and also to the primitive Turko-Tataric race. It was known also to the united Indo-Iranians, whose home, before their separation, was in Bactria, or Eastern Iran. The name of the camel is a Semitic loan-word, and that it was unknown at first to the Slaves appears from their having transferred to it the name of the elephant, as is shown by the old Slavonic word *veliblandu*, a camel.

Neither in the pile dwellings of Switzerland or Northern Italy are there any traces of domestic fowls, which first make their appearance in the Avesta, and spread from Persia to Greece in post-Homeric times, probably about the sixth century B.C.[1] The goose had been domesticated by the Greeks before the Homeric age, but not when the Iranians and Indians separated. The Aryan names of the goose, the pigeon, and the duck must have been given to these birds while still wild. Neither the Semites nor the Finns possessed poultry before the respective linguistic separations. The nomad herdsman, with the aid of his dog and his flint-pointed spear, could drive cattle from place to place, and protect them against beasts of prey; but poultry cannot so easily be driven, and well-fenced enclosures would be necessary to protect them against their natural enemies, the fox, the weasel, the eagle, and the hawk.[2]

In the foregoing discussion it has been assumed

[1] Hehn, *Wanderings of Plants and Animals*, p. 243
[2] Schrader, *Urgeschichte*, pp. 340-353.

that the inhabitants of the Swiss and Italian pile dwellings were Aryans. Helbig has proved that the Italian pile dwellings must be Umbrian, since they are earlier than the Celtic and Etruscan invasions, and exhibit a state of culture far in advance of that possessed at a considerably later period by the Ligurians. But if the Italic settlements are Umbrian, the Swiss settlements must be Celtic or Helvetic. Dahn has maintained that the inhabitants of the Swiss lake dwellings were of Finnic race, but this conclusion Schrader rejects on the ground that the Eastern and Western Finns, before their separation, were acquainted with the dog, the cow, and the horse, but not with the sheep and the goat; whereas the oldest lacustrine people of Switzerland had tamed the sheep and possibly the goat, but not the horse.

Moreover, as has already been shown, the Swiss pile dwellings were inhabited continuously till the iron age, and some of them even down to the Roman period,[1] when we know that the country was inhabited by a Celtic-speaking people. From this fact, taken together with the resemblance of the Helvetic skull to that of the Romans and the round barrow people of Britain, there can be little doubt that we are dealing with a civilisation which must be classed as Aryan and not Finnic.

§ 5. *Husbandry.*

The fact that the German *herbst*, autumn, means the "harvest" time may remind us that among an agricultural people the time for the ingathering of the crops. is the most important as well as the most

[1] Keller. *Lake Dwellings*, p. 283.

festive season of the year. But the significant fact that in the Aryan languages there is no primitive term for autumn, and that it was the last of the four seasons to receive a name, is by itself a tolerably clear indication that the undivided Aryans had not reached the agricultural stage of civilisation. Among the Aryans, as well as among the Ural-Altaic races, the oldest of the names of the seasons are the winter (*hiems*), the time of snow, when the cattle had to be stabled, and summer, when the herds went out to pasture.

Even in the historical period there were Aryan tribes who had not reached the agricultural stage. Tacitus describes the Sarmatians as nomads "in plaustro equoque viventibus;"[1] and Cæsar tells us that corn was not grown in the interior of Britain, but only in the south, which was inhabited by Belgic tribes which had recently immigrated from Gaul. No cereals have as yet been found in any of the British round barrows; but the querns and mealing stones, which are not infrequent, are supposed to indicate that grain was not unknown. This, however, is not decisive, as they may have been used for pounding acorns or wild oats.

Cuno ingeniously argues that the undivided Aryans must have been acquainted with cereals, because the name of the mouse, which means "the thief," is found in Greek, Latin, Teutonic, Slavonic, and Sanskrit. What, he asks, could the mouse have stolen except corn? But this argument is not conclusive, as in some of the South German lake dwellings we find no corn, but stores of hazel nuts, which might have been pilfered by the mouse.

[1] Tacitus, *Germania*, 46.

Our English word *grist*, which is related to the German *gerste*, the Latin *hordeum*, the Greek κριθή, and the Armenian *gari*, is however an indication that some kind of grain, probably barley, was known. But the cereal, whatever it was, may have grown wild; or, as the herdsmen moved to their spring pastures, a forest-clearing may have been made with the aid of fire, and grain may have been sown and gathered in the autumn; but there can have been no regular tillage, no permanent enclosures, and no property in land.

Barley, which was probably the earliest cereal cultivated by the Aryans, was succeeded by wheat and spelt. The name of flax, *linum*, is very widely spread, and may be traced in all the Aryan languages of Europe—Latin, Greek, Celtic, Gothic, and Slavonic. Hemp, as well as oats, rye, peas, beans, and onions do not however belong to the primitive Aryan epoch.

In words connected with tillage there is a great gulf between the Aryan languages of Asia and those of Europe. The Indo-Iranian languages have special terms for ploughing, sowing, and reaping, which do not extend to Europe; and we may probably conclude that the Asiatic Aryans had not advanced beyond the pastoral stage at the time of the separation.

The curious agreement between Greek and Sanskrit in words denoting weapons has been already remarked. Not less curious is the correspondence between the Latin, Greek, Teutonic, and Slavonic words which refer to agriculture, and the disagreement in these languages of terms which denote weapons. This seems to indicate that the Italic and Hellenic races must, at the time when agriculture began, have been dwelling in peaceable proximity in some more northern region, probably in Danubian lands, in contact with Slaves and Teutons, deadlier weapons of offence being required when they moved southwards to win new homes in the Mediterranean lands.

The primitive plough was doubtless a crooked branch of a tree, tipped probably with the tine of a stag's antler. The Finnic word *kar-a* designates both a plough and the branch of a tree, and the Indian name of the plough, *spandana*, also means a tree. That the Aryan plough was unprovided with a ploughshare may perhaps be gathered from the etymology of the word *sock*, which is used in provincial English to denote a ploughshare. This is the French *soc*, and the old Irish *socc*, a plough, and can only be explained from the old Irish *soc* (old Welsh *husc*), a sow. In like manner the Greek name for the ploughshare, ὕννις, ὕνη, must be connected with ὕς, a sow. The stages of meaning must have been first the sow, then the sow's snout, then the ploughshare, and lastly the plough. Now, as the pig did not belong to the earlier stages of Aryan culture, we may perhaps conclude that the primitive plough was unprovided with a snout.

The foregoing conclusions as to early Aryan agriculture are fairly in accord with the archæological evidence. In the pile dwellings at Laibach in Carniola both flax and grain are absent, but hazel nuts in enormous quantities were found, together with the kernels of the water chestnut, *Trapa natans*, which, according to Pliny, was made into bread by the Thracians.[1] At Schussenried, in Würtemberg, in addition to hazel nuts and acorns, wheat is abundant, but neither woven flax nor spindle whorls have been

[1] Keller. *Lake Dwellings*, p. 617.

discovered, the only fabric being a bit of rope made from the bark of the lime tree. At Mooseedorf, which is probably the oldest of the Swiss lake dwellings, barley and flax, as well as wheat, have been discovered. The pea is found towards the close of the stone age, while beans and lentils first appear in the bronze age; and oats have not been discovered in any settlement older than Möringen, which belongs to the end of the bronze age. Hemp has not been found at all. In the pile dwellings of the bronze age in the valley of the Po, when the pig and the horse had been domesticated, we find wheat, beans, and flax, with the addition of the vine, which has not been discovered in any of the Swiss settlements.[1]

§ 6. *Food.*

We have seen that in some of the oldest lake dwellings, notably those of Germany, the only farinaceous food consisted of hazel nuts, acorns, and the water chestnut. By the time the Aryans had reached Switzerland they had learned to cultivate barley and wheat; and in Cæsar's time corn was grown in the south of Britain, though not, as he tells us, in the centre of the island. Acorns were roasted in earthen pipkins, corn was pounded between two stones, and cakes of kneaded meal were baked in the hot ashes. Meat was roasted on spits, or baked in the ashes, but the art of boiling seems to have been unknown. The Latin *jus* (Sanskrit *yus*) is believed to have denoted the gravy and dripping from the roasted meat, rather than broth. The Germans, according to Pomponius Mela, feasted on raw flesh,

[1] Schrader, *Urgeschichte*, pp. 354-364.

but this was forbidden by the Viking laws. Horseflesh was largely eaten in the neolithic age, and even in the historic period by the Iranians and Scandinavians.

It seems difficult to believe that the art of making cheese was unknown to the northern nations till they had come in contact with Latin civilisation, but such appears to have been the case, since the name is a loan-word from the Latin *caseus*, and spread from the Teutonic to the Slavonic languages. Koumis, however, seems to have been made both by the Goths and the Lithuanians, whose nobles intoxicated themselves on a fermented beverage prepared from the milk of mares.[1]

It is very remarkable that there is no common name for fish in the Aryan tongues. The Zend and Sanskrit words agree, so do those in Latin, Celtic, and Teutonic, as well as those in Lithuanian and Armenian, while the Greek name is isolated.[2] This defect in the linguistic record is not by itself decisive, since the primitive word for "father" has disappeared from Slavonic, for "sister" from Greek, and those for "son" and "daughter" from Latin. But in the case of fish an inference may be safely drawn, as the divergence of the names is curiously corroborated by other evidence, so that we may conclude that it was only after the linguistic separation that fish became a usual article of food among the Aryans. Not only is the name for fish different in Greek and Latin, but all the terms connected with the art of fishing—the net, the line, the hook, and the bait—were independently evolved.

[1] Hehn, *Wanderings of Plants and Animals*, p. 55.
[2] Schrader, *Urgeschichte*, p. 171.

It is noteworthy that while the Greek word for fish cannot be traced in Latin, the Latin name, *piscis*, reappears both in Celtic and Teutonic, one out of many indications that the final separation between Greeks and Latins was earlier than that between Latins and Celts, or between Celts and Teutons.

There is no mention in the Vedas of fish being eaten, and only exceptionally in Homer, while "fish-eater" is used as a term of reproach by Herodotus. In the pile dwellings of the valley of the Po, which were so favourably situated for the practice of the fisherman's art, neither hooks nor any other implements for catching fish have yet been found. Fish-hooks are extremely rare in collections of prehistoric antiquities, the great museum at Dublin containing only one single specimen.[1] In the very early lake settlement at Schussenried, in Würtemberg, where the flint implements are of a type as primitive as those in the kitchen middens, hardly any fish bones have been found.

The taste for fish and the art of fishing seem to have been developed at a comparatively late period. Fish hooks have been found in the Celtic settlement of Hallstadt, in Austria, which is of the iron age, and others of the same pattern at Nidau, on the Lake of Bienne, and elsewhere, but they are more common in settlements which come down to the iron age than in those which belong to the ages of bronze or stone.

In the kitchen middens of Denmark fish, especially herrings, formed an important article of food. This fact, taken in connection with the absence of any common Aryan word for fish, and the curious

[1] Lubbock, *Prehistoric Times*, p. 33.

aversion to fish among the Indian, Hellenic, Italic, and Celtic races, is not without its bearing on the ethnic affinities of the primitive Aryans.

Oysters formed no inconsiderable portion of the food of the people of the Danish kitchen middens, and oysters were placed in the tombs of the royal personages buried at Mycenæ. The name is found in all the Aryan languages of Europe,[1] but is wanting in the Indo-Iranian family. If the Aryans originated in Europe, the loss of the word in lands where the oyster is unknown is perfectly intelligible; but if the European nations successively migrated from Central Asia, the adoption of the same designation is difficult to explain, more especially since the linguistic gulf between Greeks and Celts, or between Teutons and Latins, is more profound than that between Iranians and Slaves, or Greeks and Indians.

The vine appears to have been unknown to the lacustrine people of Switzerland. A vine stock was found in one of the pile dwellings in Italy, but the art of making wine was probably introduced by Greek colonists.[2] The name is probably a loan-word obtained from the Semites.

The earliest intoxicating drink was prepared from wild honey. Words etymologically related to our English *mead* reappear in Sanskrit, Greek, Celtic, Slavonic, and Latin, denoting either honey, sweetness, mead, wine, or drunkenness. In Northern Europe mead was replaced by beer, the English word *ale* corresponding to the old Prussian word *alu*, which means mead.

---

[1] Latin, *ostrea*; O. H. G., *auster*; Old Irish, *oisridh*; Russian, *ustersu*; Greek, ὄστρεον.

[2] Hehn, *Wanderings of Plants and Animals*, pp. 72-74.

§ 7. *Dress.*

The clothing of the Aryans of the neolithic and even of the bronze age consisted chiefly of the skins of beasts, the flesh, and perhaps the hair, having been removed by stone scrapers, which are extremely numerous, even as late as the bronze age. These skins were sewn together by means of bone needles, which are found in great abundance. Cæsar says of the Britons *pellibus sunt vestiti*, and Tacitus tells us that the same was the case with some of the Germans. In the Swiss and Italian pile dwellings fragments of leather, tanned by some rude but effective process, have been found.

Flax, whose very name implies that it was used for weaving (Latin *plecto*, German *flechten*), was spun and woven by the women of the neolithic household, as is evidenced by the spindle whorls and loom weights so abundantly found in the Swiss dwellings of the stone age. In several settlements linen fabrics have been discovered. The threads of the warp, consisting of two fibres of flax twisted together, must have been hung with weights from a horizontal bar, the similar threads of the woof being interlaced by means of needles of bone or wood. That the flax was cultivated is shown by the stores of linseed which have been found. In some of the earlier settlements in Southern Germany, where flax was unknown, ropes and mats were made of bast, prepared from the bark of the clematis or the lime. There is no evidence that hemp was known in the age of stone or even of bronze.

Curiously enough, though flax was so commonly

used for weaving in the stone age, there is no evidence in the pile dwellings of Switzerland or Italy of the weaving of wool, even in the bronze age, when sheep had become numerous. Evidently the sheep skins were worn with the wool on, as is still the case with the peasants of Central and Southern Italy. Woollen fabrics have, however, been found in Jutland, and in Yorkshire, associated with interments of the bronze age.[1] From the Rig Veda it would appear that wool rather than flax was the material employed by the weaver. Bone needles are found in early deposits of the neolithic age, as at Laibach, where flax and even cereals are absent; and our verb "to sew" can be traced in the Sanskrit, Greek, Latin, Teutonic, and Slavonic languages. The word probably denoted the stitching together of skins, since in the Swiss pile dwellings, where linen fabrics are abundant, only one hem and a pocket laced on with string have been discovered, and there is no trace either of a seam or of a cut piece.[2] Probably the texture of the linen was too flimsy to admit of cutting or sewing. The woven fabric seems to have been worn only as a wrapper, since there is no sign of any garments having been fitted to the figure. The first trace of any such advance in the art of tailoring is afforded by the word "breeks," which, as is proved by the old Irish *bracæ*, must, at the period when the Celts still inhabited Central Europe, have been borrowed from the Celts by the Teutons and the Slaves. But these "breeks" were doubtless made of skins.

No distinction seems to have been made in early

[1] Greenwell, *British Barrows*, pp. 32, 376; Lubbock, *Prehistoric Times*, p. 48.
[2] Keller, *Lake Dwellings*, pp. 56, 512.

times between the dress of the women and the men, which is itself a sign of a very primitive stage of civilisation. In Greece the *chiton* and the *himation* were worn both by men and women; at Rome the toga was originally the dress of both sexes; and Tacitus says of the Germans, *nec alius feminis quam viris habitus.*

The Agathyrsi, in Transylvania, painted or tattooed their bodies, and ruddle has been found in so many deposits of the stone age that we must assume that the practice was common, if not universal.

The antiquity of the practice of shaving has been the subject of much controversy, and affords a good instance of the way in which philological conclusions have been corrected by archæology.

Benfey argued that the primitive Aryans shaved their beards, on the ground of the identity of the Greek ξυρόν and the Sanskrit *kshurá*—words which both denote a razor; and he explains the absence of the word from the rest of the Aryan languages by the hypothesis that in the course of their wanderings the other Aryans may have lost elements of the primitive culture. But since it would be difficult to shave with a stone, however sharp, and as the Swiss pile buildings show that the early Aryans were still in the stone age, and since no razors were found in the very early cemetery at Alba Longa, Helbig argues that this word may have originally denoted the flint flakes which were used for scraping the hair off hides, found in great numbers in the earliest settlements, the name being afterwards transferred, after the invention of metals, to razors for shaving the chin.[1]

[1] Schrader, *Urgeschichte*, p. 53.

§ 8. *Habitations.*

The undivided Aryans were no longer troglodytes, but had learnt to construct huts. It has been already noticed[1] that the long barrows of the pre-Aryan population of Britain are imitations or survivals of the cave, while the round barrows of the Aryan invaders were constructed on the model of the circular hut.

These huts were of two kinds—the summer hut, constructed wholly above ground, and the winter hut, which was a circular roofed pit. As to the former, we have to rely chiefly on descriptions or pictorial representations; of the latter we have actual remains.

The pit dwellings at Fisherton, near Salisbury, and elsewhere, the remains of which are still to be seen, are proved to be of neolithic age by the absence of metal, and by the spindle whorls of baked clay and fragments of rude pottery. The pits are carried down through the chalk to a depth of from seven to ten feet, and the roofs were made of interlaced boughs coated with clay. They were entered by tunnels excavated through the chalk, sloping downwards to the floor. We learn also from Tacitus that in the winter some of the German tribes lived in similar holes dug in the earth, the roofs being plastered with the dung of cattle.[2]

That the undivided Aryans also constructed huts above ground, with roofs, doors, and door-posts, is proved by the linguistic evidence. The Latin word *domus* reappears in Sanskrit, Greek, Celtic, and

---

[1] See p. 78, *supra*.
[2] Tacitus, *Germania*, cap. 16.

THE NEOLITHIC CULTURE. 175

Slavonic, while the German *dach*, roof, which has become *thatch* in English, may be traced in Greek, Latin, Celtic, and Lithuanian. Our English word *door* is the same word with the Sanskrit *dvara*, the Greek θύρα, the old Irish *dorus*, and the Latin *fores*, while the name for the door-posts, in Latin *antæ*, appears also in Zend and Sanskrit.

For the real character of these houses, whose existence throughout the whole Aryan region is established by the foregoing linguistic facts, we have to rely on the archæological evidence, which proves beyond contention that they were not houses, in the modern sense of the word, but mere huts of the rudest kind.

Even in the bronze age, as late as the eleventh century B.C., the Umbrians, who among the Aryan peoples were second only to the Hellenes in the civilisation they had attained, possessed no better habitations than wattled huts, from nine to twelve feet in diameter, daubed with clay and thatched with reeds. No trace of masonry or mortar has been discovered in their settlements.[1]

According to the testimony of Strabo, which is borne out by the evidence of the carvings on the column of Marcus Aurelius at Rome, the Celtic or Teutonic tribes on the Danube, even as late as the second century A.D., lived in reed-thatched huts of wood or wickerwork. They were undoubtedly ignorant of the use of mortar, as also were the Germans in the time of Tacitus.

Even imperial Rome must at one time have contained nothing better than such huts, as is proved by two venerable survivals. The *Casa Romuli* on the

[1] Helbig, *Die Italiker in der Poebene*, p. 47.

Palatine was a hut of twigs and reeds; and the house of Vesta in the Forum, the oldest seat of Roman worship, long preserved under the guardianship of the sacred virgins, was a mere hut of wickerwork and straw.[1]

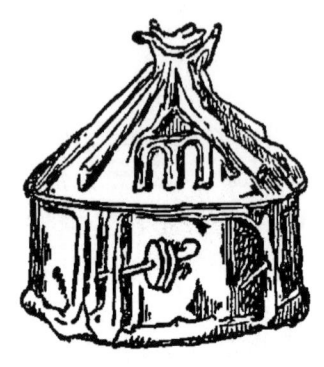

The hut urns discovered at Alba Longa doubtless represent the early abodes of the Aryan settlers in Italy.

The inhabitants of the Swiss lake dwellings had learnt to fell large trees with their stone axes, and drive the piles deep into the soft mud, and to construct on the piles platforms of beams, which were morticed together with considerable skill. On these platforms they built square or circular huts, with perpendicular walls of poles and wattle, plastered with clay, thatched with bark, straw, or reeds, and furnished with a wooden door, a clay floor, and a sandstone slab for a hearth. The modern Swiss *châlet* seems to be a survival of these pile dwellings, the living rooms being on the first floor, the lower storey merely serving as a storehouse for fuel or fodder.

HUT-URN FROM ALBA LONGA.

Even when the Rig Veda and the Avesta were composed the craft of the mason was unknown, the habitations of the Indo-Iranians long after their separation being merely huts of wood or bamboo, thatched with reeds or straw. The Iranians also constructed pit-dwellings, roofed over with poles and thatch like those of the neolithic people of Britain

Since the Gothic *gards*, which corresponds to the

[1] Helbig, *Die Italiker in der Poebene*, p. 51.

Latin *hortus*, is represented in Greek by χόρτος, which denotes primarily place for dancing, we cannot conclude from these words that the huts or seed-plots of the primitive Aryans were fenced and surrounded by enclosures.

The mason's art, and the use of mortar, are believed to have been introduced into Europe by the Phœnicians. The megalithic tombs at Mycenæ, and the huge dolmens of France and Britain, are at once a testimony to the skill of the neolithic Aryans, and a proof that the use of mortar was unknown. The vast labour of roofing these structures with enormous slabs weighing many tons would never have been undertaken if the builders had known how to construct them of smaller stones cemented together by mortar. The huge megalithic circle at Stonehenge, with its five great trilithons, one of the most impressive structures in the world, is now generally assigned by archæologists to the brachycephalic race which first introduced bronze weapons and Aryan speech into Britain, and forms an astounding testimony to the bodily and mental powers of those who planned and executed it.

§ 9. *The Boat.*

Some sort of boat, or rather canoe, must have been constructed in the primitive period, since the Latin *navis* can be traced in Sanskrit, Greek, Celtic, and Teutonic. But the word cannot at first have denoted more than the trunk of a tree hollowed out by the stone axe, with the aid of fire. This is indicated by the etymological relation of the Sanskrit *daru*, a boat, to the English *tree*, and the Celtic *daur*, an oak.

Similarly the old Norse *askr* denotes a boat as well as an ash tree. Several "dug-outs," hollowed out of a single trunk, have been found in the neolithic lake settlements of Switzerland, Italy, and Ireland. The Celtic *barca*, the old Norse *barki*, and the English *barge* and *barque* are indications that the Northern Aryans also constructed canoes of the bark of some tree, probably the birch.[1]

The canoes were propelled by oars or poles, since the Latin *remus* can be traced in Sanskrit, Greek, Celtic, and Teutonic. Sails, however, were unknown in the primitive period, as is shown by the fact that the German *segel*, our *sail*, is a loan-word from the Latin *sagulum*. Thus the Teutonic invasions of England were only made possible by previous contact with Roman civilisation.

An examination of the nautical terms in Latin yields some curious results. According to Georg Curtius, they divide themselves into three classes. We have first the proto-Aryan words *navis* and *remus;* secondly, *velum* and *malus*, which are words of Italic origin, not belonging to the general Aryan vocabulary; and thirdly, a large number of loan-words from the Greek, such as *gubernare, ancora, prora, aplustre, anquina, antenna, faselus, contus,* and *nausea*. Hence it would appear that the undivided Aryans had invented canoes and oars, that the mast and the sail were used on inland waters after the linguistic separation of the Italic and Hellenic races, while the fact that the Latin word for sea-sickness is a loan-word from the Greek may indicate that the Italic peoples did not venture to navigate the sea before they

---

[1] Kluge, *Etymologisches Wörterbuch*, pp. 18, 35.

THE NEOLITHIC CULTURE. 179

came in contact with Greek civilisation.[1] It has already been noted that while the words relating to pastoral and agricultural pursuits are to a great extent identical in Greek and Latin, those referring to fishing, such as the names of the net, the line, and the hook, are entirely unrelated.[2]

§ 10. *The Ox-Waggon.*

Indubitably the greatest invention of the primitive Aryans was the ox-waggon. The names of the wheel (Latin, *rota*), of the yoke (Latin, *jugum*), of the wain (Sanskrit, *vahana*), and of the axle (Sanskrit, *aksha*), are common to all Aryan languages. The old Irish *carr* and the Latin *carrus* may also be compared with the *karama* which Hesychius tells us was the name of the covered waggon, or tent upon wheels, in which the nomad Scythians moved from place to place in search of pasturage for their cattle.

On a Thracian coin of the beginning of the fifth century B.C., which is attributed to the Odomanti, who inhabited the pile dwellings in Lake Prasias, we have the earliest representation of the primitive Aryan ox-cart.[3] The body is of wickerwork, poised over the axle, and is drawn by means of a pole by a yoke of oxen.

A similar ox-cart, conveying three female captives,

---

[1] Schrader, *Urgeschichte*, p. 112.
[2] Helbig, *Die Italiker in der Poebene*, p. 75.
[3] Head, *Historia Numorum*, p. 180.

is depicted on a bas-relief of Shalmaneser.[1] At the beginning of the New Empire both the Egyptians and the Hittites possessed war chariots drawn by horses. The signet-ring of Darius Hystaspes represents a lion hunt, in which the king is mounted on a car of the same construction as that seen on the coin of the Odomanti, but drawn by horses instead of oxen;[2] and the Persian kings are frequently thus represented on their coins.

The primitive ox-waggon must have been constructed without metal. The wheel and the axle were probably in one piece, made out of the section of the trunk of a tree, thinned down in the middle so as to form an axle, and leaving the two ends to serve as wheels. Such waggons are still used in Portugal. They are drawn by oxen, and have two wheels only. A log is cut from the trunk of a tree, and the centre is hacked away, leaving two solid wheels united by an axle.[3] A disc of walnut wood, apparently used as a wheel, was found in an Umbrian lake dwelling at Mercurago, near Arona, in Northern Italy.[4]

§ 11. *Trades.*

In the primitive age there could have been little division of labour. The earliest trace of a trade is that of the makers of flint implements, an art which requires considerable skill. At Brandon, in Suffolk, the neolithic people obtained flints by excavating shafts and galleries in the chalk with picks made of

---

[1] Lenormant, *Histoire de l'Orient*, vol. iv. p. 197.
[2] Head, *Coinage of Lydia and Persia*, p. 31.
[3] Pösche, *Die Arier*, p. 98.
[4] Keller, *Lake Dwellings*, p. 350.

stags' antlers; and at Cissbury, in Sussex, where thousands of flint implements have been found, there must have been a regular factory of neolithic implements.[1] As the undivided Aryans were in the stone age there is no common name for the smith, whose occupation must have been specialised early in the bronze age. Down to a late period, however, bronze implements were imported into Britain from the Continent. In the Vedas only two trades are mentioned, those of the smith and the carpenter. In Homer the τέκτων is both mason, carpenter, and shipwright.

The art of pottery dates from the beginning of the neolithic period, but there is no well-recorded case of pottery being found in association with palæolithic implements.[2] The neolithic pottery was made by hand, and there is no certain trace of the invention of the potter's wheel before the later settlements of the bronze age, such as those at Concise, where wheel-made vessels have been found.[3] With the invention of the wheel the potter's art seems to have become a trade, as is evidenced by the more elaborate and conventional style of ornament which is gradually introduced.

The invention of the potter's wheel may be approximately dated by the facts that it was known when the Homeric poems were composed, while all the pottery found in the burnt city at Hissarlik is hand-made,[4] and that no wheel-made pottery has been found in any of the North Italian settlements of the

[1] Dawkins, *Early Man in Britain*, p. 276.
[2] *Ibid.*, pp. 209, 227, 229; Mortillet, *Le Préhistorique*, p. 558.
[3] Keller, *Lake Dwellings*, p. 278.
[4] Schliemann, *Ilios*, p. 329.

bronze age. In some of the amphoræ found at Hissarlik the forms seem to have been imitated from those of water skins, the handles being survivals of the fore-legs of the animal, while the navel has developed into a central ornament, which was supposed by Dr. Schliemann to represent the head of an owl.

§ 12. *Social Life.*

It has often been assumed that the Greeks brought with them into Hellas a somewhat high degree of culture, but Thucydides possessed probably a keener historical insight when he acknowledges that they were at first barbarians. The primitive civilisation of the Italians and Hellenes cannot have been higher than that of the undivided Aryans, or so high as that of the Sarmatians, Scythians, Dacians, Celts, and Teutons, as described by ancient writers. The culture of Italy and Hellas must have been the result of a lengthened process of historical evolution, stimulated, and to a great extent imparted, by contact with the higher culture of the Semites, which again was derived from the proto-Babylonian people.

It is evident that even as late as the time when the Homeric poems were composed the Greek princes lived in dirt and squalor. There were muck-heaps in the palace of Priam, and at the door of the palace of Ulysses. In the hall where the suitors carousing, the hides and feet of oxen and the offal of beasts recently slaughtered for the feast lay upon the floor.[1]

When we read that at the funeral of Patrocles Achilles slaughtered, with his own hand, twelve noble

[1] Homer, *Il.*, xxiv. 640; *Od.*, xvii. 290; xx. 299; xxii. 363.

Trojan captives, four horses, and two dogs, and when we read the description of his dragging by the heels the body of Hector thrice round the walls of Troy, it is manifest that the golden age imagined by the poets was in reality an age of brutal savagery. In the older Greek myths and legends we find traces of human sacrifice, such as prevails at Dahomé, of infanticide, of the exposure of children, of the capture and sale of wives, which must be regarded as survivals from an earlier stage of barbarism.

We find traces of the same practices among other Aryan nations. Human sacrifice prevailed among the Celts in Cæsar's time, and among all the Teutonic tribes,[1] and did not cease in Iceland before the conversion of the Scandinavians to Christianity at the close of the tenth century.

When a war galley was launched by the Vikings, men were bound to the rollers, so that the keel was sprinkled with their blood.[2] The practice of breaking a bottle of wine over a ship's stem at the launch may be regarded as a survival of this savage Scandinavian practice of "reddening the rollers," as it was called, just as the custom of leading an officer's charger before the coffin at his funeral is a survival of the old practice of sacrificing a chieftain's wives and horses at his pyre.

There is reason to believe that infanticide, human sacrifice, and even cannibalism were practised in Britain, if not by the Celts, certainly by the Iberians; and Mr. Bateman affirms, as the result of his explorations among prehistoric graves, that there is accumulated evidence to prove that wives were burnt

[1] Maclear, *History of Christian Missions*, p. 28.
[2] Vigfusson and Powell, *Corpus Poeticum Boreale*, vol. i. p. 410.

on the funeral pyres of their deceased husbands.[1] There can be no doubt that it was an early Aryan custom to kill the widow at her husband's funeral. Children were exposed, and infant daughters especially were put to death at the father's will. Among the Indians, the Iranians, the Scandinavians, and the Massagetæ, the aged were killed when they became an encumbrance.

Even the people of the Swiss lake dwellings fashioned the skulls of their enemies into drinking cups,[2] and the Greek κόμβος, which may be traced in Sanskrit and Zend, may indicate that the same savage custom was not unknown to the Indo-Iranians and the Greeks. The Sanskrit word *gola*, a round pot, reappears in Greek, and the Latin *testa* in Zend and Lithuanian.

The primitive Aryans were undoubtedly polygamists. Herodotus attributes polygamy to the Persians, and Tacitus to the Germans; and there are traces of ancient polygamy in the Vedas. But primogeniture seems to have been the Aryan custom from the first. Even at the very earliest period the Aryans had passed beyond the polyandrous stage of society. The tribal community of women, of which obscure survivals may be traced in the customs of exogamy, and of inheritance through the mother, doubtless existed among non-Aryan tribes, such as the proto-Medes, the Lycians, the Etruscans, and the Picts, and in more recent times among the Lapps, the Ostiaks, the Tunguses, and the Todas.

The curious custom of the *couvade* seems to be Iberian rather than Aryan. It is practised in Corsica,

---

[1] Lubbock, *Prehistoric Times*, p. 176.
[2] Gross, *Les Protohelvètes*, p. 107.

the South of France, the North of Spain, and in Western Africa, regions where we find traces of the Iberian race.[1]

Marriage by purchase, which prevailed among the Germans, the Thracians, the Latins, and the Vedic Indians, is a stage in advance beyond marriage by capture, of which we find traces among the ruder Dorians, and perhaps in Italy.

Only three words denoting family relationships are found in every branch of Aryan speech. These are the names for mother (*matar*), brother (*bhratar*), and father-in-law (*socer*). The last[2] is of especial value, as it affords a conclusive indication of the institution of marriage, and of orderly family arrangements among the undivided Aryans.

The primitive designation of the daughter-in-law[3] is nearly as widely spread, being wanting only among the Iranians, the Celts, and the Lithuanians. Such terms are unknown among savages, and go further than any other words that have been adduced to establish the social relations of the Aryans at the very earliest epoch.

The names for father (*pitar*), husband (*pati*), son (*sunus*), daughter (*duhitar*), as well as for sister, step-mother, and son-in-law, are also believed to be primitive, though they are wanting in one or more of the Aryan languages. But we must beware of such little idyllic pictures as that of "the father calling his daughter his little milkmaid,"[4] as it is more

[1] Lubbock, *Origin of Civilisation*, p. 18; Guest, *Origines Celticæ*, vol. i. p. 63; Tylor, *Early History of Mankind*, p. 303.

[2] Latin, *socer;* Slavonic, *svekru;* German, *schweiger;* Welsh, *chwegron;* Greek, ἑκυρός; Sanskrit, çvaçura.

[3] Latin, *nurus;* Greek, νυός; Sanskrit, *snushâ;* Slavonic, *snucha;* Teutonic, *snura*.   [4] Max Müller, *Essays*, vol. i. p. 324.

probable that *duhitar* means simply the "suckling," like the Latin *filia*, and not the milker of the cows.[1]

The unit of society was the family, comprising wives, children, and slaves; but investigations into the common Aryan names for "nation" or "tribe" yield no very definite result. Probably it was at some period later than the linguistic separation that the family grew into the gens, thorp, vicus, or φρατρία. Neighbouring *gentes* then combined for mutual protection, and some central hill, where the dead were buried, was surrounded by an earthen mound as a place of refuge in time of common peril, and the tribe was governed by the *rex*, whose chief duty was to declare the ancient customs of the tribe. The oldest words for "law" primarily denote "custom." The duty of blood revenge and the permission to atone for blood by a *wergeld* seem to have been among the earliest sanctions of customary law, and may be traced among communities so widely separated as the Afghans, the Homeric Greeks, the Iranians of the Avesta, and the Germans of the time of Tacitus.

That the primitive Aryans had nothing which we can call science may perhaps be inferred from the fact that the Teutonic word "leech," for a professor of the healing art, though found in Celtic and Slavonic, does not extend to the Southern or Eastern tongues. The Aryan words for herbs, healing drugs, poison, and magic, are mostly unrelated. The Aryan languages, however, possess common words denoting wound, vomit, cough, and heal.[2]

That the undivided Aryans had devised the decimal

---

[1] Rendel, *The Cradle of the Aryans*, p. 11.
[2] Schrader, *Urgeschichte*, p. 409.

system of notation, enabling them to count up to a hundred, is a proof that they were in advance of some existing tribes of savages, who are only able to count up to three or five. The notation was digital, as is shown by the fact that the word *five* means hand or fist. They were, however, unable to count up to a thousand, a number which is differently designated in Latin, Greek, Sanskrit, and German.

The oldest Aryan designation for periods of time was the "month," which takes its name from the moon, the universal "measurer" of time. The week is not a primitive conception, the months being divided into half-months by the light half and dark half of the moon. The names of the week and autumn were the last to be devised. The name of the "year" is not primitive. The Aryans noticed the winter, *hiems*, the time of snow, and the summer, and reckoned at first by seasons rather than by years. The Greek ἔτος is etymologically identical with the Latin *vetus*, and meant the "old" or past time. The Latin *annus* is the ring or circle of the seasons, while the Teutonic "year" is the Greek ὥρα, and meant the "season" or the "spring." It has been already noted[1] that the fact of the autumn being the last of the seasons to receive a special name is an indication that the primitive Aryans were in the pastoral rather than the agricultural stage of civilisation.

The primitive Aryan worships and conceptions of religion are so important in any estimate of the culture they had attained that their discussion must be reserved for a separate chapter.

The most widespread Aryan word for sea is *mare*, but since this only means "dead" water as dis-

[1] See p. 164, *supra*.

tinguished from running water, it does not follow that the primitive Aryans knew the sea. The word may have originally designated merely a stagnant lake or pond. Perhaps the most singular defect in the linguistic record is the want of any common word for river.

We may now briefly sum up our conclusions, which are essentially those of Hehn and Schrader, and have been obtained by correcting the earlier conclusions of philology by the safer evidence of archæology. We find the undivided Aryans were a pastoral people, who wandered with their herds as the Hebrew patriarchs wandered in Canaan, or as the Israelites wandered in the desert. Dogs, cattle, and sheep had been domesticated, but not the pig, the horse, the goat, or the ass, and domestic poultry were unknown. The fibres of certain plants were plaited into mats, but wool was not woven, and the skins of beasts were scraped with stone knives, and sewed together into garments with sinews by the aid of needles of bone, wood, or stone.

The food consisted of flesh and milk, which was not yet made into cheese or butter. Mead, prepared from the honey of wild bees, was the only intoxicating drink, both beer and wine being unknown. Salt was unknown to the Asiatic branch of the Aryans, but its use had spread rapidly among the European branches of the race. In winter they lived in pits dug in the earth, and roofed over with poles covered with turf or plastered over with cow dung. In the summer they lived in rude waggons, or in huts made of the branches of trees. Of metals, native copper may have been beaten into ornaments, but tools and weapons were mainly of stone. Bows were made of the wood of the yew, spears of ash, and shields of woven osier twigs. No metal was used in the construction of their waggons; and trees were hollowed out for canoes by stone axes, aided by the use of fire.

According to Hehn, the old or sick were killed, wives were obtained by purchase or capture, infants were exposed or killed, and after a time, with tillage, came the possession of property, and established custom grew slowly into law. Their religious ideas were based on magic and superstitious terrors, the powers of nature had as yet assumed no anthropomorphic forms, the great name of Dyaus, which afterwards came to mean God, signified only the bright sky. They counted on their fingers, and the earliest abstract conception was decimal numeration, but they had not attained to the idea of any number higher than a hundred.

§ 13. *Relative Progress.*

We have hitherto considered mainly the civilisation attained by the Aryans before the linguistic separation, but the science of linguistic palæontology yields some interesting results as to the relative progress of the different Aryan families.[1] We have already seen that the advance was unequal, some nations, for instance, being still in the stone age, while others were acquainted with bronze, and others with iron. Culture spread by means of commercial intercourse along the great trade routes, from Phœnicia to Greece and then to Italy, from Italy to the Celts, and from Celts to Germans.

It is plain from the character of the culture words

[1] See Schrader, *Urgeschichte,* pp. 74-96.

common to Zend and Sanskrit that the Indians and Iranians had before their separation advanced farther in the path of civilisation than any of the other Aryan nations. They knew themselves as a united people (Sanskrit *árya*, Zend *airya*). They had common words for bridge, column, battle, fight, sword, spear, and bowstring, and they could count up to a thousand. But the agreement in religious terms is the most striking proof of the stage of culture they had reached. They had common words for priest, sacrifice, song of praise, religious aspergation, for the sacred soma drink, for God, Lord, for heroes and demons, and for Mithra, the god of light. The chief Indian god, Indra, the god of storms, who in the Rig Veda is a beneficent deity, becomes in the Avesta a malignant power. It was formerly believed that a religious schism was the primary cause of the separation of the Indians and Iranians, but this notion is now universally given up.

Next to the Indians and Iranians the Slaves and Teutons exhibit the greatest community of culture. They have common words for gold, silver, and salt; for hoe, quern, beer, ale, and boots; for swan, herring, and salmon; for rye and wheat; and for many trees, including the aspen, the maple, the apple, and the wild cherry. They have the same name for the smith, and for many weapons; for autumn and thousand; for various maladies; as well as for lies, shame, sorrow, trouble, scorn, and, perhaps more significant than all, we discover that venal vice was accounted opprobrious.

But there are a host of culture words common to all Teutonic languages, which they do not share with their near neighbours the Slaves. In the first rank of such words are those which indicate that while the Slaves were an inland people the Teutons lived near the sea. Such are designations for sea, haven, cliff, strand, island, flood, whale, seal, gull, and many words connected with the building and steering of boats. Among trees the name of the lime; among animals those of the roe, the reindeer, the squirrel, and the fox are peculiar to the Teutons. Many names of weapons, and terms connected with metallurgy, cookery, and dress, are confined to the Teutons. Hose and shoes are peculiar to the Teutons, breeks are common to Celts and Teutons, and boots to Teutons and Slaves.

The Teutons have a special name for the horse, and peculiar terms connected with horsemanship, such as reins, spurs, and saddle. They have a new name for the house, which however was still built of wood, and new terms denoting autumn and winter, as well as for battle, victory, fame, honour, as well as for letters and the art of writing; while the names of deities and the words referring to religion are almost wholly different among the Teutons and the Slaves.

On the other hand, the undivided Slaves, after their separation from the Teutons, acquired special terms to denote iron, knife, javelin, sword, spur, needle, anchor, plough, ploughshare, corn, wheat, barley, and oats; but there are no words common to all the Slavonic dialects for steel, paper, velvet, or pavement. The still undivided Slaves cultivated the cabbage, pea, bean, lentil, leek, poppy, and hemp; they knew the oak, lime, beech, birch, willow, fir, apple, plum, and nut; they had common words for weaving and for clothes, for woodwork and ironwork; they dwelt in villages, and had huts or houses made of intertwined boughs; but all their terms connected with masonry are loan-words from foreign tongues. They had common words to designate law and rights, family and tribe, but none for inheritance or property—an indication that the land and all connected with it still belonged to the undivided house-family or *mir*.[1]

The relation between the Celts and Germans is peculiar. Linguistically they are far apart, proving that the separation dates from a very early period; but there are numerous culture words of an advanced character which seem to show that at some period subsequent to the original separation they were in geographical contact, the Celts, as the more civilised race, exercising a political supremacy over some of the Teutonic tribes. The line of contact, as has already been suggested, was probably the range of mountainous forest which separates the basins of the Elbe and the Oder from the basin of the Danube.

The connection of the Celtic and Italic languages is structural. It is much deeper than that of Celts and Teutons, and goes back to an earlier epoch. Celts and Latins must have dwelt together as an undivided people in the valley of the Danube, and it must have been at a much later time—after the Umbrians and Latins had crossed the Alps—that the contact of Celts and Teutons came about.

We have already seen that the Teutons got their knowledge of iron from the Celts, and it will be shown in the sixth chapter that Woden, the great Teutonic deity, may be identified with the Celtic Gwydion. The words for law and king are the same in the Celtic and Teutonic languages. Another indication of an early supremacy exercised by the Celts

[1] Schrader, *Urgeschichte*, pp. 90-93.

over the ruder tribes to the north of their territory is the noteworthy fact that the Celtic *ambactus*, which denotes a certain magistracy, is found as a loan-word in the Gothic *andbahts*, and also in the Slavonic *jabedniku*. We must thus explain a number of culture words common to Latin and Teutonic as words which originally belonged to the Italo-Celtic unity, which were obtained by the Teutons from the Celts, and this accounts for the curious fact that in political and legal terms Latin is nearer to German than it is to Greek. Thus the Latin *civis* is the Teutonic *hiva*, but has no connection with the Greek πολίτης. The Latin word *hostis* is the Teutonic *guest*, while the Greek word for a stranger is ξένος. The Greeks used the words νόμος and θεσμός for law, while the Latins had *lex*, and the Germans *laga*. The Greeks used the word βασιλεύς for king, while the Latins had *rex*, and the Germans *reika*.[1]

Latin words of this class, which agree with those in Greek, such as *crimen, poena, talio*, manifestly pertain to an earlier and more primitive condition of society.[2]

Other culture words which the Celto-Italic languages share with Teutonic are the Gothic *thiuds* (people), which is the Umbrian *tutu*, and the Celtic *tuath;* the Latin *ador* (spelt), which is the Irish *ith*, and the Gothic *atisk* (seed). The Latin *far* is the Irish *bairgen* and the Gothic *baris* (barley). The Latin *granum* is our corn; and the Latin *sero* is the Irish *sil*, and the Gothic *saian*.[3]

Long ago Niebuhr and O. Müller drew attention to

[1] Schrader, *Urgeschichte*, p. 75.
[2] *Ibid.*, pp. 78-80.
[3] *Ibid.*, p. 184.

the significant fact that many words relating to husbandry and peaceful avocations, the names for house, field, wood, plough, acorn, apple, fig, wine, oil, salt, honey, milk, dog, ox, bull, calf, sheep, ram, and swine, are identical in Greek and Latin.

It is, however, only the most rudimentary terms connected with agriculture which agree in Greek and Latin. The names for the various species of grain, for the various parts of the plough, for the winnowing fan, for the hand-mill, and for bread, are all different. So also are the words denoting the most elementary legal and political conceptions, as well as the words relating to metals, seamanship, fishing, and war, and the names of weapons, such as *tela, arma, hasta, pilum, ensis, gladius, arcus, sagitta, jaculum, clupeus, cassis, balteus, ocrea*, none of which can be traced in Greek.

Greek, in such matters, has more in common with Sanskrit than with Latin, the Indian and Hellenic words for the spearhead, the sling-stone, the arrow being the same. The name of the axe, πέλεκυς, is peculiar to Greek and Sanskrit. Greek also agrees with Indo-Iranian in the words for the ploughshare, the tilled field, the "fork" for digging, the spindle, town, revenge, and punishment, and in the names of three deities.[1]

We must therefore conclude that the Italic and Hellenic families separated at the very beginning of the agricultural stage, before the most elementary political ideas had been formed; before there was any conception of law, citizenship, or sovereignty; before the bow, the spear, the sword, or the shield had been invented; while the Greeks remained in contact with

[1] Schrader, *Urgeschichte*, p. 315.

the Indo-Iranians till the rudimentary forms of the later weapons had been developed.

The Indo-Iranian has several points of cultural contact with the Slavo-Lettic languages, such as the words for the master of house, marriage, holy, noon, cock, bitch, corn, and two divine names, Bogu and Perkunas.

While there is little agreement between Greek and Slavonic, yet the agreement of both with Indo-Iranian is too marked to be the result of accident. It therefore seems probable that the Indo-Iranians remained in contact on the one side with Greeks and on the other with the Slaves for some time after the final separation of Greeks and Slaves.

The Baltic and Indian languages have, however, very few culture words in common. The old Norse *âs*, god, spirit, is the Sanskrit *âsu*, life, which is plainly the primitive meaning. The old High German *ewa*, law, is the Sanskrit *eva*, custom; and the Gothic *hairus*, sword, the Lithuanian *kirwis*, axe, and the Sabine *curis*, spear, are the Sanskrit *çaru*, a thunderbolt.

The Celts share with the Slaves the words denoting winter, silver, plough, wheat, beer, yeast, wax, apple, thousand, and some words referring to tillage.

Armenian shares with Greek words for honey, salt, wine, field; with Lithuanian the name for fish, and with Latin the name of the moon.

The Celts, Albanians, Slaves, and Teutons have all borrowed the Latin *murus*, a sure indication that the art of masonry was obtained from Italy by the northern nations. The Latin *mina* and the Greek μνᾶ are Semitic loan-words, showing that weights and measures were brought to Europe by the Phœnicians. The Teutonic *pfunt* and *pfeil* are loan-words from the

Latin *pondus* and *pilum*, and the Slavonic *chlebu*, bread, is a loan-word from the Teutonic *hlaifs*, loaf.

Just as the Finns borrowed countless culture words from the Teutons and Slaves, so the Greeks borrowed no less than a hundred culture words from the Phœnicians.

As a general rule the terms relating to a pastoral life are identical among the European and Asiatic Aryans, whereas the words relating to fixed tillage differ more or less—an indication that the separation of the Indo-Iranian family from the European Aryans took place during the nomad pastoral stage of civilisation.

In any case we conclude that the undivided Aryans must have been a numerous people occupying an extensive territory before any but the rudest civilisation was developed, and that the separation began at a time when, like the Tartars at the present day, they roamed in waggons with their flocks and herds over a wide region.

CHAPTER IV.

THE ARYAN RACE.

§ 1. *The Permanence of Race.*

OUR next task is to examine which of the neolithic races has the best claim to be identified with the primitive Aryans.

It is manifest that Aryan blood is far from being co-extensive with Aryan speech. Aryan languages must have extended themselves over vast regions which are occupied by the descendants of non-Aryan races. That this should have been possible is due to the fact that change of language is more easy and frequent than change of physical type.

Broca has insisted on the fact, at one time almost forgotten, that language as a test of race is more often than not entirely misleading. He has rightly maintained that the ethnological characters of the first order of importance are physical, not linguistic.

Mixed races are not so common as is sometimes supposed. They are found, however, in some parts of Europe, especially in England, Normandy, and Central Germany, as is shown by the existence of persons combining blue eyes with dark hair.

It will, however, be impossible to do full justice to the theories of Pösche and Penka, presently to be considered, as to the extension of Aryan speech, without setting forth the reasoning by which they explain the disappearance of intrusive races, and the reversion to primitive types.

It is alleged that in the case of conquest, when two races are diverse, or where the environment favours one race more than the other, it is found that the offspring are infertile, or that there is a tendency to revert to one of the parent types. We get fertile hybrids from different varieties of the dog, or of the pigeon, but not from the dog and the wolf, the horse and the ass, the pigeon and the ringdove.

It is the same with the races of mankind. A mixed race may arise when the parent races do not very greatly differ. But this is not the case when the difference is great. Scherzer says that the child of a European father and a Chinese mother is either altogether European or altogether Chinese. According to Admiral Fitzroy, the half-castes between Europeans and Maoris are unmistakably red, without any tendency to yellow.[1] The same is the case at Tahiti, where the offspring of French fathers and native mothers are copper-coloured.[2]

A Berber, with blue eyes and no lobule to the ears, married an Arab woman who was brown, and with ears regularly formed. They had two children—one like the father, the other like the mother. An Englishman had several children by a negress, some of whom were of the European, others of the African type. I was much struck with a case I met with at Palermo. A tall, fair, blue-eyed gentleman, of the pure Scandinavian type, had married a short, swarthy, black-eyed Sicilian lady. They had three boys. The eldest was the image of the mother, the youngest of the father,

[1] De Quatrefages, *Hommes Fossiles*, p. 493.   [2] *Ibid.*, p. 494.

while the second had the eyes and complexion of one parent and the hair of the other.

But even when a half-breed race has come into existence the tendency is to revert to one of the parent types—a tendency which is powerfully aided by environment. At the close of the last century the Griquas, who are half-breeds between the Dutch Boers and the Hottentots, were numerous at the Cape, but as early as 1825 they had practically reverted to the Hottentot type.

Different races do not possess an equal faculty for acclimatisation. In the West Indies and the Southern States of North America it is said that the half-breeds between the Anglo-Saxon and negro races tend to become sterile, while the offspring of French or Spanish fathers and negro women are more fertile. Pösche affirms that his own observation, extending over many years, has led him to the conclusion that without an infusion of fresh blood no race of mulattoes has maintained itself to the third generation.[1] In Jamaica both the whites and the mulattoes become sterile, while the negroes are prolific; and hence the type is lapsing into the pure negro. The European element is dying out, not only through sterility, but by the liability to tropical diseases, which are not so fatal to the natives of the equatorial regions. The English race is doomed to disappear, leaving behind it nothing but a corrupt English jargon as an evidence of its former dominance.

Negroes succeed in the West Indies and the Gulf States, but die out in Canada and New England. The English race succeeds in the Northern States and Australia, but fails in India and the tropics.

[1] Pösche, *Die Arier*, p. 10.

The Dutch fail to naturalise themselves in Java and Sumatra; and in the third generation even the Malay half-breeds become sterile. The Dutch have left no descendants in Ceylon, but at the Cape they have large families, possessing great stature and physical power. The French succeed in Canada and the Mauritius. In the West Indies and New Orleans they can exist, but they do not increase in numbers. In Algeria emigrants from the Northern Departments of France fail to become acclimatised, while those from the Southern Departments succeed. The Spaniards, a South European race, succeed in Mexico and Cuba, and, together with Maltese and Jews, thrive better in Algiers than any other emigrants from Europe.[1]

In Egypt no foreign race has ever naturalised itself. The Egyptian Fellah still exhibits the precise type seen upon the monuments. The Ptolemaic Greeks have left no trace, the Mamelukes were unable to propagate their race, the Albanians and Turks are mostly childless, and there is great mortality among the negroes.

In India the children of Europeans fade away unless they are sent home before they are ten years old. There is in India no third generation of pure English blood. The Eurasians do not possess the vigour of their fathers, or the adaptation of their mothers to the Indian climate. Hindustan is Aryan in speech, but not in race. There are in India some 140 millions of people who speak Aryan languages, but the actual descendants of the Aryan invaders are very few. They are represented by certain Rajput

[1] Topinard, *L'Anthropologie*, p. 407.

families, and by the Brahmins of Benares and some other cities on the Ganges.

As a rule it is found that Northern races die out if transplanted to the South, and the Southern races become extinct in the North.

At St. Petersburg the deaths exceed the births, and in North Russia the Slavonic-speaking population only maintains itself owing to the blood being mainly Finnic or Samoyed.

Races become numerically predominant in localities where from physical causes the birth-rate is greatest and the death-rate least. The fair race holds the Baltic lands, the brown race the shores of the Mediterranean, and the black race holds the tropics. It is for this reason that intrusive conquest or colonisation has usually left little or no trace. The Gothic blood has nearly died out in Spain, the Lombard in Italy, and the Vandal in Northern Africa. Southern Germany was originally Celtic or Ligurian. It was Teutonised in speech by German invaders; the Row Graves of the Alemannic warriors show a mean index of 71.3, and only 10 per cent. of the skulls have an index above 80. But the dolichocephalic type of the Teutonic conquerors has now disappeared from South Germany, and the prehistoric brachycephalic type has re-asserted itself, except among the nobles who are of the Teutonic type. The mean index in the Swabian, Alemannic, and Bavarian lands is now 80. Plainly the fair northern dolichocephalic race has been unable to maintain itself, and has left little more than its Teutonic speech as an evidence of conquest.

As a rule the fair races succeed only in the temperate zones, and the dark races only in tropical or sub-tropical lands.

This has been attributed to four causes—

(1) Sterility.

(2) Infantile mortality.

(3) The tendency of an unsuitable climate to enfeeble the constitution so as to prevent recovery from ordinary disease.

(4) The liability to certain special maladies. Pulmonary affections carry off the negroes in the North, while gastric and hepatic disorders are fatal to Europeans in the tropics. Thus, while yellow fever proves deadly to the whites in the West Indies, the negroes escape, and a very slight infusion of negro blood acts as a prophylactic. Negroes succumb readily to the plague, which weeds them out in Egypt, but they enjoy comparative immunity from diseases of the liver. Italians resist malaria better than the English or the Germans.

On the other hand, feeble indigenous races are unable to maintain themselves in presence of the higher civilisation of an invading race which happens to be suited to the environment.

In the United States the Red Indians are rapidly disappearing before the whites, while in Mexico the Aztec race shows a continually increasing preponderance over the descendants of the Spanish conquerors. But the Tasmanians, Australians, Maoris, Fijians, and Sandwich Islanders have disappeared or are destined to disappear. The Arabs in Algeria are withdrawing to the Sahara, but the Berbers prosper and increase. The French conquest has resulted in one native race being supplanted by another, just as in the West Indies the European occupation has caused the Carib tribes to disappear before the more vigorous negro race which has been introduced.

These results are partly due to the destruction of former means of subsistence, the former population being unable to adapt itself to new modes of life. The wholesale destruction of the bison and the kangaroo has manifestly accelerated the extermination of the Red Indians and the Australians. The transformation from a hunting to a pastoral life, or from the pastoral to the agricultural stage, cannot rapidly be accomplished. New habits are slowly learnt.

But the introduction of new diseases is an important factor in the disappearance of native tribes. The first outbreak of measles carried off nearly half the population of Fiji, and small-pox and scarlatina have elsewhere proved nearly as deadly.

From the foregoing facts it is maintained that hybrid races are not so common as has been often assumed. When two distinct races are in contact they may, under certain circumstances, mix their blood, but the tendency, as a rule, is to revert to the character of that race which is either superior in numbers, prepotent in physical energy, or which conforms best to the environment.

The extreme cases of Haiti and Jamaica may suffice to prove that a dominant race may impose its language on a servile population, and then in the course of two or three centuries may become extinct. These considerations may prepare us to recognise the possibility that Persia, Northern India, and even some parts of Europe, may be Aryan in speech, though they may not, to any appreciable extent, be Aryan in blood.

§ 2. *The Mutability of Language.*

While race is to a great extent persistent, language is extremely mutable. Many countries have repeatedly changed their speech, while the race has remained essentially the same.

Language seems almost independent of race. Neo-Latin languages are spoken in Bucharest and Mexico, Brussels and Palermo; Aryan languages in Stockholm and Bombay, Dublin and Teheran, Moscow and Lisbon, but the amount of common blood is infinitesimal or non-existent.

In France it is probable that nineteen-twentieths of the blood is that of the aboriginal races, Aquitanians, Celts, and Belgæ; while of the later conquerors the descendants of the Teutonic invaders, Franks, Burgundians, Goths, and Normans, doubtless contributed a more numerous element to the population than the Romans, who, though fewer in number than any of the others, imposed their language on the whole country. Again, the speech of Belgium is French—a neo-Latin dialect; and yet it may well be doubted whether in Belgium there is any Roman blood at all. Coming to Italy, the south is Japygian, Sicanian, and Greek, while the north is Etruscan, Ligurian, Rhætian, Celtic, Herulian, Gothic, and Lombard; while the speech is the speech of Rome, a city which itself contained an overwhelming proportion of Syrians, Greeks, and Africans. The actual amount of Latin blood in Rome was probably extremely small, and yet the speech of Rome extends over Italy, France, Spain, Portugal, Belgium, and Roumania, as well as over a part of Canada and of the United States, and over the whole, or nearly the whole, of Central and South America.

In modern Europe the same struggle for linguistic existence is going on, and the great national languages are exterminating the small isolated tongues. English has replaced Celtic speech in Cornwall, and is encroaching on it in Wales, Ireland, and Scotland. In Brittany the Armorican will speedily become extinct; and in the Basque lands Aryan speech is, as usual, exterminating a non-Aryan language. Basque still survives near St. Sebastian and Durango, but in the neighbourhood of Pampeluna and Vittoria it has already given place to Spanish. Though the French and Spanish Basques speak dialects of the same languages, they belong anthropologically to different races, one of which must have imposed its speech upon the other. The disappearance of the Ladino of the Tyrol, and of the Romansch of the Grisons, is only a question of time.

Within the historic period German has replaced Celtic speech in the valleys of the Danube and the Main, and has more recently extinguished two Slavonic dialects, Polabian and Wend. The old Prussians spoke a sister language of the Lithuanian; they now speak German. In spite of a strong national sentiment, Hungary and Bohemia are becoming bilingual, and there can be little doubt as to the ultimate result. On the Volga, Russian is exterminating various Finnic languages, such as the Mordwin and the Wotiak. Tartaric speech is disappearing at Kasan and in the Crimea. In America all the aboriginal and local languages are doomed to extinction at no very distant time. English has replaced, or is replacing, Spanish in California, Florida, and Texas, and French in Louisiana. In Lower Canada the French-speaking population is being out-numbered by the English. English is now extending itself over large portions of the globe, as was formerly the case with Latin.

Or look at Mexico. The Spanish conquerors, few in number, succeeded in imposing on the natives their Latin speech, their religion, and their way of life; but the blood is mainly Aztec. After three centuries, the descendants of the Conquistadores are dying out, and the conquest has left its mark mainly in the Latin dialect which has been substituted for the ancient Aztec idiom, and in the allegiance to an Italian bishop.

But these very Spaniards who have imposed a Latin dialect on so large a portion of the New World, were they Latins, or even Aryans, in blood? Spain was originally Iberian or Berber. In prehistoric times the Celts wrested a large portion of the peninsula from the Iberians, the Phœnicians founded populous and important cities, the Vandals, Goths, and Suevi poured in from the north, and the Moors and Arabs from the south. The speech, and very little more than the speech, is Latin; the Romans, of whose blood the trace must be extremely small, have imprinted their language upon Spain, and the Spaniards, by reason of their speech, are often reckoned among the Latin races.

The speech of Tunis has been in turn Numidian, Phœnician, Latin, Vandal, and Arabic, and may ultimately become French. In Syria the speech was at first Semitic; it afterwards became Aryan, and is now once more Semitic.

Arabic, the local dialect of Mecca, has become the language of numerous non-Semitic peoples. A host of non-Aryan tribes in India speak neo-Sanskritic languages. The Turks in Candia almost universally speak Greek; at Damascus they speak Arabic. Many of the Papuas speak Malay dialects, and so do the Chinese in Borneo. In Africa languages of the Bantu class are spoken by races as dissimilar as the Caffres and the Guinea negroes. The Huzaras, who are pure Mongols, descendants of the followers of Ghengis Khan, still preserve their marked Mongolian physiognomy, but speak good Persian. The Tschuwash and Bashkirs, who are of Finnic race, speak Turkic dialects.

The Huns who followed Attila have left their name in Hungary, but not their speech. The Gauls who wandered from the banks of the Moselle, and finally settled in Asia Minor, left their name on the province of Galatia, but their language has become extinct. The Bulgars in Dacia acquired the language of their Slavonic subjects.

There is no reason to suppose that the political, social, and religious causes which have brought about such extensive changes of language during historic times, and which have not ceased to operate, were less effective in the prehistoric period. Aryan speech especially seems to possess the power of exterminating non-Aryan dialects. Finnic, Basque, Magyar, Turkish, are gradually, but surely, being replaced by Aryan languages in Europe. In America, North and South, in South Africa, Polynesia and Australasia, Aryan speech is rapidly extending its domain. Four hundred years ago no Aryan language was spoken on the great American continent; in much less than four hundred years hence there will not, save in the names of places, be a vestige left of any non-Aryan speech. Three thousand years ago the speakers of Aryan languages in India numbered a few thousands; now they number 140 millions. In the neolithic period Aryan languages can hardly have been spoken by more than a million persons. At the present time they are spoken probably by 600 millions—half the population of the globe.

Among the chief causes which have effected such wide extensions of certain languages are slavery, conquest, numerical superiority, commerce, political supremacy, religion, and superior culture. Slaves or serfs readily learn the language of their masters. The negroes in Haiti and the Mauritius speak French; in Cuba, Spanish; in Jamaica, English; in Brazil, Portuguese. In Mexico the pure-blooded Aztecs, who form the larger part of the population, speak Spanish, and so do the Guaranis of Paraguay.

Isolated local dialects are at a disadvantage when in contact with great national languages. To this cause we may attribute the retrocession or extinction of the Wendish and Lettic dialects in Germany, of Finnic dialects in Eastern Russia, of Etruscan, Celtic, and Greek in Italy, of Cornish in England, and of Basque in Spain. Within a measurable period all the Celtic, Euskarian, Finnic, and Turkic languages will have disappeared from Europe, and the whole continent will be Aryan in speech.

In the case of conquest it by no means invariably happens that the language of the conquerors prevails. As in the instances of the Scandinavian conquest of Normandy, of the Norman conquest of England, or of the Roman conquest of Gaul, the conquered country is for a time bilingual, but ultimately one of the two languages must infallibly supplant the other; usually, however, as we shall presently see, undergoing in the process certain modifications, partly phonetic, and partly in the direction of a simplified grammar.

The Roman conquest of Gaul and Spain, the Mahommedan conquests in Syria, Egypt, and Northern Africa, the Teutonic conquest of Southern Germany, and the Anglo-Saxon conquest of England are the chief instances in which the language of the conquerors has prevailed. But the reverse has been even more frequently the case.

Greek, which was established for a while by the conquests of Alexander as the court language at Antioch, Alexandria, Seleucia, and Samarkand, has now disappeared, leaving nothing but a few coins and inscriptions. The present inhabitants of Greece are largely a Slavonic race, which in the eighth century occupied the lands and learned the speech of the Greeks. There is probably as much of the old Greek blood at Syracuse, Salerno, or Brindisi as in some parts of Hellas. The kingdoms established by the crusading Franks have left behind them only the crumbling ruins of vast fortresses, and perhaps half-a-dozen Western loan-words which have found their way into Arabic. No vestige of Mongolic speech attests the European conquests of Attila or Genghis Khan.

The Bulgars exchanged their own Turkic speech for the Slavonic dialect of their subjects. In Normandy the Northmen acquired French, which in England they exchanged for English. The Franks, the Lombards, the Sueves, the Vandals, and the

Goths were unable to impose their Teutonic speech on the Southern lands which they overran. Dr. Hodgkin has described for us the process by which the Gothic language and nationality were extinguished in Italy. The Teutonic invaders were scattered over the land, nominally as paid protectors, really as masters, each receiving what may be designated either as salary or tribute. They became inmates of the Roman homes, enjoying half the house, half of the produce of the vineyard and the farm; they became in most cases the sons-in-law of the Roman citizens whom they protected, but their children were brought up to speak the language of their mothers. Even in Burgundy, where the conquerors were the more numerous race, as is shown by the fact that in the Department of the Doubs the racial type is Teutonic, the speech is now a neo-Latin dialect.

Plainly the laws which regulate the survival of language do not conform to the same conditions as those which regulate the survival of race. The language which prevails in the struggle for existence is sometimes that of the less numerous race, sometimes that of the race which is physically the feebler. It is sometimes that of the conquerors; sometimes it is that of the conquered. Some other law must evidently be sought. The law seems to be that the more civilised race, especially when it is politically dominant, and numerically preponderant, is best able to impose its language on the tribes with which it comes in contact. This law has been thus formulated by Professor Sayce. "We may lay it down as a general rule," he says, "that whenever two nations equally advanced in civilisation are brought into close contact the language of the most numerous will prevail. Where, however, a small body of invaders brings a higher civilisation with them, the converse is the more likely to happen. Visigothic was soon extirpated in Spain, but English flourishes in India, and Dutch at the Cape. Conquest, however, is not the sole agent in producing social revolutions extensive enough to cause a total change of language. Before the Christian era, Hebrew, Assyrian, and Babylonian had been supplanted by Aramaic. It was the language of commerce and diplomacy."[1] The influence of a powerful religious belief, especially when enshrined in the pages of a sacred book, has immense influence. The Arabs were inferior in culture to the Roman provincials of Syria, Egypt, and Northern Africa, but the language of the Koran has prevailed.

We may now apply these principles to the spread of Aryan speech in prehistoric times. As the Aryans were probably in most cases numerically fewer than the races whom they Aryanised, we must believe them to have been their superiors in culture as well as in physical force.

The Hellenes when they invaded Greece were undoubtedly more civilised than the non-Aryan aborigines; and the Umbrians were more civilised than the savage Ligurians and the Iberian cannibals whom they found in Italy. The round barrow Aryans of Britain were superior in culture to the feebler long barrow race which they subjugated and supplanted.

The Avesta affords some indications of the struggle between the Iranians and the non-Aryan indigenous tribes on whose territory they encroached; but the Vedic poems supply the best picture we possess of

[1] Sayce, *Principles of Comparative Philology*, p. 167.

the gradual advance of Aryan speech and culture which must have gone on in other lands.

The Aryan invaders, few in number, who were settled on the banks of the Upper Indus, are found gradually advancing to the south and the east in continual conflict with the Dasyu or dark-skinned aborigines, who spoke a strange language, worshipped strange gods, and followed strange customs, till finally the barbarians are subdued and admitted into the Aryan state as a fourth caste, called the "blacks," or Sudras. The higher civilisation and the superior physique of the northern invaders ultimately prevailed, and they imposed their language and their creed on the subject tribes; but the purity of the race was soiled by marriage with native women, the language was infected with peculiar Dravidian sounds, and the creed with foul Dravidian worships of Siva and Kali, and the adoration of the lingam and the snake.

The Aryanisation of Europe doubtless resembled that of India. The Aryan speech and the Aryan civilisation prevailed, but the Aryan race either disappeared or its purity was lost.

The rule that it is the more civilised race whose language prevails in the struggle for linguistic existence will incline us to discover the primitive Aryan race in the most civilised of the neolithic races. It is not probable that the dolichocephalic savages of the kitchen middens, or the dolichocephalic cannibals who buried in the caves of Southern and Western Europe, could have Aryanised Europe. It is far more likely that it was the people of the round barrows, the race which erected Stonehenge and Avebury, the people who constructed the pile dwellings in Germany, Switzerland, and Italy, the brachycephalic ancestors of the Umbrians, the Celts, and the Latins, who were those who introduced the neolithic culture, and imposed their own Aryan speech on the ruder tribes which they subdued.

§ 3. *The Finnic Hypothesis.*

The mutability of language and the permanence of race make it easy to understand that the greater part of Europe may be non-Aryan by blood, but Aryan in speech.

The neolithic races of Europe are so distinct in their anthropological characteristics that only one of them can represent the primitive Aryan race; the others must be regarded as Aryanised by conquest or contact.

The examination of the existing and prehistoric European types has led us to the conclusion that the primitive Aryans must be identified with one of four neolithic races, which, for convenient reference, may be re-enumerated as follows—

(1) The Scandinavians, a tall Northern dolichocephalic race, represented by the Row Grave and Stængenæs skeletons, and the people of the kitchen middens. The stature averaged 5 feet 10 inches. They were dolichocephalic, with an index of from 70 to 73, and somewhat prognathous, with fair hair and blue eyes, and a white skin. They are represented by the Swedes, the Frisians, and the fair North Germans.

(2) The Iberians, a short Southern dolichocephalic race, represented in the long barrows of Britain and the sepulchral caves of France and Spain. The

stature averaged 5 feet 4 inches, and the cephalic index 71 to 74. They were orthognathous and swarthy. They are now represented by some of the Welsh and Irish, by the Corsicans, and by the Spanish Basques. Their affinities are African.

(3) The Celts, a tall Northern brachycephalic race, represented in the round barrows of Britain, and in Belgian, French, and Danish graves. They were macrognathous and florid, with light eyes and rufous hair. The stature was 5 feet 8 inches, and the index 81. They are now represented by the Danes, the Slaves, and some of the Irish. Their affinities are Ugric.

(4) The Ligurians, a short Alpine brachycephalic race, represented in some Belgian caves and in the dolmens of Central France. They were black-haired, mostly orthognathous, with an index of 84, and a stature of 5 feet 3 inches. They are now represented by the Auvergnats, the Savoyards, and the Swiss. Their affinities are Lapp or Finnic.

Aryan languages are spoken in Europe by races exhibiting the characteristics of all these types; and in India and Persia by Asiatic types, Dravidian and Semitic, the Aryan blood having been merged in that of conquered races. Hence the primitive Aryans must be sought for among the four European races—Scandinavian, Celtic, Ligurian, and Iberian.

Some thirty years ago a theory which was originally propounded by Retzius, and supported by Baer and Prüner-Bey, was very generally adopted. There are in Europe two races, then believed to be autochthonous—the Finns and the Basques—whose languages do not belong to the Aryan family of speech. Retzius, assuming that both the Finns and the Basques were brachycephalous, and remarking that the Swedes were dolichocephalous, formulated his celebrated "Finnic theory," which long dominated ethnologic science, and is even now not without adherents. He maintained that the primitive population of Europe was a brachycephalic "Turanian" race, the sole survivors of which are now represented by the Finns and Basques. He supposed that this aboriginal population was overwhelmed by dolichocephalic invaders speaking an Aryan language, who are now represented in their greatest purity by the Swedes. These invaders penetrated into Europe from the East, exterminating or enslaving the "Turanian" aborigines, the Basques taking refuge in the Pyrenees, and the Finns in the swamps and forests of the North. This theory has been stated by Professor Max Müller with his habitual lucidity. He informs us that "wherever the Aryan columns penetrated in their migration from the East to the West they found the land occupied by the savage descendants of Tur."[1]

The "Finnic theory" of Retzius was very generally accepted, but little by little new facts were slowly accumulated, which proved that the proposition of Retzius must be reversed. Broca showed that the Spanish Basques, who are the true representatives of the Basque race, are dolichocephalic, and are not, as Retzius had supposed from an examination of skulls of some French Basques, brachycephalic. De Quatrefages and Hamy then proved that the supposed

[1] Broca objects, not unreasonably, to "Tur," and remarks, somewhat sarcastically, on this passage, "Voici un personage vénérable, qui fut oublié par Moïse, et qui vient s'asseoir aujourd'hui à coté des fils de Noé."—Broca, *La Linguistique et l'Anthropologie*, p. 238.

Aryan invaders were in fact the earliest inhabitants of Europe, and actually possessed a lower culture than the "savage descendants of Tur." The order in which the skulls are superimposed at Grenelle proves that both the dolichocephalic races preceded the two brachycephalic races[1] The most ancient skulls of all are those of dolichocephalic savages of the Canstadt and kitchen midden type, who subsisted mainly on shell fish, and must be regarded as the ancestors of the Scandinavian, North German, and Anglo-Saxon race. Next in order of time we find the Iberian race of savages, who subsisted on the chase, and practised cannibalism and human sacrifice, and whose descendants are found in Corsica, Spain, and Northern Africa. These Iberians were pressed back by the brachycephalic Ligurian race, who arrived in the reindeer period, and are possibly of Lapp affinities. The most recent type of skull is that of the tall brachycephalic "Turanian" people of the Finno-Ugric type, who arrived in Belgium and Britain towards the close of the neolithic age. Their civilisation was higher than that of any of the previous races. They do not seem to have been troglodytes, but were nomad herdsmen, living in huts.

The two "Turanian" races were the last to arrive. The brachycephalic Ligurian race drove the dolichocephalic Iberians to the South and West, and the brachycephalic "Celtic" race drove the dolichocephalic Scandinavians to the North. The result is that Central Europe is brachycephalic, while the North and the South are dolichocephalic. Hence the "Finnic theory," as propounded by Retzius, has been completely overthrown.

[1] See p. 116, *supra*.

The primitive Aryans—that is, those who spoke the primitive Aryan speech—may have been one of the four neolithic races, or they may have been a later intrusive race. The objection to this last hypothesis is that there is no archæological evidence for any such intrusion. The four European types may be traced continuously in occupation of their present seats to the neolithic period; and in the case of the Italic and Swiss pile dwellers, and of the round barrow people of Britain, we must believe that their speech in neolithic times was Aryan—either Celtic or Italic.

We are therefore compelled to adopt the hypothesis that one of the four neolithic races must be identified with the primitive Aryans, and that this race, whichever it was, imposed its Aryan speech on the other three.

We have now to examine in turn the claims of each of the four neolithic races to represent the primitive Aryan stock. The question cannot be considered as determined, the French and German scholars being ranged in opposite camps. All that can be done is to lay impartially before the reader the evidence, such as it is, for forming an opinion. For convenience we may commence with the two short, dark races, the Iberians and the Ligurians, with whom the difficulty is least.

§ 4. *The Basques.*

The singular Basque or Euskarian language, spoken on both slopes of the Pyrenees, forms a sort of linguistic island in the great Aryan ocean. It must represent the speech of one of the neolithic races, either that of the dolichocephalic Iberians, or that of the brachycephalic people whom we call Auvergnats or Ligurians.

Anthropology throws some light on this question. It is now known that the Basques are not all of one type, as was supposed by Retzius and the early anthropologists, who were only acquainted with the skulls of the French Basques. Broca has now shown that the Spanish Basques are largely dolichocephalic. The mean index of the people of Zarous in Guipuzcoa is 77.62. Of the French Basques a considerable proportion (37 per cent.) are brachycephalic, with indices from 80 to 83. The mean index obtained from the measurements of fifty-seven skulls of French Basques from an old graveyard at St. Jean de l'Luz is 80.25. The skull shape of the French Basques is therefore intermediate between that of the Auvergnats on the north, and that of the Spanish Basques on the south.

It is plain that the Basques can no longer be regarded as an unmixed race, and we conclude that the blood of the dolichocephalic or Spanish Basques is mainly that of the dolichocephalic Iberians, with some admixture of Ligurian blood, while the brachycephalic or French Basques are to a great extent the descendants of the brachycephalic Auvergnats.

We have seen that the South of France was, in the early neolithic age, occupied exclusively by the dolichocephalic race. It has been shown that the sepulchral caves and dolmens of the Lozère supply evidence that early in the neolithic period their territory was invaded by the brachycephalic race, which drove them towards the Pyrenees, where the two races intermingled. One race must clearly have acquired the language of the other. The probability is that the invaders, who were the more powerful and more civilised people, imposed their language on the conquered race, in which case the Basque would represent the language of the Ligurians rather than that of the Iberians. All the available evidence is in favour of the solution.

The attempt of Wilhelm von Humboldt[1] to identify the old Iberian language with the Basque is now generally held to have failed. The highest authority, Van Eys, considers that it is impossible to explain the ancient Iberian by means of Basque. Vinson comes to the same conclusion. He holds that the legends on the Iberian coins are inexplicable from the Basque language, and he considers that they point to the existence in Spain of a race which spoke a wholly different tongue. This tongue belonged probably to the Hamitic family.

We possess some two hundred ancient Numidian inscriptions which exhibit very old forms of the Berber tongue, now spoken by the Towarag and Tamaskek tribes and the Kabyles. These inscriptions suffice to prove that the Numidian belonged to the Hamitic family of speech, and that it is distantly allied to the Nubian and the old Egyptian.[2] With this Berber or Hamitic family of speech the Basque has no recognisable affinity. Many philologists of repute have come to the conclusion that Basque must ultimately be classed with the Finnic group of languages. Professor Sayce, for instance, considers that "Basque is probably to be added" to the Ural-Altaic family.[3]

---

[1] Von Humboldt, *Prüfung der Untersuchungen über die Urbewohner Hispaniens.* (Berlin, 1821.)

[2] Sayce, *Science of Language,* vol. ii. pp. 37, 180.

[3] Sayce, *Principles of Philology,* p. 98.

He says—" With this family I believe that Basque must also be grouped. Prince Lucien Bonaparte, Charencey, and others have shown that this interesting language closely agrees with Ugric in grammar, structure, numerals, and pronouns. Indeed, the more I examine the question the nearer does the relationship appear to be, more especially when the newly-revealed Accadian language of Ancient Babylonia, by far the oldest specimen of the Turanian family that we possess, is brought into use for the purposes of comparison."[1] " In spite of the wide interval in time, space, and social relations, we may still detect several words... which are common to Accadian and Basque."[2]

These philological conclusions are in accord with the anthropological evidence.

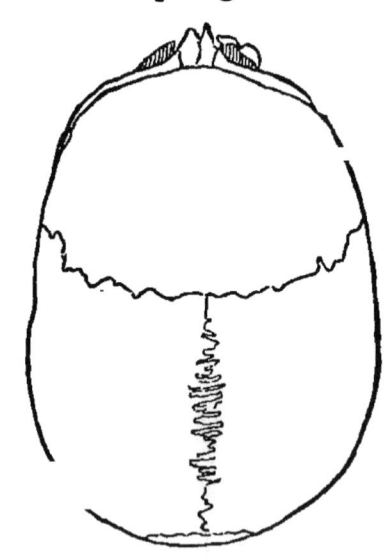

The skulls of the pure Iberian race, such as those which are found in the long barrows of Britain, or the Caverne de l'Homme Mort, are of the same type as those of the Berbers and the Guanches, and bear a considerable resemblance to the skulls of the ancient Egyptians. The skulls of the Spanish Basques present a modified form of this type, the cephalic index having probably been raised by admixture with the Ligurian invaders.

SKULL OF A SPANISH BASQUE.[3]

---

[1] Sayce, *Principles*, p. 22. [2] *Ibid.*, p. 108.
[3] Compare with this the Auvergnat skull figured on p. 111, and the Iberian skull from Gibraltar on p. 123.

We have also seen that the skulls of the Auvergnats, with whom the French Basques must be classed, belong to the Finnic or Lapp type, a fact which increases the probability that the Basque speech, whose affinities are with the Finnic group of languages, represents the primitive speech of the ancient brachycephalic inhabitants of Central France.

But at the beginning of the historic period the speech of these people, the true "Celts" of history and ethnology, differed little from the language of the Belgic Gauls, which we usually call Celtic.

Not to speak of the evidence of inscriptions, this is sufficiently established by Glück's examination of the names of Gaulish chieftains and of local names.[1] Thus in Belgic Gaul we find such names as Noviomagus, Lugdunum (Leyden and Laon), Mediolanum, and Noviodunum; while in the part of Gaul inhabited by Cæsar's Celts we find names either absolutely identical or of the same type, as Noviodunum, Lugdunum (Lyons), Mediolanum (Meillan), and Uxellodunum.

This Southern extension of the language of the Belgic Gauls is no matter for surprise, since the sepulchral caves and dolmens of the Marne and the Oise afford evidence that the Northern race gradually extended its domain to the South.

Aryan speech, as we have seen, possesses in a high degree the power of extirpating languages less highly organised. When the tall powerful Belgic Gauls extended their dominion over Central France, they would almost inevitably impose what we call "Celtic" speech upon the feebler brachycephalic Basque-

---

[1] Glück, *Die bei C. J. Cæsar Vorkommenden Keltischen Namen.* (München, 1857.)

speaking Auvergnats, who ethnologically are entitled to the Celtic name.

If so, we should expect to find that the Ligurians, who ethnologically belong to the same race as the Auvergnats, spoke a language of the Basque, and not of Celtic, type. We have only one undoubted Ligurian word, *asia,* which, as we learn from Pliny, denoted, in the speech of the Taurini, grain of some kind, probably rye or spelt, and this word has as yet been only explained from Basque sources.[1]

Helbig is of opinion that we have an undoubted Ligurian word in the name of Cimiez, near Nice, which was formerly Cimella, or Cemenelum.[2] The word "Cima," which we have in the name of several Swiss peaks, such as the well-known Cima de Jazi, must have meant a hill. Vestiges of the oldest races are commonly found in the names of mountains, and it is worthy of note that the great mountain mass of Auvergne bears the name of the Cevennes, a corruption of Κέμμενος ὄρος, afterwards known as the Cebenna Mons.

The comparison of local names is beset with uncertainties, but it may be noted that certain names in Liguria, such as Iria, Asta, Astura, and Biturgia, are identical with local names in Spain.[3]

Still more notable is Humboldt's failure[4] to discover in Spain, with the exception of names in *briga,* which may be otherwise explained, any names of the ordinary Celtic type which are so common in Gaul. The conspicuous absence of names ending in *dunum, magus, lanum,* and *dorum,* looks

---

[1] Diefenbach, *Origines Europææ,* p. 235.
[2] Helbig, *Die Italiker in der Poebene,* p. 30.
[3] Humboldt, *Prüfung,* p. 111.   [4] *Ibid.,* p. 100.

as if the "Celts" and Celtiberians of Spain did not speak what we call a "Celtic" language.

On the other hand, Celtiberian Spain, which is supposed to have been the district conquered or colonised by the Celts, contains numerous tribe names in *etani*, which is explained as the plural locative suffix in Basque, meaning "those who dwell in" the district designated by the first portion of the name. In Gaul we only find this suffix among the Aquitani, who were the ancestors of the French Basques. That the language spoken by the Aquitani, which must have been an ancestral form of Basque, was actually designated as the "Celtic" speech is indicated by a curious little piece of evidence which may be taken for what it is worth. The French Basques occupy the same territory as the Aquitani of Cæsar, the corner between the Garonne and the Pyrenees. Now Sulpicius Severus, writing in the fourth century A.D., distinguishes between the "Celtic" and "Gallic" speech. A Gaul, he says, speaks *Gallice*, an Aquitanian speaks *Celtice*.[1] Gallic was undoubtedly what we now call "Celtic," while the Aquitani, who lived in a district where "Celtic" has never been spoken, nevertheless spoke what Sulpicius called Celtic, which must be the language which we should call Basque. This would be decisive if it were not for the doubt whether the Aquitania of Sulpicius was co-extensive with the Aquitania of Cæsar, or whether it included the district between the Loire and the Garonne, which was added by Augustus to the older Aquitania for administrative purposes.

It may be as well to sum up briefly the argument set forth in the foregoing pages.

[1] See Penka, *Origines Ariacæ*, p. 106.

The tall, fair-haired Gauls were of a wholly different type from the short, dark Auvergnats. It is impossible to believe that the language of both races was originally identical, as it had become in the time of Cæsar. One of these races must have imposed its language on the other. Not only were the Belgic Gauls the conquering people, but their language had been extended to Belgium and to Britain, where no traces of the Ligurian race have been discovered. Hence it is most probable that what we call "Celtic" speech was the original speech of the Belgic Gauls, and not of the Auvergnats, the true "Celts" of Broca. Basque must represent either the speech of these true "Celts" or that of the Iberians, as no other neolithic race is found in the Aquitanian region. The race type of the Iberians was that of the Berbers, and their tongue was probably the same—a language of the Hamitic family. Hence we conclude that the language of the "Celts" is now represented by that of the Basques, who, if we may trust Sulpicius Severus, spoke a language which he calls "Celtic."

The Iberians were a feeble race, in a low stage of culture, without cereals or any domesticated animals, and their pottery is of the rudest type. On the coasts of Portugal we find shell mounds resembling the kitchen middens of Denmark, and we discover traces of cannibalism in some of their heaps of refuse. It is not probable that they were able to impose their language on the more highly civilised Ligurians. We therefore conclude that the language of the Silurian or Iberian race which occupied Britain, Gaul, and Spain at the beginning of the neolithic age was akin to that of the Hamitic race, to which they belong anthropologically, its nearest congener being that of the Numidian inscriptions.

Towards the close of the reindeer period a short, dark brachycephalic race of Finnic or Lapp blood, who are the Ligurians of modern ethnologists and the "Celts" of Cæsar, speaking a Euskarian language which is believed to belong remotely to the Ural-Altaic class, made their appearance in Western Europe. They found Gaul occupied by a short, dark dolichocephalic people, Silurians or Iberians, who retreated southwards to the region of the Pyrenees. Here the Ligurians amalgamated with them to some extent, and imposed on them their language. This mixed race is known as Basque or Celtiberian.

Later in the neolithic age a tall, xanthous, brachycephalic race, belonging to the Ugric type, and speaking an Aryan tongue which philologists call Celtic, made their appearance in Belgium, north of the Sambre and the Meuse, and gradually drove the Ligurians before them out of Belgic Gaul. Throughout Central France the Ligurians acquired the Aryan speech of their conquerors, while south of the Garonne they retained their own language, which we know as Basque, but which is called Celtic by Sulpicius and Cæsar. Thus of the three neolithic races of Gaul, it seems most probable that the original speech of the Iberians was an Hamitic language, akin to the Numidian; that of the Ligurians was Euskarian, a Ural-Altaic language; while that of the Gauls was Celtic, an Aryan language.

Hence we conclude that neither of the southern races, the Iberians or the Ligurians, can be identified with the primitive Aryans. It remains now to examine the claims to the Aryan name of the two northern neolithic races, the Celto-Latin people of the pile dwellings, and the Scandinavian people of the kitchen middens.

§ 5. *The Northern Races.*

If, as seems probable, the speech of the Iberians was Hamitic, and that of the Ligurians was Euskarian, neither of these races can be identified with the primitive Aryans. Two possibilities remain to be discussed. The introducers of Aryan speech must have been either the dolichocephalic Row Grave race, now represented by the Swedes, the Frisians, and the North Germans; or, in the alternative, the brachycephalic round barrow race represented by the Lithuanians, the Slaves, the Umbrians, and the Belgic Gauls.

The question has been debated with needless acrimony. German scholars, notably Pösche, Penka, Hehn, and Lindenschmit, have contended that the physical type of the primitive Aryans was that of the North Germans—a tall, fair, blue-eyed dolichocephalic race. French writers, on the other hand, such as Chavée, De Mortillet, and Ujfalvy, have maintained that the primitive Aryans were brachycephalic, and that the true Aryan type is represented by the Gauls.

The Germans claim the primitive Aryans as typical Germans who Aryanised the French, while the French claim them as typical Frenchmen who Aryanised the Germans. Both parties maintain that their own ancestors were the pure noble race of Aryan conquerors, and that their hereditary foes belonged to a conquered and enslaved race of aboriginal savages, who received the germs of civilisation from their hereditary superiors. Each party accuses the other of subordinating the results of science to Chauvinistic sentiment.

Thus Pösche, in somewhat inflated language, writes:—" The true scientific theory, which uplifts itself, calm and clear, like the summit of Olympus, over the passing storm-clouds of the moment, is that a noble race of fair-haired, blue-eyed people vanquished and subjugated an earlier race of short stature and dark hair. In opposition to this is the new French theory, without scientific foundation, originating in political hatred, which asserts that the primitive Aryans were a short and dark people, who Aryanised the tall, fair race."[1]

M. Chavée, on the other hand, contends that the intellectual superiority lies with the other race. Look, he says, at the beautifully-formed head of the Iranians and Hindus, so intelligent and so well developed. Look at the perfection of those admirable languages, the Sanskrit and the Zend. The Germans have merely defaced and spoilt the beautiful structure of the primitive Aryan speech.

Ujfalvy says " if superiority consists merely in physical energy, enterprise, invasion, conquest, then the fair dolichocephalic race may claim to be the leading race in the world; but if we consider mental qualities, the artistic and the intellectual faculties, then the superiority lies with the brachycephalic race."

De Mortillet also is strong to the same effect. The civilisation of Europe is due, he contends, to the brachycephalic race.[2]

---

[1] Pösche, *Die Arier*, p. 44.
[2] De Mortillet, *Le Préhistorique*, p. 629.

The disputants seem, however, to have forgotten that neither the French nor the Germans, any more than the English or the Americans, can claim to be an unmixed race. North-eastern France, from Normandy to Burgundy, although of Latin speech, is largely of Teutonic blood, while Central and Southern Germany are occupied by brachycephalic races which have acquired Teutonic speech.

The claimants who have the best pretensions to a pure Aryan pedigree are the dolichocephalic Swedes and the brachycephalic Lithuanians, neither of which has played any very prominent part in history. It is rather the orthocephalic people, found alike in Germany, France, England, and the United States, who, having acquired their physical endowments from the one race, and their intellectual gifts from the other, have reached the highest standard of perfection.

The French cannot claim to be descended from the Gauls any more than the Germans can claim to be descended from the Teutons. When Niebuhr, from the pages of Diodorus and Polybius, described the Gauls who invaded Italy, with their " huge bodies, blue eyes, and bristly hair,"[1] he received a letter from France complaining that he had described not Gauls but Germans. In like manner the Teutonic tribes, Alemanni, Suevi, and Franks, who Teutonised Southern Germany, differed altogether from the existing type. In the Row Graves, which are the tombs of these invaders, the mean cephalic index is as low as 71.3. The nobles, descended from these invaders, are still blue-eyed and dolichocephalic, but the burghers and peasants are brachycephalic, with a mean index of 83.5.

[1] Niebuhr, *Lectures on the History of Rome*, p. 262.

THE ARYAN RACE. 229

In order to determine the affinities of the primitive Aryans we must go back to an earlier time, and compare the Row Grave race, who were unmixed Teutons, dolichocephalic and platycephalic, with the round barrow people, who were pure Celts, brachycephalic and acrocephalic.

The types are so different, and can be traced so far back into the neolithic age, that they cannot be identified. One only can be Aryan by blood, the other must be merely Aryan in speech.

On this question experts differ in opinion, according to their nationality. The problem is difficult, possibly insoluble. No very confident decision can be given, but the arguments on either side, such as they are, may be placed before the reader.

The German writers urge that the dolichocephalic Swedes, whom they claim as the representatives of the primitive Teutons, are the purest race in Europe, and that it is difficult to suppose that they could have acquired a new language without some admixture of blood, whereas Swedish graves, from the neolithic period down to the present day, exhibit precisely the same type of skull. They moreover contend that while the peasantry and middle classes over the greater part of Europe are brachycephalic, the nobles and landed proprietors approximate rather to the Teutonic type. This, they say, is a proof that a brachycephalic autochthonous people was conquered and Aryanised by Teutonic invaders.

It has, however, been already shown[1] that it is not the speech of the conquerors but the speech of the more numerous and more civilised people that usually prevails, and in the case of the Normans,

[1] See p. 210, *supra.*

the Goths, and the Burgundians, Teutonic conquerors have acquired the speech of the more civilised subject races. This argument cannot therefore be considered as conclusive.

Penka has also accumulated a considerable body of evidence, which has already been summarised,[1] to prove that when a Northern race comes under the influence of Southern skies it tends to die out, and he thus accounts for the fact that there is now no trace in Greece or Italy of the tall, fair, blue-eyed Scandinavian type, which he believes was originally that of the Greeks and Romans, as well as of the Persians and Hindus.

Since Penka's theories have met with wide acquiescence in Germany, and have obtained in England the adhesion of such influential scholars as Professor Rendel,[2] Professor Sayce,[3] and Professor Rhys,[4] it is less needful to repeat them at full length than to state the difficulties which must be met, and to examine certain arguments on the other side which, as yet, have hardly received the attention they deserve.

In determining which of the two Northern races has the best claim to represent the primitive Aryans two kinds of evidence have to be taken into account. One is linguistic, the other archæological.

It will be shown in the next chapter that when any race abandons its old language and adopts another, the acquired speech is liable to undergo certain changes, both phonetic and grammatical, owing to the difficulty of pronouncing unaccustomed sounds, and of learning the niceties of an elaborate

[1] See pp. 199-203, *supra*.
[2] Rendel, *The Cradle of the Aryans*, pp. 49, 63.
[3] Sayce, *Report of the British Association* for 1887, p. 890.
[4] Rhys, *Race Theories*, p. 4 (*New Princeton Review*, Jan. 1888).

grammar. Hence a language which has lost many of the primitive inflexions, and also exhibits extensive phonetic changes, is more likely to be an acquired speech than a language which in these respects has suffered little change.

Judged by this standard the Lithuanian, among European languages, has the best claim to represent the primitive speech. More perfectly even than Greek, far more perfectly than Gothic, it has preserved the original inflexions as well as the original sounds.

The Teutonic languages, on the other hand, have undergone extensive mutilation. They have lost many of the old inflexions which have been preserved in the Slavo-Lettic languages, and more especially in Lithuanian. Gothic has lost the dual, the old ablative, and nearly all the old datives. In conjugation it has lost the aorists, the imperfect, and the future, and has only preserved the present, and a very faint trace of the reduplicated perfect. Lithuanian has retained the dual and all the old cases, as well as the present and the future; while the South Slavonic has retained the aorist and the imperfect. In all these points the Slavo-Lettic languages are nearer to the proto-Aryan speech.

The Lithuanian phonology is also the more primitive, as will be seen by comparing the Lithuanian *dalptan* with the Teutonic *delfan*, to delve; *gibanti* with *giban*, to give; *woazis* with *ask*, an ash; *lomiti* with *lam;* *pulkas* with *folc;* *klente* with *hrind;* *kiausze* with *haus;* *kaistu* with *heito*, *heiz* and *hot;* *gladuku* with *glat;* *tukstantis* with *thusandi* and *thousand*.[1]

[1] See Schmidt, *Verwandtschafts verhältnisse der Indo-Germanischen Sprachen*, pp. 36-45.

If the Teutons are not Aryans by blood, but only Aryanised, how did they acquire Aryan speech? Geographically they were hemmed in by the Celts and the Lithuanians. The relations between Celtic and Teutonic speech are not so intimate as to make it probable that either could have been derived from the other. But with the Lithuanian it is different. The Lithuanians belong to the great brachycephalic race, the Teutons to the dolichocephalic. The two races are, and as far as we know have always been, in geographical contact, and Teutonic speech is nearer to Lithuanian than to any other Aryan language. According to Penka's theory, the ancestors of the Lithuanians acquired Aryan speech from the ancestors of the Teutons; according to the other theory, the ancestors of the Teutons acquired it from the ancestors of the Lithuanians.

It is difficult to believe that the Teutonic, which has lost so many of the primitive inflexions, which has mutilated so many Lithuanian words, and has degraded the primitive phonology, can represent the mother-speech from which Lithuanian was derived; whereas there is no such insuperable difficulty in supposing that Teutonic may have been obtained from some older form of Slavo-Lettic speech. Moreover, on Penka's hypothesis a still greater difficulty has to be met. It will have to be explained how the speech of the brachycephalic Celts and Umbrians, to say nothing of that of the Greeks, the Armenians, and the Indo-Iranians, was obtained from that of the dolichocephalic Teutons; how a people which in neolithic times was few in numbers, and in a low stage of culture, succeeded in Aryanising so many tribes more numerous and more civilised.

We have now to consider the other department of the evidence—the evidence of archæology and of linguistic palæontology. We have already seen[1] that the general law is that when two races in different stages of culture are in contact the speech of the more cultured is likely to prevail in the struggle for linguistic existence. This rule has a most material bearing on the question. If with Penka we are to believe that the Teutons were by blood the only pure Aryan race, which Aryanised all the rest, their relative culture should be high. But if we go back to the early neolithic period, the time when, if at all, the Teutons must have imparted Aryan speech to the other race, we find that the dolichocephalic people of the Baltic coast were in the lowest grade of savagery, while the brachycephalic races of Central Europe had made no inconsiderable progress in civilisation, and had reached the nomadic pastoral stage.

Coming down to a much later period, we find that at the close of the neolithic age the Teutonic race was the more backward, since their culture words are largely loan-words from the contiguous Slavo-Lettic and Celtic languages. This is the case even with words referring to agricultural and pastoral life.

As M. d'Arbois de Jubainville and other writers have shown, Celtic, in its fundamental morphological structure, is more closely related to Latin than it is to Teutonic. The relations between Celtic and Teutonic date from a comparatively late period, and are valuable as showing the relative civilisation which had been attained by both peoples. Several Celtic

[1] See p. 210, *supra*.

loan-words which have found their way into Teutonic relate to matters of civil and military administration. They can hardly be later than the time of the Gaulish empire founded by Ambigatos in the sixth century B.C. We gather from them that at this, or some earlier period, the culture and political organisation of the Teutons was inferior to that of the Celts, and that the Teutons must have been subjected to Celtic rule. It would seem from the linguistic evidence that the Teutons got from their Celtic and Lithuanian neighbours their first knowledge of agriculture and metals, of many weapons and articles of food and clothing, as well as the most elementary, social, religious, and political conceptions, the words for nation, people, king, and magistrate being, for instance, loan-words from Celtic or Lithuanian.

The hypothetical Aryanisation of Europe by Teutonic conquerors which Penka's theory demands must be referred to a very remote period, long before the rudiments of civilisation had been imparted to the Teutons by contact with the more civilised Celts. It is difficult to suppose that the Teutons, several millenniums before they had acquired the conception of sovereignty, of a nation, of an army, or of a state, could have Aryanised by conquest the ancestors of peoples so much more advanced in social organisation and the arts of life as the Indians and the Iranians, or the Homeric Greeks and the people of Mycenæ and Tiryns.

These hypothetical Teutonic conquests must have taken place very early in the neolithic age, or how can we explain the Aryan speech of the Celts and Umbrians, who erected Stonehenge and Avebury, and constructed the lake dwellings in Southern Germany, Switzerland, and Italy.

We must inquire whether at so remote a time the dolichocephalic people of the Baltic coasts had arrived at a stage of civilisation which would make it probable that they could have conquered and Aryanised all the brachycephalic Southern races.

We learn from the science of linguistic palæontology that the undivided Aryans were a neolithic people who had reached the pastoral stage, and may have practised some rude form of sporadic agriculture. It is certain that they had domesticated the ox, and probably the sheep, following their herds in waggons, and constructing huts with roofs and doors, but they were probably unacquainted with the art of catching fish, which they did not habitually use for food.

With this linguistic evidence as to the grade of civilisation attained by the undivided Aryans, we may compare the archæological evidence as to the civilisation of the neolithic ancestors of the Teutons and the Celts.

It has already been shown that the neolithic people of the shell mounds of Sweden and Denmark represent the ancestors of the Scandinavians and Teutons, while the neolithic people of the pile dwellings of Southern Germany, Switzerland, and Northern Italy are to be identified with the brachycephalic ancestors of the Celto-Latin race.

At the earliest period to which our knowledge extends the valley of the Danube was occupied by dolichocephalic savages of the Canstadt race, who sheltered themselves in caves. They were replaced, in the early neolithic age, by the brachycephalic people whose remains are found in the mound graves of this region, and who are believed to belong to the same race as the round barrow people of Britain. To this race the pile dwellings must be assigned. In the peat bogs and lakes of Carniola, Austria, Bavaria, Würtemberg, and Baden, we find the remains of pile dwellings which are the prototypes of the later pile dwellings of Switzerland and Northern Italy, and which to all appearance were constructed by races essentially the same, who extended eastward to Dacia and Thrace. According to Herodotus, there were pile dwellings in Lake Prasias, in Thrace. The Dacians were an Aryan people akin both to Thracians and Celts, and a representation of a Dacian pile dwelling may be seen on Trajan's column at Rome.[1] Remains of pile dwellings, belonging to the neolithic age, have also been found in the Lithuanian region. The practice of erecting pile dwellings seems therefore to have been common to the Aryan-speaking peoples of Central Europe.

One of the oldest pile dwellings hitherto discovered, coeval it is believed with the Danish shell mounds,[2] has been disinterred from a peat moss at Schussenried, on the Feder See, in Würtemberg. The stage of culture here disclosed is precisely that which linguistic archæology proclaims to have been possessed by the primitive Aryans. The people lived mainly by the chase. The bones of the stag are more plentiful than those of any other animal, but those of the wild boar are common. The dog, the ox, and the sheep had been domesticated, but no bones of the goat or of the horse have as yet been found. The implements were

---

[1] Helbig, *Die Italiker in der Poebene*, p. 56.
[2] Keller, *Lake Dwellings*, vol. i. p. 589.

of stone, horn, and bone. Mealing stones were found, and charred wheat, but cereals are less abundant than stores of hazel nuts, beech mast, and acorns. Linseed was found, but no linen, the only fabric being a bit of rope made of twisted bast. It is to be noted that no fishing implements of any kind were discovered; there were a few vertebræ of a pike, but the extreme rarity of fish bones is remarkable.

Remains of a somewhat later settlement exist in the Lake of Starnberg, in Bavaria. Here the bones of the dog, the ox, the sheep, and the goat are numerous, together with hazel nuts and barley.

It will be noticed that the civilisation disclosed in these settlements, and in some similar ones on the northern shore of the Lake of Constance, agrees very remarkably with that of the primitive Aryans.

Older probably, if we may judge from the absence of cereals, is the very ancient lake dwelling which has been disinterred from the peat bog on Laibach Moor, in Carniola, about fifty miles north-east of Trieste.[1] That this region was occupied by a Celtic-speaking people is indicated by the fact that the moor is intersected by a river which bears the common Celtic name of the Isca, which was also the ancient name of the Devonshire Exe and the Monmouthshire Uxe. The inhabitants of this settlement were in the pastoral stage; they possessed cows, sheep, and goats, but lived principally by fishing and the chase, their food consisting chiefly of the flesh of the stag and the wild boar. They cultivated no cereals, but laid up stores of hazel nuts and water chestnuts (*Trapa natans*), which they pounded in stone mortars. They were in the neolithic stage, the implements are chiefly of stags' horn,

[1] Keller, *Lake Dwellings*, vol. i. pp. 606-618.

the stone implements are rude, not superior to those of Denmark. They were wholly ignorant of agriculture; neither grain, flax, nor linen, which are common in the Swiss settlements, have been found. The only woven fabric yet discovered was a piece of bast matting, manufactured from the bark of some tree.

The Laibach settlement was not abandoned till the age of metal had begun, a store of copper or bronze implements having been discovered on one spot—a fact which connects the settlement with the historical occupation of this region by the Latovici, who, according to Zeuss, were Celts.[1]

By this route, through Carniola, which forms the easiest passage across the Alps, the Umbrians, the near congeners of the Celts, may have penetrated into Italy. The other route, by the Brenner, was occupied by the Rhætians, who were probably of Ligurian race.

The Celts of the British round barrows and of the Belgian caves were in much the same grade of civilisation as the Celts of the earlier pile dwellings.[2] The round barrows of the stone age were the sepulchres of a pastoral people, who had domesticated the ox, the sheep, the goat, and the pig.[3] Though no remains of corn have been discovered, the mealing stones, which are not uncommon, are believed to prove that they used cereals of some description.[4] In all essential points the civilisation of the neolithic Celts of Britain was identical with that of the undivided Aryans as disclosed by linguistic archæology.

[1] Zeuss, *Die Deutschen*, p. 257.
[2] Greenwell, *British Barrows*, p. 114.
[3] *Ibid.*, pp. 168, 130, 132.
[4] *Ibid.*, p. 114.

We now turn to the people of the Danish shell mounds, who belonged to the tall dolichocephalic type now represented by the North Germans and the Swedes. This type has been so confidently identified by recent German writers — Lindenschmit, Penka, and Pösche—with that of the primitive Aryans, that the question of the grade of civilisation which they had attained has become an important factor in the discussion as to the ethnic affinities of the Aryans.

The vast mounds called *Kjœkkenmœddings*, which line portions of the Danish and Swedish coasts, have already been described.[1] They are manifestly the refuse accumulated during long ages by a race of savages. They are composed chiefly of the shells of oysters and other mollusks, but contain also numerous bones of wild animals, of birds, and of fish. Implements of stone are numerous; they are mostly rude, but in some instances carefully worked. Bone pins and implements of horn are found, but pottery, so abundant even in the oldest lake dwellings, is extremely rare. The rudeness of the stone implements and the rarity of pottery show that during the immense period required for the accumulation of these mounds the people who formed them had made little progress in the arts of life.

We now apply to these mounds the same linguistic tests which have been applied to the lake dwellings. They contain bones of the stag, the beaver, the bear, the otter, the hedgehog, the lynx, the fox, and the wolf, all of which, according to Schrader's linguistic investigations, were known to the primitive Aryans. This, however, is not decisive, since the bones of the horse, the hare, and the squirrel, animals also known

[1] See p. 61, *supra*.

to the undivided Aryans, are absent. Still more important is the absence of the bones of animals which, on linguistic grounds, are believed to have been domesticated before the separation of the Aryans. There are no remains of the goat, the sheep, or even of the ox, but only a few bones of the urus, which doubtless belonged to the wild animal, slain in the chase. The absence of the bones of the reindeer, which are found in the caves of the brachycephalic people of the Lesse, is an evidence of the comparatively recent date of the kitchen middens, and may also indicate that the Lapps had already retired farther to the North.

The only animal that had been domesticated was the dog, who was occasionally eaten when other food was scarce. The domestication of the dog has been established by Professor Steenstrup, who, as we have already seen, found by experiment that certain bones of birds, and certain portions of the bones of quadrupeds, which are invariably absent from the refuse heaps, are precisely those which are eaten by dogs, while those bones which do occur are those which dogs habitually reject.[1]

Now, the evidence of the Stængenæs skull identifies the kitchen midden people with the Scandinavian race, while the earlier pile dwellings are believed to be as old as some of the kitchen middens. The stage of civilisation disclosed by the earlier pile dwellings agrees with that which on linguistic grounds we must attribute to the undivided Aryans, while the civilisation of the kitchen middens was far ruder; not higher than that of the Fuegians or of the Digger Indians of Oregon.

[1] Lubbock, *Prehistoric Times*, p. 240; and see p. 130, *supra*.

Virchow, Broca, and Calori agree that the brachycephalic or "Turanian" skull is a higher form than the dolichocephalic. The most degraded of existing races, such as the Australians, Tasmanians, Papuas, Veddahs, Negroes, Hottentots, and Bosjemen, as well as the aboriginal forest tribes of India, are typically dolichocephalic; while the Burmese, the Chinese, the Japanese, and the nations of Central Europe are typically brachycephalic. The fact that the Accadians, who belonged to the Turanian race, had, some 7000 years ago, attained a high stage of culture, from which the civilisation of the Semites was derived, is a fact which makes it more probable that the language and civilisation of Europe was derived from the brachycephalic rather than from the dolichocephalic race.

There was an essential difference in the mode of life of the two races. The Aryans, before the linguistic separation, were a pastoral people, who had invented the ox-waggon, and had therefore certainly domesticated the ox, but were unacquainted with the art of fishing, since the words for the net, the line, the hook, and other fishing implements, differ in most of the Aryan languages; while fish-bones and hooks are absent from the older pile dwellings in Germany and Italy. The kitchen midden people, on the other hand, had not domesticated the ox, but subsisted chiefly on oysters, mussels, cockles, and periwinkles, varied by the products of the chase. They were, however, very skilful fishers, as the bones of the herring, the dorse, the dab, and the eel are extremely numerous in the shell mounds. If the Aryans are descended from the kitchen midden people, it is difficult to understand how they should have lost the taste for fish, or have relinquished their chief art—that of the fisherman.

It is not less difficult to believe that the repulsive savage of the kitchen middens, with his narrow brow, his retreating forehead, his low skull, his prognathous jaw, his prominent orbital ridges, and his animal propensities so clearly indicated by the occipital development, a mere nomad hunter, without fixed abode, and making use of no regular sepulchres, could have been the ancestor of the noble Aryan race. It is easier to believe that the Aryan civilisation originated with the broad-headed race of Central Europe, which possessed the skill to construct, with rude stone tools, the pile dwellings of Switzerland and Italy.

It may be urged that the two civilisations were not synchronous, and that the accumulation of the shell mounds ceased long before the earliest of the pile dwellings were erected. This, however, does not seem to have been the case. The two periods are believed to have overlapped for some two or three thousand years, while the types of the flint implements found in the lake dwellings at Schussenried are thought to be more archaic than some of those from the kitchen middens.[1] Moreover, there are reasons for believing that the mode of life of the shell mound people lasted down to the historic period. Virchow, as we have seen,[2] claims to have discovered the descendants of the ancient Frisians in the platycephalic inhabitants of certain islands in the Zuider Zee, whose skulls are of the low Neanderthal type. It must be the inhabitants of these islands who are

[1] Keller, *Lake Dwellings*, vol. i. pp. 584, 589.
[2] See Chapter ii., section 6.

described by Cæsar as the fierce barbarians who lived at the mouth of the Rhine, and subsisted on fish and the eggs of birds.[1]

If these islanders were, as Virchow maintains, the ancestors of the Frisians, whose language preserves an archaic form of Teutonic speech, we must believe that they were an isolated survival of the pure Teutonic race. In their skull form they agree more nearly with the Swedes than with any other European race; while their manner of life in Cæsar's time corresponds to that of the people of the kitchen middens, whose skulls are also of the dolichocephalic Swedish type. But if in Cæsar's time these fish-eating Frisian coast tribes were still mere savages, it is hardly possible to identify them with the primitive fish-loathing Aryans, who, before the linguistic separation, had reached the pastoral stage, had domesticated the ox, if not also the sheep; and who had invented the ox-waggon, in which they travelled as their herds moved in search of pasture.

We have already seen that when two races are in contact the probability is that the speech of the most cultured will prevail. It is an easier hypothesis to suppose that the dolichocephalic savages of the Baltic coast acquired Aryan speech from their brachycephalic neighbours, the Lithuanians, than to suppose, with Penka, that they succeeded in some remote age in Aryanising the Hindus, the Romans, and the Greeks.

[1] Describing the Rhine, he says :—" Ubi Oceano appropinquat, in plures diffluit partes, multis ingentibusque insulis effectis, quarum pars magna a feris barbarisque nationibus incolitur (ex quibus sunt, qui piscibus atque ovis avium vivere existimantur), multisque capitibus in Oceanum influit."—Cæsar, *De Bello Gallico*, iv. 10

Physically the Teutonic race is taller, larger-limbed, and more powerful than any other. The Swedes, their purest representatives, are the tallest race in Europe, averaging 5 feet 7½ inches in height. The Stængenæs man reached 5 feet 10 inches. The Scandinavian skeleton found at Aspatria in Cumberland must have been 7 feet in stature. Sidonius Apollinaris also describes the gigantic Burgundians as 7 feet high. But the skull is of a low type. The index of the Engis skull is 70.52, of the Hohberg type, which represents the Burgundian conquerors of Switzerland, 70.7, of the Row Grave type, 71.3; while the descendants of the Frisians have a lower cranial vault than any other European race.

The pure Teuton is phlegmatic in temperament, and somewhat dull of intellect; but is brave, warlike, and given to field sports and athletic exercises. He is a tall, flaxen-haired, large-limbed giant, fat and stupid, like the Goths and Burgundians whom the Roman provincials regarded with fear, mingled with contempt.

It is a result of Teutonic conquest that the landed gentry of Europe are largely descended from this race—Goths, Lombards, Normans, Franks, Saxons, Angles—and they preserve with singular persistency the physical characteristics and the mode of life of their remote ancestors. It is, as an acute writer has remarked, "a strange result of the wealth and intelligence of the modern world to give the upper classes the pursuits of the savage, without the necessity which is the excuse for them. They are barbarians armed with the complicated appliances of civilisation. Their greatest glory is to have killed a large quantity of big wild beasts." "Field sports are good for keeping up the energy of semi-barbarous aristocracies."[1]

Matthew Arnold's fair-haired "young barbarians," cricketers, deer-stalkers, or fox-hunters, but destitute of intellectual tastes, are noble types of the Teutonic race, but they are not the "children of light." Owing to their strength, bravery, and stature, the Teutons have been a great conquering race, but the Goths and their kinsmen had not the genius to rule the kingdoms they had won. The Saxons, the Angles, the Goths, developed no high civilisation of their own. The Scandinavians and Frisians have little intellectual culture. The genius of Germany comes from the other race, to which Luther and Goethe both belonged. "Philippus Zaehdarm, Zaehdarmi Comes, qui quinquies mille perdrices plumbo confecit," was a representative of one race, Teufelsdröckh and his biographer of the other.

The qualities which have enabled the Teutonic races to play their wonderful part in the history of Europe are well displayed in the twelve valiant sons of Tancred of Hauteville—William Iron Arm, Robert Guiscard, Roger, and the rest—who carved out kingdoms for themselves in Apulia and Sicily. They were a vigorous race, large of limb, stout of heart, tenacious in will, with abundant physical energy, taking their pleasure in drinking and hunting. They had broad shoulders, fair hair, and blue eyes, as we see from Anna Comnena's portrait of the son of Robert Guiscard, Bohemond, Prince of Tarentum, who was "a cubit taller than the tallest man known, fair, with blue eyes, his cheeks tinted with vermilion."

The energy, the self-will, the fondness for adventure,

[1] Hamerton, *French and English*, pp. 61, 265.

and the love of combat which have enabled the Teutonic peoples to extend their rule over the world, come from the dolichocephalic race; but the intellect and genius of Europe, the great writers, and more especially the men of science, belong rather to the brachycephalic race which has so profoundly modified the physical type in Germany, France, Italy, and England.

Pösche and Penka[1] have drawn attention to the curious fact that though the lines of linguistic demarcation in Europe have small relation to race, the religious division adheres very closely to the racial frontiers. The reason they assign is that religion depends more intimately than language on the fundamental ethical character of the race. No European nation is Mahommedan, or even any Aryan nation, except to some extent the Persians, and in Persia we find only the Shiah sect, which has altogether transformed the innermost tenets of Islam. The Shiahs are essentially mystics, and they have found themselves able to read into the Koran doctrines which approximate very curiously to those of Swedenborg, Tauler, and other Teutonic mystics.

The Jews speak everywhere the language of the land in which they sojourn, but everywhere they have clung tenaciously to the doctrines of their Oriental faith. And so the Christianity of the New Testament, with its peacefulness, its submissiveness, and its resignation, in which it agrees with Islam and other Oriental faiths, was contrary to the inner genius of the Teutonic race, with its inde-

[1] The following pages are little more than a summary of the somewhat speculative remarks of these writers. See Pösche, *Die Arier*, p. 210; Penka, *Origines Ariacæ*, p. 115.

pendence, its self-will, its free life, and its contentiousness. Hence the Teutonic races, in which these Aryan characteristics are the most strongly developed, were the last to submit to the yoke of the Gospel. It was only when the Goths had settled within the bounds of the Roman empire that they were converted, and when they were converted it was to a rationalistic form of Christianity; it was Aryanism and not Catholicism which they were willing to accept.

And now that Christianity has spread over Europe, it is divided into two opposed camps—the Catholic and the Protestant, the Church of Authority and the Church of Reason, the line of division coinciding very closely with the line which separates the two great races of Aryan speech. The dolichocephalic Teutonic race is Protestant, the brachycephalic Celto-Slavic race is either Roman Catholic or Greek Orthodox. In the first, individualism, wilfulness, self-reliance, independence, are strongly developed; the second is submissive to authority and conservative in instincts. To the Teutonic races Latin Christianity was never congenial, and they have now converted it into something very different from what it was at first, or from what it became in the hands of Latin and Greek doctors. The Teutonic peoples are averse to sacerdotalism, and have shaken off priestly guidance and developed individualism. Protestantism was a revolt against a religion imposed by the South upon the North, but which had never been congenial to the Northern mind. The German princes, who were of purer Teutonic blood than their subjects, were the leaders of the ecclesiastical revolt. Scandinavia is more purely Teutonic than Germany, and Scandinavia is Protestant to the backbone. The Lowland Scotch, who are more purely Teutonic than the English, have given the freest development to the genius of Protestantism. Those Scotch clans which have clung to the old faith have the smallest admixture of Teutonic blood. Ulster, the most Teutonic province of Ireland, is the most firmly Protestant. The case of the Belgians and the Dutch is very striking. The line of religious division became the line of political separation, and is conterminous with the two racial provinces. The mean cephalic index of the Dutch is 75.3, which is nearly that of the Swedes and the North Germans; the mean index of the Belgians is 79, which is that of the Parisians. The Burgundian Cantons of Switzerland, which possess the largest proportion of Teutonic blood, are Protestant, while the brachycephalic Cantons in the East and South are the stronghold of Catholicism. South Germany, which is brachycephalic, is Catholic; North Germany, which is dolichocephalic, is Protestant. Hanover, which is Protestant, has a considerably lower index than Cologne, which is Catholic. The Thirty Years' War was a war of race as well as of religion, and the peace of Westphalia drew the line of religious demarcation with tolerable precision along the ethnic frontier.

Wherever the Teutonic blood is purest—in North Germany, Sweden, Norway, Iceland, Ulster, the Orkneys, the Lothians, Yorkshire, East Anglia—Protestantism found easy entrance, and has retained its hold, often in some exaggerated form. In Bohemia, France, Belgium, Alsace, it has been trodden out. In Galway and Kerry it has no footing. The Welsh and the Cornishmen, who became Protestants by political accident, have transformed Protestantism into an emotional religion, which has inner affinities with the emotional faith of Ireland and Italy. Even now Protestantism gains no converts in the South of Europe, or Catholicism in the North. Roman Catholicism, or the cognate creed of the Greek and Russian orthodox churches, is dominant in all those lands where the brachycephalic race prevails; Protestantism is confined to the dolichocephalic Teutonic region. The neighbourhood of Toulouse, which was the headquarters of the Albigenses, is more dolichocephalic than any other part of Southern France, and Toulouse was the Visigothic capital. In no city of France were the Huguenots so numerous as at Nimes, another stronghold of the Visigoths, and Nimes is still largely Protestant in creed. England, which is orthocephalic, is neither Catholic nor Protestant, but Anglican. It is not to be supposed, however, that religious belief is a function of the shape of the skull, but that the shape of the skull is one of the surest indications of race.

Those who are curious in such matters may refer to Cæsar's contrast between the religions of the Germans and of the Gauls.[1] The same essential contrast in the religious genius of the two races prevailed then as it does now. The Gauls had a Pope. "His autem omnibus Druidibus præest unus, qui summam inter eos habet auctoritatem." The priests are judges in public and private concerns, and disobedience to their decrees is followed by an interdict. "Si qui aut privatus aut publicus eorum decreto non stetit, sacrificiis interdicunt. Hæc poena apud eos est

[1] Cæsar, *B. G.*, Bk. vi., cap. 13 and 21.

gravissima. Quibus ita est interdictum, ii numero impiorum ac sceleratorum habentur; iis omnes decedunt; aditum eorum sermonemque defugiunt: ne quid ex contagione incommodi accipiant; neque iis petentibus jus redditur, neque honos ullus communicatur."

This might be taken as a picture of a Roman interdict in the Middle Ages, or even of modern boycotting in Ireland.

With this we may compare the picture of the religion of the Germans—"Germani multum ab hac consuetudine (Gallorum) differunt; nam neque Druides habent, qui rebus divinis præsint, neque sacrificiis student."

CHAPTER V.

THE EVOLUTION OF ARYAN SPEECH.

§ 1. *The Aryan Languages.*

FORTY years ago it was believed that relationship of language implied relationship of blood, and it was the fashion to talk of the Aryan family and the Aryan race.[1] The pendulum then swung in the opposite direction, and Oppert lays it down that "there are Aryan languages, but there is no Aryan race." It may be questioned whether the reaction has not gone too far. It may be admitted that the word "Aryan" should be primarily regarded as a linguistic rather than as an ethnic term, and that though the Aryan languages may be traced to a common source, the speakers of those languages have for the most part no community of blood. But since Aryan speech must have originated with some one of the races among which it now prevails, it is legitimate to inquire by which of them it was probably evolved.

The undivided Aryans doubtless roamed as nomad hunters and herdsmen over a considerable territory, gradually multiplying in number and incorporating other tribes. The modifications of the primitive

[1] See p. 3, *supra*.

speech are believed to be largely due to the acquirement of Aryan speech by these non-Aryan races.

From anthropological and archæological considerations we have seen that of the four neolithic races of Europe two must be excluded from any claim to represent the primitive Aryans, and that of the remaining two the balance of evidence inclines in favour of the brachycephalic race of Central Europe. The linguistic evidence has now to be taken into account, and we have to consider the mutual relations of the Aryan languages, to ask how they became differentiated, how the primitive Aryan speech could have been evolved, and whether it could have been the speech of that race which, on other grounds, seems to have the best claim to represent the primitive Aryan stock.

There are nine existing families of Aryan speech —the Indian, the Iranian, the Armenian, the Hellenic, the Italic, the Celtic, the Teutonic, the Lithuanian or Lettic, and the Slavic. Besides these there are several which have become extinct, such as the Phrygian, the Dacian, and the Thracian.

Some of the more closely-related families may be grouped together, giving six families instead of nine —the Indo-Iranian, the Armenian, the Hellenic, the Celto-Italic, the Teutonic, the Letto-Slavic.

Zend and Sanskrit are so closely allied that we may postulate the existence of a common mother-tongue for both, which, for convenience, we may call the Indo-Iranian. In like manner, Lithuanian is closely related to Slavonic on the one hand, and less closely to Teutonic on the other.

The old traditions of classical philology, dating from a time when only two ancient Aryan literatures were

THE EVOLUTION OF ARYAN SPEECH. 253

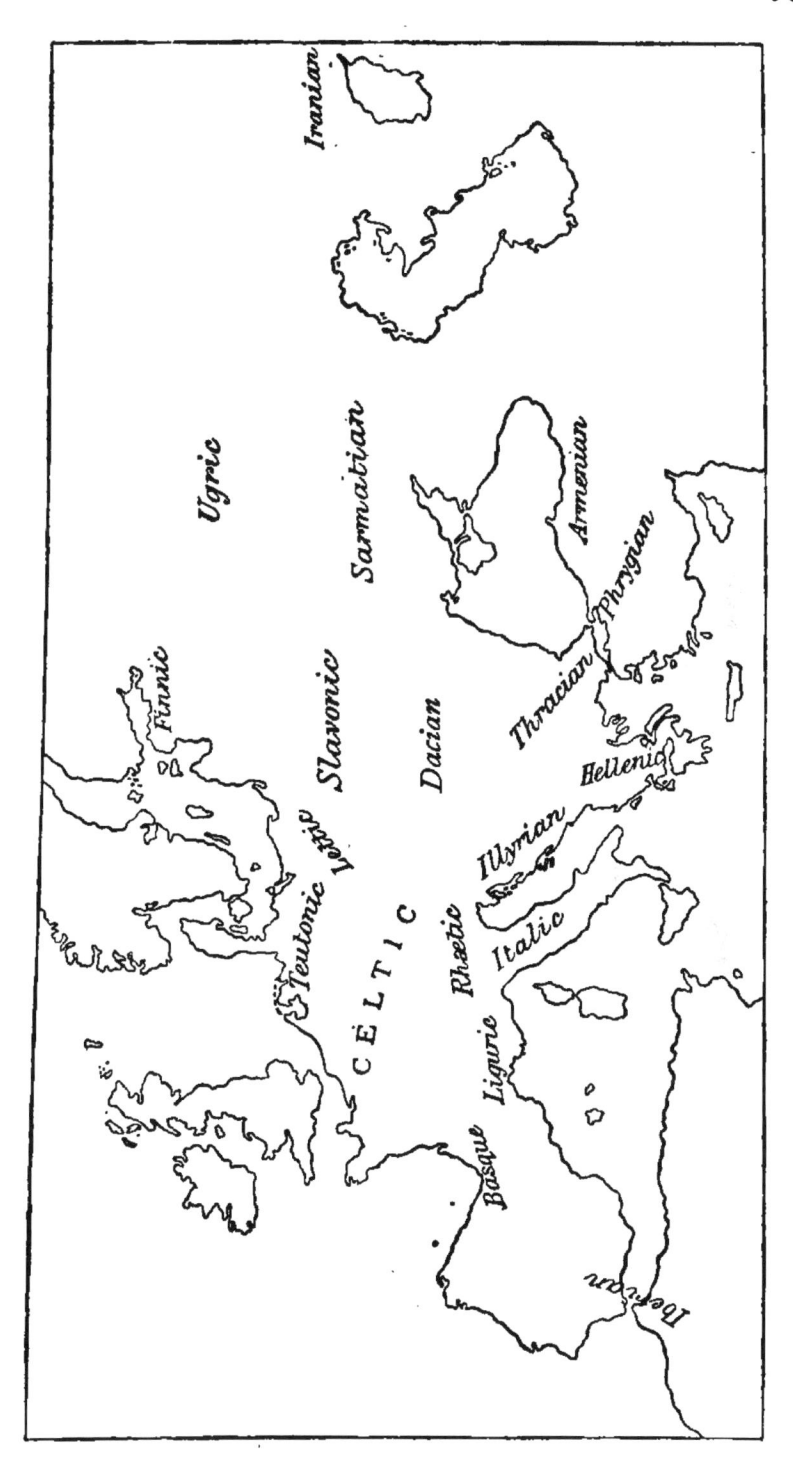

known, gave rise to a belief that the two classical tongues, Greek and Latin, were sister languages, very closely allied; but this opinion has now given place to the belief that the closest affinities of the Italic languages are with Celtic, and those of Greek with Indo-Iranian and Armenian.

Schmidt catalogues ninety-nine words which occur only in Greek and Indo-Iranian, and one hundred and thirty-two which are found only in Greek and Latin. Some of these, however, are culture words, or the names of animals and plants, which may probably not be primitive. Of more importance is the fact that the augment and the reduplicated aorist are confined to Greek and Indo-Iranian, while they also possess peculiar forms of the infinitive. The names of six Greek deities can be explained from Sanskrit, while only three are common to Greek and Latin.

We have seen[1] that while certain words relating to the pastoral life, and to rudimentary agriculture, are common to Greek and Latin, the names of weapons differ, the Greek names agreeing for the most part with Sanskrit, and the Latin names with Celtic. The relative dates of the linguistic separations are also indicated by the numerals. The undivided Aryans could only count up to a hundred. The word for a thousand is common to Greek and Indo-Iranian, but is not shared by Latin. Latin and Celtic have the same word for a thousand, and so have Lithuanian and German. We conclude, therefore, that the separation of Greek and Latin, and of Latin and Lithuanian, was comparatively early; but that the separation of Latin and Celtic, of Greek and Indo-Iranian, of Lithuanian and German, was comparatively late.

[1] See p. 194, *supra*.

On other grounds it appears that the Italic languages are much more intimately related to Celtic than to Greek. The Umbrians, the northernmost of the Italic peoples, were in geographical contact with the Celts, but must have been separated from the Hellenes by the Illyrians. The Thracian and Dacian languages, which are lost, probably formed links between Greek and Celtic.

Bacmeister,[1] by the aid of local names, has traced the ancient domain of Celtic speech. It included the valleys of the Rhine, the Main, and the upper Danube, together with Belgium, Britain, and portions of Switzerland and France. Celtic territory formed the great central region of Aryan speech. It extended on the east to the frontiers of Dacia, if indeed Dacian was not itself a member of the Celtic group.

Lugdunum, a characteristic Celtic name, is found at Laon, at Leyden on the lower Rhine, at Lyons on the Rhone, and on the upper Garonne at the foot of the Pyrenees. We find Batavodurum at the mouth of the Rhine, and Boiodurum at the junction of the Danube and the Inn.

That Southern Germany, before it was Teutonised by northern conquerors, was occupied by the Celts is proved by the Celtic names in the valley of the Danube and even of the Save.[2] Through Carniola, the great highway by which so many of the invaders of Italy have passed, the Umbrians, a people whose language is intimately related to the Celtic, may have reached the plains of Northern Italy.

[1] Bacmeister, *Allemannischen Wanderungen* (Stuttgart, 1867).

[2] The theory that the Celts extended themselves at a comparatively recent period from Gaul down the valley of the Danube is now very generally abandoned.

Some of the oldest and deepest morphological changes in Aryan speech are those which affect the Celto-Italic languages. Such are the formation of a new passive, a new future, and a new perfect. Hence it is believed that the Celto-Italic languages may have separated from the rest while the other Aryan languages remained united. The Celto-Italic union is less apparent than the Indo-Iranian or the Slavo-Lettic because it dates from an earlier period.

The relations of Celtic with Teutonic are less profound than those with Latin. They affect the culture words rather than the morphological structure, and point to late political supremacy and geographical contact rather than to primitive organic unity.

The relations of the Teutonic family to the Slavo-Lettic are more deep and continuous, as they affect not only the culture words but the grammar. The final separation of the Slaves and Teutons must have been comparatively late. The Slavic and Teutonic languages agree largely in metallurgic terms, but differ in the words relating to weapons, agriculture, and navigation. An intimate connection between Slavo-Lettic and Teutonic is also indicated by the fact that they agree in changing a primitive *bh* to *m* in certain case endings, a change which is not found in the other Aryan languages. On the other hand, a connection between Indo-Iranian and Slavo-Lettic is shown by the fact that in some sixteen words they agree in changing a primitive *k* to *s*, a change which has not occurred in Teutonic. The Iranian name, *bhaga*, for the supreme deity, is also common to the Slaves and Phrygians, but is not found in either Greek or Latin. Hence the Slavo-Lettic family forms a link between the Iranian and the Teutonic, while the relations of Greek are with Indo-Iranian on the one hand and with Italic on the other.

It is now generally admitted that the European languages are not less archaic than the Asiatic, due allowance being made for the fact that the literary monuments of Sanskrit reach back to an earlier time than those of the European tongues. Zend, as we have it, may date from the sixth century B.C., and Sanskrit from the tenth. But modern Persian preserves less of the primitive Aryan grammar than any other Aryan language except English. It has got rid of declension altogether, and though it has preserved some of the personal suffixes of the verb, it has lost the old tenses. The neo-Hindu languages, which arose out of the Prakrits, or vernacular dialects, about the tenth century A.D., have lost most of the archaic features which distinguish Sanskrit. The neuter gender has disappeared, a new plural and new case endings have been substituted for the old forms, and the inflexions of tense have been replaced by new forms derived from the participles. It cannot be doubted that this destruction of old forms has been accelerated, if not altogether caused, by the acquirement of Aryan speech in India by non-Aryan tribes.

Among the Lithuanians the opposite has been the case. The language has not extended itself, and those who now speak Lithuanian are probably the direct descendants of those who spoke it two or possibly three thousand years ago. Hence there has been less destruction of grammatical forms than in any other existing Aryan language. Alone among existing languages it has preserved the dual and the old declension. Its phonetic system is inferior only to Sanskrit, and is in some respects even more archaic, despite the fact that the Sanskrit literature is older by nearly 3000 years than the Lithuanic, which dates only from the beginning of the eighteenth century.

On the whole the Latin, Celtic, and Lithuanian have kept most closely to the primitive system of consonants. The Slavonic and Indo-Iranian languages have developed numerous sibilants and fricatives. The primitive Aryan speech had only one sibilant and two nasals, but the Sanskrit has four sibilants and five nasals. The cerebrals or linguals which are peculiar to the Indian languages are believed to be due to early Dravidian influences. It was formerly thought that the primitive Aryan had only one sound for *r* or *l*, but it is now believed that there were two, the European languages in this respect being more primitive than the Asiatic. In like manner, it was formerly considered that the Indian vowel system was more primitive than the European, but the opposite opinion now finds favour with scholars. Greek has preserved the old tenses better than Latin, and retained the dual. Sanskrit has normally replaced by the genitive the old ablative, which is seen in the Latin *senatu-d* and the Oscan *fructu-d*, and which has disappeared from all the other Aryan languages except Zend. Latin, however, has formed three new tenses—the future in *-bo*, the imperfect in *-bam*, and the perfect in *-vi*, which we have in *amabo, amabam,* and *amavi*. The Italic languages, like the Celtic and the Lithuanian, have also created a new middle voice, which afterwards became a passive.

In the retention of the old intransitive voice, of the dual, and of ancient tenses and declensions, Greek is more archaic than Latin. The Doric and Æolic dialects are more archaic than classic Greek, doubtless because the Ionian Greeks were less purely Aryan by race. The loss of the digamma and the tendency to Zetacism among the Ionians may be due to an admixture with the pre-Aryan population from which the Dorians were free. Latin, however, was more faithful than Greek to the primitive consonantal system. Thus Latin has kept the primitive guttural which Greek often changes to *p* or *t*. Thus while Latin has *quis* and *quinque*, Greek has τίς and πέντε or πέμπε. Again Latin keeps the initial sibilant which in Greek lapses into an aspirate. Thus Latin has *sex*, *septem*, and *socer*, while Greek has ἕξ, ἑπτά, and ἑκυρός.

We find the same change of *qv* to *p* in Welsh and Gaulish, but not in Irish or Latin. Thus the Latin *quatuor* is *cethir* in Irish, and *pedwar* in Welsh. The change also occurs in Oscan and Umbrian, as in *pan* for *quam* and *pis* for *quis*. Latin also preserves the old semi-vowel *y* (represented by *j*), which Greek changes into *h* or *z*. Thus we find *jecur* and *jugum* instead of ἧπαρ and ζυγόν.

Hence, in spite of the greater antiquity of the Sanskrit literature, it would appear that some of the European languages in their morphological structure, and still more in their phonetic system, are as archaic as the Asiatic.

On the whole, the Lettic languages have changed the least, and the Teutonic the most. In almost every respect the languages of the brachycephalic people of Central Europe—Lithuanian, Slavonic,

Celtic, Umbrian, Latin, and Doric Greek—have adhered more closely to the primitive type than Teutonic, the language of the dolichocephalic people of the Baltic coast. Thus it would seem that the Lithuanians have the best claim to represent the primitive Aryan race, as their language exhibits fewer of those phonetic changes, and of those grammatical losses which are consequent on the acquirement of a foreign speech.

§ 2. *Dialect and Language.*

The origin of the Aryan languages is veiled in the remote past, and the causes which gave rise to their divergences must be to a great extent a matter for conjecture. But the unknown can often be explained by the known, and the genesis of modern dialects throws considerable light on the obscure genesis of ancient languages.

The method which Darwin has used to explain the origin of species may be applied to explain the origin of languages. Darwin began by showing the origin of varieties—a process which is now in progress in the case of pigeons, dogs, and rabbits. He then argued that species may have arisen out of varieties, and genera out of species. Species became distinct owing to the survival of the fittest, and the extinction of intermediate varieties in the struggle for existence. The families of Aryan speech are analogous to genera, the individual languages to species, and dialects to varieties. Of the origin of languages, as well as of the origin of species, we have no direct knowledge, while the origin of dialects, like the origin of varieties, is less obscure. Hence the study of the origin of dialects can hardly fail to throw light on the origin of languages.

The causes which have led to the formation of dialects can be well studied in the case of Germany. The dialects of German have already become so diverse that a Swiss is unintelligible to a Holsteiner, or a Frisian to a Transylvanian; yet they all speak German. All these dialects are connected by a series of intermediate links — Swabian, Bavarian, Austrian, Hessian, Franconian,—affording a continuous passage from one extreme to the other. If these had been extinguished, we should call the speech of Uri, Holstein, and Transylvania separate languages; as it is, we call them dialects of German. No German dialect is altogether isolated. Each agrees in some respects with one or more of its immediate neighbours, and differs in other respects. The Franconian or central dialects, for instance, share certain phonetic peculiarities with the Low German dialects to the north of them, and others with the High German dialects on the south. The East Franconian differs from the Alemannic more than it does from the Bavarian.

A probable cause can be assigned for some of these dialectic variations. We know that within the historic period German has extended its domain over large districts which are not Teutonic by blood. By race the north-west region of German speech is largely Teutonic, the eastern Lithuanian and Slavonic, the central region is Celtic, and the southern is Ligurian. When toward the close of the second century of our era, the Goths, the Burgundians, and other Teutonic tribes began to move southwards to the Danube, and thence into Italy, Gaul, and Spain, the

Slaves pressed forward from the East into the lands which had been left vacant, and took possession of the valleys of the Vistula, the Oder, the Elbe, the Saale, the upper Main, and the middle and lower Danube. In the sixth century, as the local names clearly testify, Oldenburg, Mecklenburg, Saxony, Lauenburg, Pomerania, Silesia, the south-eastern part of Hanover, and the Altmark were peopled by Slaves. Slavonic dialects were spoken at Kiel, Lubeck, Magdeburg, Halle, Berlin, Leipzig, Dresden, Salzburg, and Vienna.

During the last thousand years German speech has been slowly winning back its lost provinces, but without displacement of population. The Slavic tribes have not been expelled, but only Teutonised, and the brachycephalic Slavic type remains.

In like manner Eastern Prussia, which is Lithuanian by blood, was Germanised by the Teutonic Knights. The Celtic lands of central Bavaria, the land of the Boii, as well as Würtemberg, Baden, and Hesse, were Germanised in the fourth century by Alemannic, Suevic, and Frankish tribes. In several Swiss cantons the blood is Rhætian but the speech Burgundian. It is therefore no matter for surprise that in all these regions the Low German speech of the conquerors was modified when it was acquired by the native tribes. The primitive Low German dialects are only spoken in those Frisian and Dutch districts which are Teutonic in blood as well as speech.

We may now go a step further and examine the case of the neo-Latin dialects which have now become languages. French, Spanish, and Italian are called languages, but they arose out of dialects; and if the connecting dialects be taken into account, the sharp line of separation which divides the literary languages disappears in the case of the vernacular speech.

Beginning at the North, and excluding the literary languages, we find a series of mutually intelligible dialects of the Langue d'oïl, such as Walloon, Picard, Norman, Burgundian, and Savoyard, which shade off gradually into the dialects of the Langue d'oc, such as Limousin, Auvergnat, Gascon, and Provençal; and these again into Catalan, Navarrais, Castilian, and Andalusian, while Savoyard forms the transition to Piedmontese, through which we successively arrive at Lombard, Venetian, Tuscan, Corsican, Neapolitan, Calabrese, Sicilian, and Maltese, Sardinian forming a link between Spanish and Italian.

Owing mainly to political causes, the Tuscan, Castilian, and Parisian dialects have become literary languages, and with the spread of education are rapidly extinguishing the provincial vernaculars. If it had so happened that all the intermediate dialects between Walloon and Sicilian had been extinguished, the speech of France and Italy would be almost as different as Sanskrit and Zend. In the case of the Aryan languages there has been an extensive extinction of intermediate dialects. Instead of an inclined plane of speech, such as that which extends from Uri to Holstein, or from Picardy to Calabria, we have, as it were, a staircase—the inclined plane has been broken up into irregular and disconnected steps.

The process by which the primitive Aryan speech first became extended over a vast region, and then broke up into dialects which became the parents of the Aryan languages, must be analogous to the process by which in historic times the Latin language, the dialect of one city, Rome, spread over the whole Roman empire, and then broke up into the neo-Latin languages. The neo-Latin languages arose out of the local vernacular dialects, which existed side by side with the literary Latin. These dialects owe their origin to the fact that the Latin of the legionaries was acquired by the conquered races, whose languages were extinguished, but left their mark on the acquired speech.

Thus the Latin speech when acquired by Ligurians gave rise to the Langue d'oc, by Gauls to the Langue d'oui, by "Celts" to Castilian, by Iberians to Portuguese, by Celtiberians to Aragonese. In the Alps there are three Ladino dialects which may owe their peculiarities to the influence of the old Rhætian language on the acquired Latin speech. Roumanian has doubtless been infected by the speech of the ancient Dacians, among whom the Roman colonists lived. In several cases the vowels have acquired a nasal sound, or have been converted into diphthongs. The article has become a suffix; we have, for instance, *omu-l* (*homo ille*), the man. The fact that this peculiarity is found also in Bulgarian, a Slavonic language, and also in Albanian, makes it probable that this usage may have been derived from the old Illyrian family of speech to which Dacian probably belonged.

Italian is nearer to Latin than Provençal, and Provençal than French, because there was a smaller foreign element in Italy than in Southern Gaul, and in the south of Gaul than in the north. The change of speech is phonetic rather than lexical, and largely due to the foreign accent with which Latin was spoken by those to whom it was an acquired language.

The dialect of the Isle de France has become the literary language of France owing to the accident that the Capets came to fix their capital at Paris. Umbrian, Oscan, and Messapian gave place to Latin because the Roman republic subdued the rest of Italy. Because Athens was the intellectual centre of the Hellenic world, because Castilian was spoken at Madrid, because Mahommed was born at Mecca, the local dialects of Attica, Castile, and Mecca have become the literary languages which we call Greek, Spanish, and Arabic.

When a literary language has been established, local dialects tend to disappear. Owing probably to political causes, the dialects which must once have bridged over the gulf between Slavonic and Iranian, Armenian and Greek, Latin and Celtic, have been extinguished It is thus that we must explain the growth of local dialects into languages, and the extinction of intermediate varieties.

It has often happened that the dialect which has succeeded in the struggle for existence has been one which has incorporated the most numerous foreign elements. Latin was by no means the purest of the Italic dialects. Attic Greek was further from the primitive Hellenic speech than Doric or Æolic. Literary English is the mixed language of the Danelagh, rather than the pure Saxon speech of Wessex or the pure Anglian of Northumbria, and Frisian is nearer to the primitive Teutonic speech than literary German.

§ 3. *The Lost Aryan Languages.*

The tendency of vernacular dialects to disappear, thus accentuating the distinctions between those which survive, will help to explain the extinction of linguistic families which must formerly have been the missing links between existing languages.

In some cases we are able to form probable conjectures as to the nature of the languages which have been exterminated, and which might have bridged over the gulf between divided families of Aryan speech.

The Armenians are believed to have been an eastern extension of the Phrygians, who themselves have been identified with the Briges of Thrace. Thus of the few Phrygian words which we possess, Βαγαῖος, the Phrygian name of the supreme God, is the Iranian *Bhaga*, and the Slavonic *Bogu*.[1] Hence we may conjecture that Phrygian and Thracian might supply some of the missing links between Greek, Armenian, Slavonic, and Iranian. Between the last two Sarmatian and Scythian were probably interposed. There can be little doubt that several Iranian languages have disappeared. The existing Iranian languages—Pushtu, Persian, Kurd, and Baluchi—resemble the patches of Bagshot sand which crown the heights near London, remnants of a once continuous formation now extensively destroyed by denudation.

The ancient Dacian, our only knowledge of which is derived from geographical names and a few plant names preserved by Dioscorides, was conterminous,

[1] Renan, *Langues Sémitiques*, p. 47.

or nearly so, with Celtic, Illyrian, Thracian, and Lithuanian. The Dacian name of the cinquefoil, *propedula*, reminds us of the Celtic *pempedula*. Dacian probably belonged to the Thraco-Illyrian family, and if it had come down to us would doubtless have supplied a valuable link between Celtic, Albanian, Greek, and Lithuanian. Albanian again is the descendant of the old Illyrian. Its linguistic position is doubtful. Hehn thinks it approaches most nearly to Greek, Blau believes it was nearer to Iranian; but as Greek has closer relations with Indo-Iranian than with any other family, the old Illyrian, if it had been known to us, might have helped to bridge over the existing gulf. Illyrian, however, has left its mark in the region which it once occupied. Albanian, as we have seen,[1] like Roumanian and Bulgarian, possesses a definite declension, obtained by means of a suffixed article, a peculiarity probably derived from the old Illyrian, which may have been a link between the Italic, Hellenic, and Lettic languages.

Thus it would appear that three links—the Dacian, Illyrian, and Thracian—are wanting between the European languages. The Dacian and the Thracian might have formed the transition between the Slavonic to the East, the Celtic to the West, and the Greek to the South. Phrygian and Thracian might have bridged the gulf between Armenian and Greek; Sarmatian between Slavonic and Iranian.

The destruction of so many of the central links may help to explain why the northern and southern languages of Europe have so little in common. If

[1] See p. 263, *supra*.

the lost languages had survived, the probable connections between the Aryan languages might be represented by the following diagram.

[Diagram: overlapping ovals labeled Teutonic, Celtic, Lettic, Slavonic, Scythic, Sarmatian, Dacian, Thracian, Illyrian, Italic, Hellenic, Phrygian, Armenian, Iranian, Indian]

§ 4. *The Wave Theory.*

Reason has been shown for believing that the Aryan languages were evolved out of dialects, much in the same way that the Teutonic dialects or the neo-Latin languages have been formed.

The probability that the Aryan languages were evolved, so to speak, *in situ*, has been demonstrated by Schmidt in a tract to which reference has already been made.[1] Schmidt's "wave theory" has, however, so important a bearing on the question of the region where Aryan speech originated that a few pages must be devoted to setting it forth in greater detail.

Relying on certain words and forms which are confined to the European Aryans, Fick and Schleicher had maintained that there was an early and fundamental separation between the European and Asiatic

[1] See p. 35, *supra.*

Aryans; while Grassmann, Pauli, Sonne, and Spiegel contended that Greek was nearer to the Asiatic languages than to Latin or Teutonic; and Bopp and Pott in like manner urged the close phonological resemblances between the Slavonic and the Indo-Iranian languages.

Schmidt showed that all the Aryan languages formed links in a chain, that Slavonic can be severed neither from German on the one side nor from Iranian on the other, while Greek forms the connecting link between Sanskrit and Latin.

Assuming the close connection of Zend and Sanskrit, which is admitted by all scholars, and regarding them as sister languages, Schmidt showed that the three Baltic families—Teutonic, Lettic, and Slavic—are united by 143 verbal links, all three being joined together by 59 links, Teutonic and Slavic by 50, and Teutonic and Lettic by 34. He then showed that the Indo-Iranian, or Eastern group, is united to the Baltic, or Northern group, by 90 links, of which 61 specially connect it with the Slavo-Lettic family, and only 15 with the Teutonic. While the intimate connection of the three Baltic families is evidenced by 143 links, there are nearly as many, 132, which unite the two Mediterranean families—Italic and Hellenic; the Asiatic group being united with the Mediterranean by 123 links, of which 99 connect it with the Hellenic family, only 20 with the Italic, and 4 with both. There are also 10 links uniting the Slavo-Lettic, Indo-Iranian, and Hellenic families.

These links are only in the vocabulary, but there are others in the grammatical structure. Thus Teutonic and Slavo-Lettic agree not only in the words for silver, rye, wheat, beer, and thousand, but in the change of a primitive *bh* to *m* in certain case endings. Lettic and Teutonic replace *d* by *l* in the numerals e*l*even and twe*l*ve. Slavo-Lettic agrees with Indo-Iranian in the designation of the supreme deity, Bogu, in the word for marriage, and in several numerals; and also in two cases of the noun, four forms of the verb, and certain forms of the pronoun. Greek shares one form of the verb (the *futurum exactum*) with Latin, and three with Indo-Iranian. Iranian, Greek, and Slavonic change *s* into *h* between two vowels, and Iranian and Greek replace an initial *s* by *h*. In many culture words and in several grammatical forms Latin is nearer the Northern languages than it is to Greek. The close agreement of Latin with Celtic has already been pointed out. They have both formed a new passive and three new tenses in the same way. The morphological peculiarities of Lithuanian are shared partly with the European, and partly with the Asiatic languages. Thus in the word *melzu*, "I milk," the *e* is European, the *z* Asiatic. In *des-ina-mus*, a dative plural feminine, the vowel of the root is distinctively European, the stem suffix is Indo-Iranian, and the case suffix distinctively Slavo-Teutonic. Hence we see that the great families of Aryan speech, Indo-Iranian, Hellenic, Celto-Italic, Teutonic, and Slavo-Lettic, are indissolubly bound together. Slavo-Lettic can be no more torn from its connection with Teutonic on the one side than from Iranian on the other. Greek is linked with Sanskrit as closely as with Latin.

The way the Aryan languages are interlinked seems to prove that there could have been no successive migrations from Asia[1] The European

---

[1] See the diagram on p. 22, *supra*.

languages could only have arisen in Europe, at a time when the Aryan nations occupied much the same relative positions as in the historic period. The Slaves, for instance, must from the first have been between the Iranians and the Germans, and the Greeks between the Latins and the Indo-Iranians. The more remote languages are from each other, geographically, the fewer are the peculiarities which they share in common. Thus Schmidt has shown that the connection of Indo-Iranian with Slavonic is closer than its connection with Teutonic in the proportion of more than 10 to 3. In like manner, the connection of Indo-Iranian with Greek is closer than its connection with Latin in the proportion of nearly 5 to 1.

Schmidt maintains that the Aryan linguistic area was at one time homogeneous. In various portions of this domain he supposes that tendencies to variation arose, and spread like undulations from the centre of disturbance. Thus in one spot a tendency may have arisen to change the primitive guttural tenuis into a sibilant, a tendency which affected the regions occupied by the forefathers of the Indo-Iranians, the Armenians, and the Letto-Slaves, so that the Greek ἑκατόν, which is *cét* in old Irish, *centum* in Latin, and *hund-* (=*kunt*) in Gothic, corresponds to *çata-m* in Sanskrit, *sate-m* in Iranian, *suto* in old Slavonic, and *szimtas* in Lithuanian.

At some other time and in some other region we may suppose that there was a tendency to change the primitive *bh* in the case endings -*bhi*, -*bhis*, -*bhya(m)s*, to *m*, a tendency which only extended to the ancestors of the Slaves and Teutons, so that in place of the old Irish *fera-ib* and the Latin *hosti-bus* we get *vulfa-m* in Gothic, and *vluko-mu* in old Slavonic.

At a third point a new passive was formed, which extended to the Celtic and Italic languages, and perhaps more remotely to the Lithuanian, giving us the old Irish *bera-r* and the Latin *fero-r*. In the same way, Celtic and Teutonic were possibly affected by a tendency to denote past time by prefixes. Other changes affected the whole European region and included the Armenian, others merely the Italo-Hellenic domain.[1]

In like manner, we find certain primitive worships extending over contiguous regions. Bhaga, as the name of the supreme deity, is found among Iranians, Slaves, and Phrygians; Woden only among Celts and Teutons; Juno and Vesta are confined to Greeks and Latins; Uranus to Greeks and Indians; Mithra to Indians and Iranians.

These facts are clearly inconsistent with any theory of the migration of the Aryans from Asia to Europe at any time subsequent to the period of linguistic unity. The Aryan languages must have originated when the Aryan nations occupied much the same relative positions which they now hold.

§ 5. *Language and Race.*

The intimate interlinking of the Aryan languages which Schmidt has established proves that the linguistic separation must have taken place at a time when the Aryan races occupied nearly the same relative positions as at the beginning of the historical period. But Schmidt assigned no cause for the local dialectical disturbances or tendencies to variation which he assumed to have taken place.

[1] Schmidt, *Verwantschaftsverhältnisse*, p. 17.

This has been done by the anthropologists—more especially by Penka. We have already seen that Aryan languages are spoken by at least four European races, only one of which could have been Aryan by blood. The others must have exchanged their primitive tongue for Aryan speech. The evidence adduced by Penka and Pösche to prove the mutability of speech and the comparative stability of race has also been summarised. We have also seen that the peculiarities which distinguish the neo-Latin languages may be due to the acquirement of Latin speech by Iberians, Gauls, Rhætians, or Dacians. The origin of the dialects of ancient Italy and Greece, and of the modern provincial dialects of France, Spain, Germany, and England, may to some extent be explained in the same way.

We are therefore entitled to extend this principle as a *vera causa*, which may account for the origin of the dialects out of which grew the Aryan families of speech. In other words, we may attribute many, if not all, of the differences which distinguish the Aryan languages to the Aryanisation of non-Aryan races.

In some cases the influence of a foreign idiom can be definitely traced. Thus Spiegel has shown the influence of Semitic grammar on Persian, and of Dravidian grammar on Sanskrit. It is the same with Sanskrit phonology; the linguals and cerebro-dentals, which are so characteristic of Sanskrit, belonged to the tongue of the subjugated Dravidians, and have infected Aryan speech in India, but in no other land.

It is not impossible that some of these phonetic changes may be due to causes purely organic. Duncan Gibb has proved that in extreme types, such as the negro and the European, there are actual differences in the structure of the larynx, which may suffice to explain why negroes find it is so difficult to utter certain sounds which come easily to ourselves. A negro finds it almost impossible to pronounce the English *th*, which he transforms into *d*, while a Swiss turns it regularly into *z*. A Russian, on the other hand, turns it into *f*, the name Theodore, for instance, becoming Feodor. We have a similar change in Latin, *fumus* answering to θυμός, and *rufus* to ἐρυθρός.

There are many such phonetic tests of race. On the night of the Sicilian Vespers the French fugitives, with the sword at their throats, were bidden to say the word *ciciri*, and if the *c* was pronounced as *s*, and not like our *ch*—if they said *sisiri* instead of *chichiri*—they were recognised as Frenchmen, and killed.

Again, when the Mamelukes in Egypt exterminated the Arabs of the Said they made them say the word *dakik* (flour), in order to ascertain whether the guttural was pronounced as a *k* or a *g*.

The men of Gilead said *shibboleth*, but the men of Ephraim " could not frame to pronounce it right, and said Sibboleth," and were slain at the fords of Jordan (Judges vii. 6).

The Polynesians are unable to say " Mary," which they change to *Mali*. The Chinese have turned Benares into *Po-lo-nai*, Brahma into *Fan*, and Christ into *Ki-li-sse-tu*. The Caffres of the Cape pronounce the word " gold " as *igolide*, and " sugar " as *isugile*, while they are able to catch some of the difficult Hottentot clicks which an Englishman finds impossible, even after long practice—*experto crede*. These are extreme cases, but we may take it as an axiom that whenever a new language is acquired by foreigners or by subject races there will be certain classes of sounds which will be pronounced with difficulty, and will therefore as a rule be evaded or be inaccurately reproduced. This is especially the case with the soft and aspirated mutes. Thus when Aristophanes brings barbarians on the stage he makes them replace the difficult sounds of the Greek aspirated tenues, φ, θ, χ, by the simple tenues π, τ, κ. The same difficulty was felt by the Goths. Ulphilas represents the Greek χ by *k*. The Ugrians find the soft mutes *b, g, d*, difficult to pronounce, and change them to *p, k, t*. Thus a Magyar speaking German says *pinter* instead of *binder*, *pek* instead of *beck*, and *pleh* instead of *blech*. Shakespeare's foreigners do the same. Fluellen in "Henry V.," and Sir John Evans, the Welsh parson in the "Merry Wives of Windsor," substitute *p* for *b*, *t* for *d*, and *f* for *v*, and introduce peculiar idioms and a simplified form of English grammar. "Pragging knave, Pistol, which you and yourself and all the world know to be no petter than a fellow, look you now, of no merits: he is come to me, and prings me pread and sault yesterday, look you, and bid me eat my leek." "It is that ferry person for all the 'orld." "The tevil and his tam." Dr. Caius, the Frenchman, is unable to pronounce our *th* and *w*. Mrs. Stowe's negroes, Mr. Black's Highlanders, and Lever's Irishmen encounter similar difficulties, phonetic and grammatical, when they speak English. The pidgin-English of a Chinaman differs from that of a Malay or a Chinook.

It may therefore be regarded as probable that racial tendencies may explain, to some extent, the differentiation of the Aryan languages. This hypothesis derives support from the existence of similar phonetic tendencies in French and Welsh. Two Aryan languages, Latin and old Celtic, have been modified in similar ways. The French, like the Welsh, find a difficulty in pronouncing the initial double consonants *sc, sm, sp, st*, and in both cases the difficulty is overcome in the same way by prefixing a vowel. The Welsh have made the Latin *schola* into *yscol, spiritus* into *yspryd*, and *scutum* into *ysgwyd*. Similarly the Latin *schola* became *escole* in old French and *école* in modern French; *spiritus* became *esprit; sperare* became *espérer; species* became *espèce* and *épice; spada* became *espée* and then *épée; scabellum* became *escabeau; scala* became *eschelle* and then *échelle*.[1] We find other regular phonetic changes, such as *n* for *m*, *r* for *l*, and *ch* for *c*, as in *rien* from *rem, sente* from *semita, orme* from *ulmus, chef* from *caput*.

In some of these words we see another characteristic common to French and Welsh. This is the Celtic tendency to the mutilation of unaccented syllables. The accented syllable is preserved, the short atonic syllables are suppressed. Thus the Latin words *pórticus, ásinus, septimána, liberáre*, and *régula* have become in modern French *porche, âne, semaine, livrer*, and *regle*, and *semetipsissimum* has become *même*. In like manner the Latin *benedíctio, papílio*, and *córpus* became *benditt, pabell*, and *corff* in Welsh, and *Caerleon* represents *Castra Legionum*.

In French as well as in Welsh this tendency to contraction has played havoc with the declensions. In Welsh there are hardly any remains of the old

[1] See Max Müller, *Lectures*, vol. ii. pp. 195, 196.

suffixes which indicated case, and prepositions have to be used instead. French has in like manner lost its cases, which have been replaced by the same device as in Welsh, and we have to say *à la ʾfemme, de la ʾfemme, pour la ʾfemme*. Similar ethnic tendencies produce similar results on language. If we were ignorant of the history of the French language we might probably be led to connect it too closely with Welsh, owing to the superficial resemblance due to these common tendencies.

In certain words the aspirated tenues in Greek, Sanskrit, and German answer in Latin, Celtic, and Lithuanian to the corresponding unaspirated tenues, and it is found that the Slaves and Roumanians, who also belong to the brachycephalic race, make the same change when they speak German. In South Germany and Switzerland, which were originally Celtic, and where the Celtic skull-type has reasserted itself, we find that the North German *kh*, *th*, and *ph* are frequently changed to *k*, *t*, and *p*.

During the historic period Aryan speech has been extending itself over Finnic territory. Scattered over the valley of the Volga, the linguistic map of Russia[1] shows sporadic settlements of Finns—Mordwins, Wotiaks, and Tscheremiss—who are gradually acquiring Slavonic speech. Moscow in the tenth century lay in Finnic territory; it is now the heart of Russia. In the seventh century the whole valley of the Dvina was Finnic; it is now almost wholly Slave. Over one-half of Russia the blood is probably Finnic, and we may therefore expect to find peculiarities of Ugro-Finnic phonology in Russia. Now Anderson

[1] See the map in the *Suomalais-Ugrilaisen Seuran Aikakauskirja*, part i. (Helsingfors, 1886.)

has collected a number of instances of the tendency in the Finno-Ugric languages to change a guttural into a sibilant.[1] It is worthy of note that this change is found also in the Slavo-Lettic languages, which are spoken by races which come nearer than any other Aryans to the physical type of the Ugro-Finns. The same sibilation of gutturals is found also among the Indo-Iranians. This may be explained by the hypothesis of Penka that the Indo-Iranians were originally Aryanised Ugrians. But while the Indo-Iranian languages share in common this peculiarity of the Finno-Ugric phonology, the Iranian languages, which are so closely related to the Indian, are entirely free from the characteristic Dravidian sounds, the cerebrals, and linguo-dentals, which are found in no Aryan language except Sanskrit. These peculiarities in the phonology of Sanskrit are indications of its migration from Finno-Ugric to Dravidian territory.

Anderson has also collected instances of the Ugric fondness for inserting a parasitic *j* or *v* after explosives,[2] owing to which *k* becomes *č, t,* or *t'*. We may detect similar tendencies among the brachycephalic Aryans, which may explain the equivalence of *kis, quis, tis,* and *pis;* of *keturi, quatuor* and *petuar,* and of *pankan, quinque,* and *pimp.*

From the foregoing instances it may be concluded that when the language of conquerors is acquired by subject races the more difficult sounds will be more or less modified. In such a case there will also be a difficulty in learning the more elaborate grammatical inflexions, which are not easy to catch and remember. A destruction of grammatical forms will ensue, new formations will be developed, and the simplified

[1] Anderson, *Studien,* p. 184.   [2] *Ibid.,* p. 185.

grammar will ultimately be adopted by the conquerors in their intercourse with their more numerous subjects.

Of this process we have actual instances. Mr. Kington Oliphant has shown the result of the Danish Conquest in breaking up the old Anglian inflexions. He has shown how, except in the case of a few plurals like *oxen*, the genitive and plural in *es* swallowed up the old genitives and plurals in *an*, and uncoupled the preposition from the verb.[1] The grammar was simplified and made more easy to acquire. Mr. Oliphant has also shown the influence of the Norman Conquest in causing certain French prefixes and suffixes to be tacked on to the English stems.[2]

The Teutonic conquest of Gaul had a similar result. As early as the fifth century four of the six cases of the noun were lost, and replaced by prepositions. A new future was formed from *habeo*. Instead of *amabo* we find *j'aimer-ai*, equivalent to *ego amare habeo*, the pronoun being prefixed to make the new formation intelligible, and then, when this had become familiar, a more emphatic form, *je vais aimer*, was invented.[3] But even *amabo* was not the old Aryan future. In Umbrian, Oscan, and Celtic the old future in *s* was altogether lost, and there are only faint traces of it in Latin.[4] The new future in *bo* was formed from the auxiliary verb *fuo;* so that *ama-bo* is "I am to love."

In the Slavo-Lettic languages the old perfect has disappeared without a trace, and it is nearly lost in

---

[1] Oliphant, *Standard English*, pp. 47-52.
[2] *Ibid.*, pp. 241, 247.   [3] Sayce, *Principles*, p. 29.
[4] Schleicher, *Compendium*, pp. 821, 822.

the old Irish.[1] In Bulgarian, a Slavonic language acquired by a Turkic tribe from the conquered Slaves, very few of the old grammatical forms have been retained, while the Servians and Croats, who are more purely Slave in blood, have kept the old aorists and imperfects. But even the Old Church Slavonic, which has kept the aorist and the present, has lost the primitive imperfect and the reduplicated perfect. It has acquired three new sibilants and two nasals, it prefixes a euphonic *y* to words beginning with a vowel, it has lost the final consonants, and has changed the primitive diphthongs into simple vowels. In like manner Bulgarian, Roumanian, and Albanian have acquired, probably from the old Illyrian or Dacian, a suffixed article.

The Celts, when they invaded Britain, found the country in possession of the Silurian race, whose descendants can be traced in Denbighshire and Kerry. Professor Rhys believes that he has detected the influence of this race on the Celtic tongues. He thinks that the incorporation of the pronouns between the Irish verb and its prefixes and the inflexion of the Welsh prepositions, as *erof* "for me," *erot* "for thee," *erddo* "for him," is due to the influence on Celtic speech of a pre-Aryan population.[2]

Hence it seems probable that many of the phonetic and grammatical distinctions which differentiate the Aryan languages are due to the fact, with which the researches of the anthropologists have already made us familiar, that the Aryan-speaking nations belong not to one race but to several, who have in remote times abandoned their primitive speech for that of Aryan conquerors.

[1] Schleicher, *Compendium*, p. 746.   [2] Penka, *Origines Ariacæ*, p. 212.

§ 6. *The Genesis of Aryan Speech.*

Many years ago Professor Max Müller affirmed his belief that " in the grammar of the Aryan and Semitic languages we can discover the stamp of one powerful mind, once impressed on the floating materials of speech, at the very beginning of their growth, and never to be obliterated again in the course of centuries."[1]

The doctrine of evolution, which has so profoundly affected the physical sciences, has now been applied to the science of language, and it is more in accordance with modern scientific principles to suppose that language has been slowly developed during the lapse of innumerable ages, and that the Aryan inflexions, instead of being invented by "one powerful mind," were unconsciously evolved out of some ruder form of speech.

What this form was can only be matter for conjecture, but we may legitimately examine the non-Aryan languages with the object of discovering which of them approaches most closely to the primitive Aryan, and whether any probable hypothesis can be formed as to the nature of the mother-speech from which the Aryan languages were evolved.

The Aryan territory is circumscribed by three other linguistic families—the Hamitic, the Semitic, and the Ural-Altaic. Among these its nearest congener must be sought, all other families of speech being too remote, both geographically and structurally.

The Iberians, as we have seen, were probably non-Aryan by race and language. Their physical type

[1] Max Müller, *Survey of Languages*, p. 86.

was that of the North African tribes, who spoke Numidian dialects belonging to the Hamitic family, and remotely akin to the old Egyptian.

Many philologists of repute are of opinion that the inflexional Semitic languages were evolved out of some tongue of the Hamitic class,[1] and they have pointed out striking grammatical agreements between the Semitic and the old Egyptian.

But all attempts to connect Aryan and Semitic speech have conspicuously failed. Both, it is true, are inflexional, but the inflexion is of a wholly different character. The verbal roots are also different, the formative elements are different, and are employed in a different manner. There is an impassable abyss between the Semitic and Aryan languages. It is impossible to conceive that the one could have been evolved out of the other.

There are no white races except the Ural-Altaic and the Semitic from which the white Aryan race could have originated. In physical character the Mediterranean dolichocephalic Aryan-speaking race resembles the Semites; while the Central European brachycephalic race agrees with the Finno-Ugric type. But there is no such impassable gulf between Ural-Altaic and Aryan speech as there is between Aryan and Semitic.

The Semitic languages have prefixes and infixes, whereas the Aryan and Ugro-Finnic languages possess only suffixes. Hence there is an agreement in their fundamental structure. It is true that the Ugro-Finnic languages are agglutinative, but in some

[1] F. Müller, *Allgemeine Ethnographie*, pp. 32, 527; Sayce, *Introduction to the Science of Language*, vol. ii. p. 178; Hovelacque, *Science of Language*, pp. 152, 174.

of them, as in the West Finnic class, the agglutination has almost reached the inflexional stage, differing little from the primitive stage of flexion which we discover in the more archaic Aryan languages. There is no absolute line to be drawn between agglutination and inflexion. Isolating languages tend to become agglutinative, agglutinative languages to become inflexional; inflexional languages tend ultimately to lose their flexions, and become analytic. Chinese is monosyllabic; Tibetan shows a tendency to agglutination. The Ural-Altaic languages are in the agglutinating stage; but Finnic, the most advanced of this class, has almost reached the stage of inflexion. Aryan languages are inflexional, but in Persian, French, and English the inflexions have almost disappeared, and the analytic stage has been nearly reached.

The farther we go back into the history of Aryan speech the more agglutinative and less inflexional is the character of the grammar. The more archaic Aryan languages, such as the Lithuanian, approach the most closely to the transparent Ugro-Finnic grammar, which is simple and logical; while in other Aryan languages the grammatical forms are degraded and obscure. On the other hand, the more developed Finnic languages have become less agglutinative and more inflexional. Professor Max Müller admits that in the Finnic grammar we find a closer approximation to the Aryan than can be elsewhere discovered. He goes so far as to say that "we might almost doubt whether the grammar of this language (Finnic) had not left the agglutinative stage and entered into the current of inflexion with Greek and Sanskrit."[1] Dr.

[1] Max Müller, *Lectures*, vol. i. p. 319.

Schrader admits that it cannot be denied that the Aryan languages exhibit traces which show that they have emerged from a lower stage of development, nearer to that of the Ural-Altaic languages.

The Finnic, which is the most advanced of the Ural-Altaic languages, also approaches the Aryan languages in requiring the adjective to agree with the substantive in number and case. Moreover, in the Finnic and Aryan languages the ultimate verbal roots are largely the same in sound and meaning, the pronominal and other formative elements are largely the same, and are used in the same way, and with the same import.

There has been a constant tendency to assimilate the forms of the Aryan cases and to obliterate the distinction of the grammatical forms, while the recuperative power of producing new forms seems to be now lost. At the same time, while cases and tenses have disappeared, there has been a tendency to multiply declensions and conjugations. But primitive Aryan speech possessed only two forms of declension and conjugation, those belonging to the vocalic and consonantal stems, and these probably are ultimately reducible to one. In this it agreed with the primitive Ural-Altaic speech, which primarily possessed only one form of declension and one of conjugation.

The Altaic languages still possess the power of developing cases with great readiness, a power which Aryan speech must have once possessed but has now lost. The primitive Aryan speech was rich in cases, which were formed by agglutinated postpositions. Latin kept five, the mediæval langue d'oïl kept two, modern French has lost them all. As these cases fell into disuse it became necessary to supply the defect by prepositions. In the proto-Aryan speech there were certainly seven and probably nine cases—a genitive, a dative, and an accusative, two locatives, two instrumentals, and two ablatives. With them we may compare the nine cases in Yakut and the fourteen in Finnic, which possesses illative, prosecutive, and mutative cases. We have seen that some Aryan languages, such as Sanskrit and South Slavonic, have developed numerous consonants which the primitive speech did not possess. The Ugro-Altaic phonetic system seems to be a simple stage out of which the Aryan system might have been evolved. It possesses only one guttural, *k*, while the Aryan has six; one dental, *t*, while the Aryan has three; and one labial, *p*, while the Aryan has three.

It is however alleged that there are three radical distinctions which separate the Aryan and Finnic languages. They are gender, the formation of the plural, and the law of vocalic harmony.

The vocalic harmony, which is such a characteristic feature of the Ural-Altaic languages, has been adduced as the most fundamental difference by which they are distinguished from Aryan languages. But some of them, as the Tscheremiss and the Wotiak, possess only faint traces of it. M. Adam supposes that they have lost it. If so, the Aryan languages might have lost it also. M. Hovelacque, on the other hand, believes that the vocalic harmony is of comparatively recent origin, and that the Tscheremiss and Wotiak have only imperfectly acquired it.

The next great difference is in the formation of the plural. The Aryan and Ural-Altaic languages have three numbers—singular, dual, and plural. In this they agree, but we have to face the formidable difficulty that though the dual is formed in the same way, the structure of the plural is altogether different. In the Finnic languages the sign of the plural is inserted between the stem and the pronominal or postpositional suffixes, whereas in Aryan languages the sign of the plural comes last. But this difference, fundamental as it may seem, may rather be regarded as a sign of primitive unity. Professor Sayce has shown reasons for believing that in the primitive Aryan speech there was no plural, but only the singular and the dual. "Nothing," he says, "seems to us more natural, nay, more necessary, than the existence of the plural; we might suppose that its roots go deep down into the very beginnings of language, and yet there are two facts which militate most clearly and decisively against such an opinion."[1] One is the occasional survival of the dual, which would have been needless if the plural had been in existence, as we see by the fact that the existence of the plural has caused the dual to be dropped. "The dual," he says elsewhere, "was older than the plural, and, after the development of the latter, survived only as a useless encumbrance, which most of the Aryan languages contrived to get rid of."[2] The same was the case in the Finnic languages, which originally had a dual, as is proved by its survival in Ostiak, Lapp, and Samoyed, while in the more cultured languages it has disappeared. The second fact is that many families of speech possess a dual, but have not yet developed a plural. The Accadian and Basque possess the plural only in an imperfect and rudimentary form. That the plural was a late formation in the

[1] Sayce, *Principles*, p. 258.
[2] Sayce, Article "Grammar" in the *Encyclopædia Britannica*.

Ural-Altaic languages is proved by the fact that they have not all adopted the same plural suffix. It is *t* in Finnic, *k* in Magyar, *lar* in Turkic, and *nar* in Mongolic.[1] The Aryan and Finnic languages form the dual in the same way. In both the dual suffix follows the case ending or the pronominal suffix. The dual suffix is also believed to be identical in its origin, having been constructed out of the same pronominal elements in Samoyed, Lapp, and Ostiak as in those Aryan languages which have retained the dual.

But while the formation of the dual is the same in the Aryan and Finnic languages, that of the plural is different. In the Aryan languages it was formed on the model of the dual, the plural suffix simply taking the place of the dual suffix. In the Finnic languages it is formed by a plural suffix, *t*, inserted before the pronominal or postpositional suffixes, just as in English we tack on the sign of the genitive in such words as *man* and *men*, and say "the man's boots" or "the men's boots," a formation which corresponds to that in the Finnic languages; whereas in primitive Aryan speech the sign of case comes first, as in the word *nobis*, where *bi* is the sign of the case, and *s* of the plural. In a Finnic language the order of these suffixes would be reversed.

Hence from the agreement in the formation of the dual, and the disagreement in that of the plural, we see that Aryan speech might have been evolved out of a language of the Finnic class at a time when both were still in the stage which Professor Sayce assigns to the primitive Aryan speech, that is when,

---

[1] Kellgren, *Die Grundzüge der Finnischen Sprachen*, p. 59.

like the Hamitic languages, they possessed only the singular and the dual.

The third difference between Aryan and Finnic languages which has been thought fundamental is that the Finnic languages, like the rest of the Ural-Altaic class, are destitute of gender. Dr. Schrader considers that the absence of gender is the point in which the Ural-Altaic languages are most decisively distinguished from both the Aryan and Semitic. But here again Professor Sayce maintains the probability that the primitive Aryan speech agreed with Finnic in the absence of gender. He considers gender a later formation, "the product partly of analogy, and partly of phonetic decay." "There are many indications," he continues, "that the parent Aryan at an early stage of its existence had no gender at all." "The terminations of father and mother, *pater* and *mater*, for example, are exactly the same." Feminines like *humus*, or masculines like *advena*, "show that there was a time when these stems indicated no particular gender, but owed their subsequent adaption, the one to mark the masculine, and the other to mark the feminine, to the influence of analogy."[1]

We therefore conclude that the language out of which Aryan speech was evolved must have agreed with the Ural-Altaic in being destitute of gender.

It appears, therefore, that none of the differences which have been adduced as fundamental distinctions between the Aryan and Ural-Altaic languages are really primitive. Aryan inflexion arose out of agglutination, and it must at one time have been more simple and more regular; the Aryan cases must originally have been more numerous; the genders and the plural are

[1] Sayce, Article "Grammar" in the *Encyclopædia Britannica*.

new formations; and in the Ural-Altaic languages the vocalic harmony cannot be regarded as an essential law. Thus while the differences which distinguish the Aryan and the Semitic languages go down to the very foundations of speech, those which divide the Aryan from the Ural-Altaic languages are not radical. They are all neologisms—new formations which in the course of many millenniums might be expected to arise.

On the other hand, there are points of structural agreement which can only be explained as due to a primitive unity. These have been set forth by Diefenbach, Cuno, Anderson, and above all by Weske,[1] and the conclusions of these scholars must now be briefly set before the reader.

The agreements in the vocabulary are numerous, but as a rule are not primitive. They are largely, as has been shown by Thomsen, Ahlqvist, and Schrader,[2] culture words borrowed from the Swedish, Slavonic, and Iranian languages.

But when we penetrate deeper, and come to the verbal roots out of which the vocabulary has been framed, we find, as Anderson and Cuno have shown, that the roots are to a large extent identical, and that these verbal roots have been built up into word-stems by the same processes, and by aid of identical

[1] Diefenbach, *Origines Europææ* (Frankfort, 1861); Cuno, *Forschungen im Gebiete der Alten Völkerkunde* (Berlin, 1871); Anderson, *Studien zur Vergleichung der Indo-Germanischen und Finnisch-Ugrischen Sprachen* (Dorpat, 1879); Weske, *Ueber die historische Entwickelung der Finnischen Sprachen im Vergleich mit der Indo-Germanischen* (Dorpat, 1875).

[2] Thomsen, *Ueber den Einfluss der Germanischen Sprachen auf die Finnish-Lappischen* (Halle, 1870); Ahlqvist, *Die Kulturwörte der West Finnischen Sprachen* (Helsingfors, 1875); Schrader, *Sprachvergleichung und Urgeschichte*.

formatives. To take an example, we have both in Aryan and Finnic the verbal root *kar*, to run, to move. From this we get in Finnic the word *ker-ap*, a carriage, and in English the word *char-iot*. Here, from the same root, words of similar meaning have been independently constructed.

These identical verbal roots are numerous. To give a few instances, we have both in Aryan and Finnic languages the verbal roots *kad*, to fall; *kak*, to bend, with the secondary meaning to excrete; *kap*, to hold; *kam*, to bend; *kar*, to work, to do, with the secondary meaning to work evil or injure; *kas*, to praise; *kal*, to be cold; *ku*, to swell out; not to speak of certain resemblances in the roots of the numerals, which have been set forth by Cuno.[1]

In the next place, both in Aryan and Finnic, identical formative suffixes are attached to the verbal roots to form stems. Thus the formative *ma* is employed in the same way both in Aryan and Finnic for the construction of verbal nouns.[2] In Finnic, combined with the verbal root *san*, to say, it gives *san-o-ma*, a message; combined with the root *juo*, to drink, it gives *juo-ma*, drink; with the root *tek*, to do, it gives *tek-e-ma*, a deed; and many similar words, such as *luke-ma*, reading, and *laulo-ma*, song. In Aryan languages this formative is identically employed. Thus from the root *ghar*, to burn, we have in Sanskrit *ghar-ma*, warmth; and from *dhu*, to move, we have *dhu-ma*, smoke. In Lithuanian, from *vaz*, to carry, we have *vaz-ma*, carriage; from *aud*, to weave, we have *aud-i-ma*, a web. In Latin, from *fa*, to say (*fa-ri*), we have *fa-ma*, a report; and in Greek such

[1] Cuno, *Forschungen*, p. 52.
[2] Weske, *Entwickelung*, p. 5; Anderson, *Studien*, p. 108.

words as τιμή and γνώμη. The comparison might be extended to other formative suffixes which are employed both in the Aryan and Finnic languages, such as *na, ja, va, la, ka, ta,* and *mine.* To take a few instances, we have in Finnic the formative *na*, which combined with the verbal root *koh,* to drink, gives *koh-i-na,* drunken. In Sanskrit this suffix combined with the verbal root *svap,* to sleep, gives *svap-na,* sleep, and *sap-na,* sleep, in Lithuanian. In like manner the formative *ja* gives in Finnic *lug-e-ja,* a reader, from the root *lug,* to read; *laulo-ja,* a singer; *kakarda-ja,* a dipper; while in Lithuanian it gives *zyn-ja,* a magician, from the root *zin,* to know, and *sta-ja,* a position or place, from the root *sta,* to stand.[1]

When the stems have thus been built up by means of roots and formatives which are largely identical, and used in precisely the same way, conjugation and declension are effected by the same processes, declension by suffixed prepositions, and conjugation by tense signs attached to the stem, and followed by pronominal suffixes.

Some of the tense stems are the same. Thus both in Aryan and Finnic we have tense stems formed by *sk* and *ja,* and perfect stems by *s.*

The identity of the pronominal suffixes is still more important. For the first person the pronominal suffix was originally *ma,* which means "I" or "me," both in Aryan and Finnic. In modern languages, both Aryan and Finnic, this has become *m* or *n,* or has disappeared altogether. Thus from the verbal root *bhar,* to bear, we have in Sanskrit *a-bhar-am,* I bore,

[1] For other instances see Anderson, *Studien zur Vergleichung der Indo-Germanischen und Finnish-Ugrischen Sprachen,* pp. 107-109.

and in Greek ἔ-φερ-ον. The Old High German *tuo-m*, I do, and *ga-m*, I go, have become *thu-e* and *geh-e* in New High German. In Finnic the same pronominal suffix *ma* has undergone the same changes. Thus in Tscheremiss "I come" is *tola-m*, in Suomi it is *tule-n*, and in Esthonian *tul-e*. "I live" is *äle-m* in Lapp, *ale-n* in Suomi, and *el-ä* in Esthonian. The first person singular present from *lukea*, to read, is *luge-n* in Veps, *luga-n* in Lapp, *luda-m* in Tscheremiss, and in Wotiak *lugo*, where the pronominal suffix has disappeared as completely as in the Latin *lego*. The pronominal suffix for the second person is *ta* in Finnic, which becomes *ti* and *t;* while in Aryan it is *tva*, which becomes *ta, tha, ti,* and *s*. Thus in Suomi we have *tule-t*, thou comest, and in Sanskrit *dadi-tha* (Latin *dedis-ti*), thou hast given.[1]

In the plural, as has already been explained, the order of the suffixes has been reversed, but their identity in Aryan and Finnic can be recognised. Thus in Finnic the suffix of the second person plural is *t-te*, as in *tule-t-te*, ye come. Here *t*, the plural sign, is followed by *te* (= *ta*), the pronoun of the second person. In Aryan, the order being reversed, the suffix of the second person plural was *ta-si*, where *ta* is the pronoun, and *si* the sign of the plural. Thus in the Latin *ama-ti-s*, ye love, *ti* is the pronoun, and *s* the plural sign, the Finnic plural suffix *t* being probably the archaic form of the Aryan plural suffix *s*.

Thus the verb is conjugated in the same way in the Aryan and Ural-Altaic languages, the formation in both being, stem + tense + personal suffix;

---

[1] Weske, *Entwickelung der Finnischen Sprachen*, p. 7; Papillon, *Comparative Philology*, p. 161.

the Sanskrit future of the first person, *dat-as-mi*, giver-am-I, being constructed in the same way as the Ostiak future, *pan-de-m*, or the Turkic *yaz-ar-im*.

It is the same with the declension of the nouns. The case signs in Finnic arose out of suffixed prepositions, as in the Aryan languages. Thus we have a Finnic ablative in *ta* or *t*,[1] which corresponds to the Aryan ablative in *at* or *t*; a Finnic locative in *ti*,[2] which corresponds to the Aryan locative in *dhi*; and a Finnic genitive in *n*, of which there are traces in Aryan genitives in *n* and *m*; and a Finnic accusative in *am* or *m*,[3] which is identical with the Aryan accusative. Thus in Tscheremiss we have the accusative *vida-m* from the stem *vida*, water, and in Sanskrit the accusative *pati-m*, master, from the stem *pati*.

These deep-seated structural agreements between the Aryan and Finnic languages are, as Penka admits, too profound to be explained by geographical contiguity, commercial intercourse, inroads, wars, or political supremacy. Penka accounts for them[4] by the supposition that Finnic is a mixed speech which has been influenced by Aryan in much the same way that English has been influenced by Norman-French. But this hypothesis will hardly suffice to account for the fundamental agreement in the pronouns, the declensions, the conjugations, and the formatives. An explanation at once more simple and more satisfactory would seem to be that the Finnic languages

[1] Donner, *Die gegenseitige Verwandtschaft der Finnisch-Ugrischen Sprachen*, p. 62.
[2] *Ibid.*, p. 93.
[3] *Ibid.*, p. 73; Weske, *Untersuchungen zur Vergleichenden Grammatik des Finnischen Sprachstammes*, p. 39.
[4] Penka, *Origines Ariacæ*, p. 68.

exhibit a survival of the primitive form of speech out of which the Aryan languages were developed; the archaic semi-agglutinative Lithuanian approaching most closely to the Finnic, which is semi-inflexional.

Of the four neolithic European races one only can have been the primitive Aryan race. Two of them, the Slavo-Celtic and the Ligurian, are, like the Ugro-Finnic race, brachycephalic.

On archæological grounds we have arrived at the conclusion that the culture of the Slavo-Celtic race, as exhibited in the round barrows of Britain, and the pile dwellings of Central Europe, comes nearest to that of the primitive Aryans as disclosed by linguistic palæontology. We have also seen that, anthropologically, this race belongs to the same type as the Finno-Ugric tribes of Eastern Europe and of Central Asia.[1] This conclusion is also in accord with the philological tests, which make it possible that Aryan speech may have been evolved out of a language of the Ural-Altaic class; the grammatical resemblances pointing to a primitive unity of speech, just as the physical resemblances point to a primitive unity of race. There must have been some ruder form of speech out of which the elaborate Aryan inflexion was evolved, and there is no other known form of speech, except the Ural-Altaic, which can possibly be regarded as the germ out of which the Aryan languages may have sprung.

One possibility remains to be considered. Since the colour of the hair and eyes are more variable than the shape of the skull, some anthropologists of repute, as we have already seen, are inclined to believe that the two brachycephalic races, the short, dark Ligurians, and

[1] See p. 91, *supra*.

the fair Celto-Slavic race, may be ultimately identified. We have also seen that the Basque probably represents the primitive speech of the former, and that it is also believed to belong ultimately to the Ural-Altaic family. We have also come to the conclusion that the Celto-Slavic race best represents the primitive Aryans, whose speech may have been evolved out of a language of the Ural-Altaic class. We may therefore conjecture that at the close of the reindeer age a Finnic people appeared in Western Europe, whose speech, remaining stationary, is represented by the agglutinative Basque, and that much later, at the beginning of the pastoral age, when the ox had been tamed, a taller and more powerful Finno-Ugric people developed in Central Europe the inflective Aryan speech. By this hypothesis many difficulties would be reconciled.

Ahlqvist has constructed a picture of the civilisation of the undivided Finnic race by first eliminating the culture words which have been borrowed from the Aryans, and then distinguishing those which belonged to the Finns before their separation, by the test of their being the common possessions of the Western or Baltic Finns, and the Eastern Finns of the Ural and the Volga. His reconstruction of the primitive Finnic civilisation does not differ greatly from that which, on linguistic and archæological grounds, has been assigned to the undivided Aryans.

He comes to the conclusion that the undivided Finns were in much the same stage of culture as the Woguls, or the Ostiaks on the Obi, as described by modern travellers. They were nomad hunters and fishers, whose chief domesticated animal was the dog. The cow was not altogether unknown, but the art of making butter and cheese had not been acquired. The domestication of the sheep, the goat, and the pig was later than the contact with the Aryans. The name of the horse is an Aryan loan-word. Tillage was merely sporadic, a patch of forest may have been cleared by fire, and a crop of barley grown. The dwelling, *sauna*, was a pit dug in the earth and roofed over, or a conical hut, *kota*, made of poles leaning against each other, or supported by a tree, and covered in winter by skins. These dwellings had a door, and a hole in the roof, through which the smoke escaped. The fire was built on a few loose stones in the middle of the hut, but there was no flooring and no window, light entering through the door or the smoke-hole in the roof The women, with bone needles, made clothing from the skins of animals, and spun thread with spindles from the fibres of plants, while the men fabricated canoes, snow-shoes, and implements for hunting and fishing. If they had any knowledge of metals it must have been confined to native copper.

It was only after the separation of the Eastern and Western Finns that they became acquainted with the sheep, and the art of preparing yarn from its wool. They had no towns, or judges, or hereditary chiefs.[1]

It will be seen that Ahlqvist's picture of the civilisation of the undivided Finno-Ugric race, as derived from linguistic materials, differs little from that which Schrader has drawn of the culture of the undivided Aryans.[2]

According to Vambéry, the culture of the un-

[1] Ahlqvist, *Kulturwörter der West Finnischen Sprachen*, p. 264.
[2] See p. 188, *supra*.

divided Turko-Tartaric family was higher than that of the undivided Finns, but we must remember that the separation was much later. They knew the horse, the ox, the ass, the camel, and the sheep, as well as the dog, and they cultivated wheat and millet as well as barley.

CHAPTER VI.

THE ARYAN MYTHOLOGY.

NOT less remarkable than the silent revolution which has overthrown the once universally accepted hypothesis as to the successive migration of the Aryan nations from Central Asia, is the general abandonment of the expectation which was at one time entertained that India would interpret for us the meaning of the Teutonic, Roman, and Greek mythologies. We were told that "the Veda is the real theogony of the Aryan nations,"[1] and that "the mythology of the Veda is to comparative mythology what Sanskrit has been to comparative grammar." It was confidently proclaimed that the discovery of "the common origin of Greek and Sanskrit mythology" had already been made. It was compared to "the discovery of a new world;" and it was predicted that "the science of comparative mythology will soon rise to the same importance as that of comparative philology."[2]

The Sanskritists confidently produced their identifications. Aphrodite, Eurydice, Athena, Daphne, and Brynhild were all pronounced to be dawn maidens, and were identified with Urvasi; Heracles, Ares, Achilles, Meleager, Orpheus, Balder, and Sigurd were solar heroes, and identified with Pururavas; the

[1] Max Müller, *Essays,* vol. i. p. 381.   [2] *Ibid.*, p. 449.

Greek Charites were the Indian Harits; and the Indian Maruts became the Roman Mars.[1]

No importance was attached to the objection that the Harits, the nine horses of Indra, did not in number, sex, form, or function bear any resemblance to the three Graces, the Charites of Greek mythology. Helen, a dawn maiden stolen by Paris, was identified with the Vedic Sarama, who, instead of being himself stolen, recovers for Indra his stolen cows, which are the clouds of heaven. Professor Max Müller actually suggests that Achilles, a bright solar hero, is the Indian Ahalya, who is the goddess of the night beloved and destroyed by Indra.[2]

All such difficulties were overlooked, and we were told that the riddle of Aryan mythology had at last been solved. But these confident expectations have been doomed to be disappointed. Scholars were not more agreed as to the explanations from Sanskrit sources of the names of the Greek divinities than as to the order in which the Aryan nations started on their march from Central Asia. The explorations of neolithic graves, followed by the pamphlet of Johannes Schmidt, rendered untenable the hypothesis of the successive westward migrations of Aryan tribes; and in like manner George Smith's discovery of certain cuneiform tablets in the mounds of Nineveh upset the conclusions of the comparative mythologists, and falsified the confident prophecies which had been adventured by the too eager Sanskritists.

The key to the Greek mythology has indeed been found, but it has been discovered, not as was anti-

[1] Cox, *Mythology of the Aryan Nations*, vol. i. pp. 32, 395-445.
[2] Mahaffy, *Prolegomena to Ancient History*, p. 51.

cipated, on the banks of the Ganges, but on those of the Tigris. Much of the mythology of ancient Greece, instead of having a common origin with that of India, proves to be essentially non-Aryan, and must have been obtained from Babylonia through Phœnician channels. As might have been expected, the greater part of the Greek mythology proves to have been derived from the same source as the first elements of Greek culture. The rude barbarians of Hellas obtained their knowledge of gold and bronze, of weights and measures, of textile fabrics, spices, and jewellery, of the art of writing, and of the alphabet itself, from the Phœnician merchants who visited their shores; and in like manner, we now find that they obtained many of their deities and a considerable portion of their mythologic tales from the more cultured Semites. Mythologists were unable to explain why, if so many of the Greek myths were, as they affirmed, the common heritage of the Aryan race, so few of them could be traced in Italy or Germany. This riddle is now solved. They were not, as was supposed, a part of the common Aryan inheritance, but merely a foreign importation, at a comparatively late date, and confined to those portions of the Aryan territory which were frequented by Phœnician traders.

The clue, once obtained, has been followed up with marvellous success.

The great Semitic goddess Istar, primarily the moon, and afterwards the planet Venus, bore two characters, the chaste warrior-maiden, and the voluptuous deity of love. The Phœnician mariners brought her, in the latter character, and under the name of Astarte or Ashteroth, to Cyprus, whence, as the sea-born Aphrodite, her worship spread among the Greeks; while, probably by the land trade route through Asia Minor, the Babylonian Istar came to Ephesus as Artemis. Thus Aphrodite, instead of being an Indian dawn maiden rising from the sea, is now found to be the Babylonian moon goddess brought in Phœnician ships to Cythera and Cyprus.

When once the identity of Istar with Aphrodite and Artemis was established, it became easy, with the help of the Babylonian epic of the descent of Istar, recovered from the clay tablets of the library of Assur-banipal, to explain the significance of a considerable number of obscure Greek myths. The Phrygian myth of Atys and Cybele, and the corresponding Greek myth of Adonis and Aphrodite, was recognised as a mere Western version of the Phœnician myth of Tammuz and Astarte, the story of the moon mourning over the death of her lost spouse, the sun, and the name of Adonis was seen to be merely the Semitic Adonai, the "lord" of heaven. And when Artemis was also identified with Istar, the Greek Amazons were seen to be the priestesses of the Asiatic goddess, the Galli were her eunuch priests, Istar being represented in Assyrian art with a quiver and a bow, just as Artemis is represented in the art of Greece.[1]

The bull, whose form was assumed by Zeus in order to carry off Europa, a Phœnician damsel, was seen to be the bull of Anu, the Semitic Heaven god, the same bull which we recognise in the constellation Taurus, and Europa, the "broad-faced" maiden, is only another form of Istar, the broad-faced moon, instead of being identical with Urvasi, the Vedic

[1] Sayce, *Hibbert Lectures*, p. 271.

dawn maiden.[1] The identity of the names was maintained on the ground that a Sanskrit *s* occasionally corresponds to a Greek *p*, though a suspicion that the Europa myth was of Phœnician and not of Indian origin might have been aroused by the fact that Europa is called the daughter of Phœnix—only another way of saying that the myth was derived from the Phœnicians.

Another myth, seemingly so diverse—the story of the slaying of the dragon by Perseus and the rescue of Andromeda—was localised by the Greeks on the Phœnician coast. It proves to be a lunar eclipse myth, ultimately Babylonian, a Greek translation of the Phœnician version of the combat of Bel Merodach with the dragon Tiamat, and the rescue of the moon goddess Istar from the black dragon who threatened to devour her.[2]

Another Tiamat myth is preserved in the Greek legend of the mutilation of Uranus by his son Cronus. This myth, which seems to us so repulsive, is merely a misunderstood translation from the Babylonian cosmogony, which represents Bel Merodach, the Semitic sun-god, cutting asunder his parent Tiamat, the primordial chaos from which he had sprung.

Ares, the warrior-god of the Greeks, has been identified by Professor Sayce[3] with Uras, the warrior-god of the Babylonians, whose title, "the lord of the pig," helps to explain an obscure Greek myth which tells us that Ares slew Adonis by taking the form of a wild boar, the sun-god being slain by the tusk of winter.

[1] Max Müller, *Essays*, vol. i. p. 406.
[2] See Sayce, *Hibbert Lectures*, p. 102.   [3] *Ibid.*, p. 153.

The bold attempt of the Sanskritists to identify Mars (stem, *mart*) with the Vedic Maruts, who are the winds, presented the difficulty that the name of Mars was unknown to the Greeks, and even to the Iranians. It is, at all events, less plausible than the new explanation which identifies him with Mâtu or Martu, the Babylonian god who ruled the tempest, and was worshipped as Rimmon by the Syrians.

The theory of the Indian origin of the great Dionysiac myth was shaken by Lenormant's comparison of Dionysus with the Assyrian sun-god who bore the name of Dianisu; and this was confirmed by Dr. Neubauer's identification of his mother Semele, daughter of Cadmus the Phœnician, with the Phœnician goddess Semlath, and with the Edomite " Semlah of the Vineland."

One of the greatest reproaches which the Sanskrit school of Comparative Mythologists had to bear was that in the Vedic hymns no trace could be found of Apollo, the great Hellenic sun-god, a deity reverenced more than any other by the Greeks. None of the myths of Apollo resembled the myths of any of the Indian sun-gods, and no explanation of the name was forthcoming from the resources of Aryan philology. If the Greek and Indian mythologies were parts of the common inheritance of the Aryan nations, it was strange that the name and worship of Apollo should be confined to those lands which were visited by the Phœnicians. But these mysteries have been at last explained. The oldest epigraphic form of the name of Apollo is Aplu, which corresponds to the Semitic Ablu, the "son" of heaven, which was one of the titles of Tammuz the Syrian sun-god. Heracles, again, is the Semitic sun-god under another aspect. His

THE ARYAN MYTHOLOGY.

twelve labours are the twelve labours of Isdhubar, the Accadian hero, whose story may be read in the fragments of the great Chaldean epic which was redacted into a single whole many centuries before the Vedic hymns were first composed. The name of Heracles is of Greek invention, but Melicertes, the name which he bore in the Phœnician settlement at Corinth, is merely a Greek transliteration of the name of Melcarth, the Phœnician sun-god.

The very foundations of the Sanskritic school of interpretation being thus rudely shaken, scholars began to question other explanations which had been received with general acquiescence. Professor Max Müller, for instance, had identified Athena, the great deity of the Ionian Greeks, with the Vedic *dahana*, the "dawn" creeping over the sky. The philological difficulty was considerable, and scholars are now inclined to believe that Athena was not the dawn but the lightning. Even the identification of the Centaurs with the Vedic Gandharvas has been questioned, owing to the discovery of Centaurs sculptured on Babylonian monuments.

Perhaps the greatest of the difficulties which beset the attempt to explain the Aryan mythology from Vedic sources was the almost complete discordance between the names of Greek and Roman deities. Juno and Hera, Venus and Aphrodite, Mars and Ares, Mercury and Hermes, Diana and Artemis, Neptune and Poseidon, Ceres and Demeter, are plainly unrelated names. If the Rig Veda explains so insignificant a portion of the mythology of the Greeks, whose language approaches Sanskrit much more closely than Latin does, it could hardly be expected that the mythology of Italy could be explained by that of India.

But it is now seen that many of the myths which were formerly supposed to prove the common origin of the Greek and Roman mythology are merely late and arbitrary transferences of mythic stories to wholly unrelated deities. Thus the adventures of Heracles, the Greek solar hero, which, as we have seen, are merely the borrowed adventures of the Babylonian Isdhubar, were assigned to Hercules, the old Italic god of enclosures, who has nothing in common with Heracles except an accidental phonetic resemblance of the name,[1] while Saturnus, the Italic god of agriculture, was identified with Cronus, merely because his emblem, the sickle of the husbandman, resembled somewhat the sickle of Cronus, which is the curved scimitar with which Bel Merodach, the prototype of Cronus, combats the powers of darkness.

In like manner, the Greek myths relating to Aphrodite, which are mainly of Semitic origin, were boldly transferred by Ovid and other adapters to Venus, a purely Italic deity, of whose existence no trace can be discovered in Homer, Hesiod, the Avesta, or the Rig Veda, although the mere name can be explained as Aryan by help of the Sanskrit word *vanas*, which denotes that which is pleasant, especially pleasant drink,[2] and also sexual desire Greek myths relating to Poseidon were also transferred to Neptune, whose name can be explained by help of the Iranian word *napat*, water. In old Irish we have the word *triath*, which means the sea, and helps to explain the Greek Triton, the Sanskrit *trita*, and the Zend *thrita*. In all these cases the linguistic

---

[1] Sayce, *Science of Language*, vol. ii. p. 262.
[2] Mommsen, *Romische Geschichte*, vol. i. p. 16.

elements of the later mythologic names are primitive, but not the mythology itself.

These examples may serve to show that while there was a common inheritance of language, any inheritance of a common mythology must be reduced to very small proportions. The names of the Aryan deities may be primitive words, but the mythological conceptions must be referred to a period later than the linguistic separation.

Setting aside the great Indian triad of Brahma, Siva, and Vishnu as being manifestly of late date, we find the Vedic gods of the first rank are Indra and Agni, after whom come Varuna and Mitra, Ushas and Surya. The great Hellenic gods are Zeus, Apollo, and Athena, followed by Poseidon, Hera, Aphrodite, Artemis, Hermes, Ares, Heracles, Demeter, and Dionysus. The great Italic deities are Jupiter, Juno, Mars, Minerva, Janus, Neptune, Diana, Pluto, Vulcan, Mercury, Venus, Hercules, Bacchus, and Ceres. The Teutonic deities were Thor, Odin, Freya, Baldr, Tiu or Tyr, the god of war, and Frigga the Earth, who is the wife of Woden the Heaven. Among the Celts we have Ogma, Maponos, Segomo, Camulos, Toutates, Taranucos, Esus, Taranis, Cernunnos, and Nuada. The Letto-Slavic deities were Bogu, Perkunas, Perunu, Radegast, Swantowit, Potrimpos, and Picullas.

The diversity of these names is very striking, especially when we consider that they are all elemental. The Aryan nations, and many which are not Aryan, have personified the Heaven and the Earth and the Ocean, the Sun and the Moon, the Storm, the Thunder, the Lightning, the Dawn, the Fire, and the Wind. For these phenomena of Nature there were common names in the primitive Aryan speech, and hence the real matter for surprise is not that there is here and there a resemblance in the divine names of the different nations, but that the diversity should be so great.

They all reverenced and personified as the supreme deity the protecting vault of Heaven, but it was worshipped under different names, by the Indians as Varuna, by the Greeks as Zeus, by the Celts as Camulos, and by the Teutons as Woden. They all reverenced Mother Earth, the spouse of Heaven, but she was called Prithivi by the Indians, Gæa or Demeter by the Greeks, and Nerthus, Frigga, or Jördh by the Teutonic nations.

There is not a single power of Nature which can be proved to have been worshipped under the same primeval name by all the Aryan peoples.

The mythologists who affirm that the Greek and Indian mythologies have "a common origin," and that "the Veda is the real theogony of the Aryan nations," are encountered by two great difficulties. The first, as we have seen, is the fact that the mythologic names in Greek and Latin, and Latin and Celtic do not agree; the second is that though the connection of the Indians and Iranians is very close, the mythologic conceptions supposed to be common to the Indians and the Greeks are not also common to the Greeks and the Iranians.

As a rule the Celtic divine names are confined to the Celts, the Latin names to Italy, the Slavonic names to the Slaves. Words relating to religion have a more restricted currency than those which refer to cattle, agriculture, and weapons. This leads to the presumption that the Aryans before their separation did not possess what can properly be called any common system of mythology. But this result is in accordance with the probabilities of the case. It has been shown that the primitive Aryans were not, as was formerly supposed, a semi-civilised race who, in the bronze period, some fifteen centuries B.C., migrated from Asia into Europe, but that they were rather the lineal descendants of the neolithic people who had occupied Europe for unnumbered ages. Can it be supposed that these rude barbarians, clad in skins, ignorant of agriculture and metals, unable to count above a hundred, who practised human sacrifice, were capable of elaborating a complex and beautiful mythology? or if they had invented it, is it likely that the names and adventures of dawn maidens and solar heroes could have been handed down orally in recognisable form through so many millenniums during which the art of writing was unknown? It is a question if there was any idolatry properly so called among the primitive Aryans. On the earliest monuments of the Egyptians and Babylonians we find sculptured representations of the gods. But there is no word for "idol" common to the Aryan languages, and no idols or objects of worship have been found in neolithic tombs,[1] or in the Swiss and Italian pile dwellings,[2] and even the Scandinavians had originally no images of their gods.[3]

The Greeks owed to the Phœnicians the notion of representing the gods under human form,[4] and images

[1] See, however, De Baye, *L'Archéo'ogie Préhistorique*, p. 95.
[2] Helbig, *Die Italiker in der Poebene*, p. 24.
[3] *Corpus Poeticum Boreale*, vol. i. p. 406.
[4] Di Cesnola, *Cyprus*, Plate vi.

of the gods at Rome were first made by Etruscan artists. The earliest objects of Aryan worship seem to have been fetishes, such as sacred trees, belemnites, or meteoric stones.[1] The Jupiter Lapis of the Fetials at Rome was probably a belemnite. Artemis was worshipped at Ephesus as the stone which fell from heaven, and the many-breasted representations of the goddess may have been suggested by the bosses found on meteoric stones. Zeus Cassius is represented as a stone on coins of Seleucia in Syria, and the Paphian Venus appears under the form of a conical stone on coins struck in Cyprus.[2]

The earliest shrine of Greek worship was at Dodona, and here the object of worship was an oak, on whose branches charms and talismans were hung, and the whisperings of the wind in the leaves were regarded as the oracular voice of heaven. It is plain that the culture of the undivided Aryans has been immensely overrated by the mythologists who have endeavoured to prove that the theological conceptions of the Vedas, of the Edda, and of the Homeric poems were handed down from a pre-ethnic source.

The hypothesis of common traditions transmitted from the holoethnic period is not necessary to explain such resemblances as may exist in the mythological conceptions of the Aryan nations. It is more probable that somewhat similar myths were independently evolved as explanations of recurring natural phenomena. In all countries the day succeeds the night, the sky hangs over the earth, the sun and the moon pursue each other through the heavens, and the

---

[1] Lang, *Myth, Ritual, and Religion*, vol. ii. pp. 219, 235; *Custom and Myth*, p. 223.

[2] Evans, *Ancient Stone Implements*, p. 9.

uprising of the sun is heralded by the tender dawn. Hence in all mythologies the day and the night, the heaven and the earth, the sun and the moon, the sun and the dawn, are represented as man and woman, either as lovers, or as husband and wife, or as brother and sister.

It is natural to represent the sun as a bridegroom coming out of his chamber in the east, and the dawn as a blushing maiden. Hence few mythologies are altogether free from the loves of solar heroes and dawn maidens. But it is not necessary to suppose that such myths are primitive.

The Indian *Ushas*, the Iranian *Ushanh*, the Greek ἠώς, the Latin *Aurora*, and the Lithuanian *Auszra*, all denote etymologically the glow of the rosy dawn, which was personified by Greeks and Romans, and deified by the Indians, but there are no common myths. The Vedic Surya, the spouse of Ushas, is etymologically the same as the Greek Helios, the Latin Sol, and the Welsh Heul (Howel), but Eos is associated in Greek myth with Kephalos and Tithonus, and not with Helios. The connection is merely linguistic, not mythologic, and the solar heroes and dawn maidens were plainly evolved after the Aryan separation.

The divine names which go back to the primitive period are all names of the powers of nature, and in dealing with such early words it is impossible to say whether the names may not have referred merely to the phenomena of nature rather than to any divine personifications, which may have arisen independently at later periods.

Scanty as are the mythologic names common to any two of the Aryan families of speech, the significance of these few agreements tends to disappear on closer examination. Indra and Agni are the deities who occupy the highest places in the oldest Indian mythology. This is evident from the fact that of the most ancient hymns in the Rig Veda 265 are addressed to Indra, and 233 to Agni, and not more than 60 to any other god.[1] But supreme as is the position of these two deities in the most ancient records of Aryan religion, their worship is practically confined to India. In the European mythologies their place is taken by Zeus and Woden, Apollo, Thor, and Balder. In the Avesta there is barely a vestige of the great name of Indra, nor can it be traced in any of the European languages.

In the Vedic hymns Agni is second only to Indra in importance, and much has been made of the etymological identification of the name of Agni with the Latin *ignis* and the Lithuanian *ugnis;* but this amounts to very little. It merely proves that the undivided Aryans were acquainted with fire, but it does not prove that fire was an object of worship. The inference is rather that the worship of the sacred fire arose after the separation of the Aryans. We find that in India Agni was a chief object of worship at the earliest time of which we have any cognisance of Aryan religion, but there is no reason to believe that fire was ever worshipped under this name by Latins or Lithuanians.

The presumption is rather the other way, since the Roman fire-worship was addressed to Vesta, the tribal fire of the domestic hearth, while Agni among the Indians was quite another thing—the sacrificial or celestial fire.

[1] Keary, *Outlines of Primitive Belief*, p. 126.

The Greek Hestia, it is true, agrees in name and function with the Latin Vesta,[1] and this is the most striking of all the correspondencies between Roman and Greek mythology, more especially since there is reason to believe that Vesta was the oldest of the deities of Rome. But there is no trace of this venerable worship in India. In Sanskrit the name only exists as *vastu*, which merely means the house or dwelling place.

The very fact that the Vesta worship is the most indubitable of the correspondencies between the Greek and Roman mythologies is itself a proof of the rudimentary nature of their common civilisation. Only among the rudest of existing savage tribes, such as the Australians, is it held a duty to keep alight the fire of the tribe, which if extinguished has to be obtained from some neighbouring tribe, as they are ignorant of the means of rekindling it. The Chippeways and Natchez Indians had an institution for keeping alight the tribal fire, certain persons being set aside and devoted to this occupation;[2] and the incorporation and endowment of the Vestal Virgins at Rome seems to be a survival of a similar practice, the social duty, originally devolving on the daughters of the house, obtaining a religious sanction as the service of the perpetual flame.

The name of Prometheus, who, according to the Greek myth, brought fire from heaven to mortals, may be explained by the Sanskrit *pramantha;* but this word did not become a mythological term among the Indians, but merely denoted the

[1] Preller, *Griechische Mythologie*, vol. i. pp. 227-333; *Romische Mythologie*, p. 532.
[2] Lubbock, *Prehistoric Times*, pp. 464, 537.

drill by which fire was obtained by friction. Here clearly the mythological conception is later than the separation of Greeks and Indians, and we are only entitled to conclude that the fire-drill was known before the linguistic separation. Hence the whole of the evidence tends to the belief that the most primitive of all worships—that of fire—does not belong to the earliest period, but was independendently evolved among the Eastern and Western Aryans.

The gulf between the Teutonic and Celtic languages is much wider than that between Indian and Iranian; but, as has been already shown, the culture words prove that the relations of the Celts and Teutons were those of later geographical contact and political supremacy. There are reasons for supposing that a considerable portion of the Teutonic mythology may have been obtained from Celtic sources, as that of the Greeks was obtained from the Semites. Professor Rhys believes that the myths relating to Woden, the great Teutonic sky-god, may be traced to a Celtic origin, and he compares the name of Woden with the Celtic Gwydion.[1] But as no parallel name and no parallel myths are to be found among the Italic races, who stand in a much closer linguistic relation to the Celts than the Celts do to the Teutons, these myths probably date not from the time of the Celto-Teutonic unity, but from the much later period when the Teutons lived under the political supremacy of the Celts.

Thor or Dunar, the Teutonic thunder-god, may also be compared with the Celtic thunder-god Taranucus (Welsh *taran*, thunder), and Professor Rhys

---

[1] Rhys, *Hibbert Lectures*, p. 283.

finds Toutiorix, the Gaulish Apollo, in the legends of the German solar hero Theodoric, and he connects the Gaulish Esus with the Teutonic Anses and the Norse *æsir*, a word which is applied to the gods generally, and may be etymologically explained by the Sanskrit *asus*, the breath of life. He also compares the Teutonic Mars, Tiu, the "glorious" or splendid one, with Llud (King Lud), who is Nuada of the silver hand under another name. The name Nuada, originally Nodens, may be compared with the Italic Neptune, which is written Nethuns on an early mirror. The Celtic heaven-god Camulos corresponds etymologically to the Teutonic Himmel, and his functions are those of the Greek Uranus, but Heaven was worshipped by the Teutons as Woden and not as Himmel.

Kuhn thinks that Sarama, the messenger of Indra, was the wind; Professor Max Müller, with less reason, claims him as the dawn; and he may perhaps be identified, at least etymologically, with the Greek Hermes, the messenger of Zeus. The Vedic Ushas, the morning red, is etymologically the Greek Eos and the Latin Aurora, and the Vedic Surya is etymologically the Latin Sol.

Other suggested identifications between mythological beings in Greece and India are between Phlegyas and Bhrgu, Trita and Triton, Phoroneus and Bhuranyu, the Centaurs and the Gandharvas, and between the lovely Saranyus, who is the morning dawn, and the gloomy Erinyes, the implacable Furies of the Greeks.

But some of these identifications are etymological rather than mythological, and others are rejected by the best scholars. It is possible, however, that there may be a connection between Janus and Ζάν, Juno and Διώνη.

Professor Max Müller has attempted to identify the Indian Maruts with the Roman Mars. But in the Greek mythology, or even in the Iranian, which is so much closer than the Latin to that of the Indians, we have no trace of Mars or Maruts, and we are driven to conclude that the evolution of the Maruts was subsequent to the separation of the Indians and the Iranians, and indefinitely later than the separation of the Italic and Indian races, and the identification of Mars (Martis) with the Babylonian storm-god, Mâtu or Martu, is, to say the least, as probable as is any connection with the Indian Maruts. Not only the Maruts, but Rudra and the other Indian deities associated with Indra are unknown in the Avesta. Brahma, who afterwards replaced Indra as the supreme Indian god, appears in the Rig Veda, and so also does Vishnu; but Siva and Kali, who now occupy such a prominent position in Indian worship, are unknown, and are probably of Dravidian origin.

When we have diligently read all the bulky volumes which have been written with the object of identifying the deities of India and Europe, it is surprising to find how scanty are the actual results which are accepted by all scholars. This has been well put by Mr. Lang,[1] who says that Mannhardt, after having been a disciple of the Sanskritist school, has been obliged to confess that comparative mythology has not borne the fruit that was at one time expected, and that those gains of the science which may be considered certain, reduce themselves to the scantiest list of parallels—namely, the Indian Varuna and the

[1] Lang, *Myth, Ritual, and Religion*, vol. i. p. 23.

Greek Uranus, the Indian Bhaga and the Slavonic Bogu, the Indian Parjanya and the Lithuanian Perkunas, and finally, the Indian Dyaus and the Greek Zeus. Mannhardt adds that a number of other equations, such as Sârameya and Hermeias, Saranyus and Erinys, Gandharvas and Kentauros, will not stand criticism, so that these ingenious guesses will prove mere *jeux d'esprit* rather than actual conclusions of science.

But even the four identifications which Mannhardt believes to be actually established are more or less illusory. If Varuna, Bhaga, Parjanya, and Dyaus were deities worshipped by the undivided Aryans, we should expect to find these names in the whole circle of the Aryan languages, just as we find the names for mother, wife, and daughter, for dog, cow, waggon, and wheel, for five and ten. But this we do not find. Dyaus is the only name which is at all widely spread, and even in the case of Dyaus, the strongest of all, there are reasons which may make us doubt whether he can ever have been the supreme god of the undivided Aryans.

The case of the Sanskritists rests on these four Indian names, Bhaga, Parjanya, Varuna, and Dyaus. The real significance of these four names will therefore have to be examined more closely.

The Norse Fjörgyn was identified by Grimm[1] with the Lithuanian thunder-god Perkunas, and probably with the old Slavonic Perunu; but Professor Rhys considers as futile the attempt to connect them with the Sanskrit Parjanya, the god of rain and thunder. The Mordwin thunder-god Porguini is doubtless the same as Perkunas, but this may be set down as a case of

[1] Grimm, *Deutsche Mythologie*, p. 156.

mythological borrowing, and there is no trace of such a deity in Greek or Latin.

In the Slavonic languages Bogu denotes the supreme deity. The word is found in the Rig Veda as *bhaga*, which means the distributor of gifts, especially of food, and is used as an epithet of the gods, and also, seemingly, as the name of a subordinate deity. In the Avesta the word has attained a larger significance, and is applied as an epithet to Mithra, and also to Ahura-Mazda, who is called Bhaga-Bhaganam, god of gods.[1] The word only became the name of the supreme deity among the Slaves, and among the closely-related Phrygians, with whom, according to Hesychius, the word Βαγαῖος was the equivalent of Zeus. The inscription, *Jovi Baginati*, inscribed on a Gaulish altar found in the Department of the Isère, was probably a dedication by Persian or Phrygian mercenaries, as there is no other indication that such a name belonged to the Celtic Pantheon.[2]

Bogu and Perkunas must therefore be set aside as divine names which had only a limited geographical currency, and may be ranged with other culture words of late date which are common to the Iranian and Slavo-Lettic languages.[3]

The comparative mythologists who assert that the undivided Aryans were in possession of a common mythology before their separation have therefore to rest their case on two equations—that of the Indian Varuna and the Greek Uranus, and of the Indian Dyaus with the Greek Zeus, the Latin Jupiter, and

---

[1] See Cook, *Origins of Language and Religion*, p. 69.
[2] Rhys, *Hibbert Lectures*, p. 54.
[3] See p. 195, *supra*.

the Teutonic Tiu.[1] The identification of Varuna and Uranus, although from an etymological point of view it leaves nothing to be desired, fails to prove the contention, because it is confined to Sanskrit and Greek, and we have already seen that the Greeks and Indians share late culture words, such as those for certain weapons, and for implements of tillage, which are not found in other Aryan languages—an indication of a geographical contact posterior to the linguistic separation of the Aryans. But there is this great difference, that while the Indo-Greek culture words are found also in Iranian, the Indo-Greek mythologic names are significantly wanting. This defect in the Iranian record is the more specially significant because the separation of the Indians and Iranians was later than that of any of the other Aryan families, and also because the religious ideas of the Rig Veda agree in so many minute particulars with those of the Avesta. The Indians and Iranians, as we have already seen,[2] had a common religious ritual, they had common names for priests, sacrifices, sacred chants, for the soma drink, and for religious aspergation—a clear proof that an organised system of worship had been developed before the separation. There are no such ritualistic agreements between any of the other Aryan families. The agreement in the mythologic system is also so close and striking that if we find mythologic names in Greek and Sanskrit but not in Iranian, it is difficult to believe they are really primitive, and not evolved independently by Greeks and Indians.

[1] See, for instance, Max Müller's article on "The Lesson of Jupiter" in the *Nineteenth Century*.
[2] See p. 190, *supra*.

To give a few instances, we find that in the Avesta Mithra's club is called Vazra, while in the Veda Indra's club is Vajra. The cloud demon slain by Indra is Vritra, the demon slain in the Avesta is Verethra. In the Avesta, Vayu, the wind, rides in a golden chariot; in the Veda, Vayu is Indra's charioteer. Azhi-dahaka, the biting serpent of the Avesta, is the serpent Ahi of the Veda. The Thrita and Thraetona of the Avesta are the Trita and Traitana of the Veda.[1] The mighty warriors and far-ruling kings of the Avesta are in the Veda the ancient spirits of the sky.[2] Yama, who was originally merely the setting sun, is, like the Egyptian Tum, exalted in the Veda to be the king of the dead, while in the Avesta he has become the first legendary Iranian monarch. The Indian sun-god Mitra became among the Iranians the gracious Mithra, the "friend" of mankind. Mitra is associated with Varuna as Mithra is with Ahura. Ahri-man, the destructive spirit, appears in the Veda as well as in the Avesta.

Asura and Mazda are titles given in the Veda to Varuna, but in the Avesta these two titles are combined as the proper name of the supreme God, and we have the magnificent conception of Ahura Mazda (Ormuzd), the "Lord Omniscient," whose all-seeing eye is the glowing orb of day, whose son is the fire, while the robe which clothes him is represented as the vast starry firmament, which also is the garment of the Indian Varuna.

It is plain that while the lower mythological ideas of the Indians and Iranians agree, the higher religious conceptions, involving the name of the king all

[1] Duncker, *History of Antiquity*, vol. v. p. 42.
[2] *Ibid.*, p. 44.

glorious above, "whose robe is the light, whose canopy space," were the creations of a later time, when Indians and Iranians had separately advanced out of the earlier barbarism to a higher and nobler intellectual culture.

But Ahura Mazda, the supreme deity of the Iranians, was not the supreme deity of the Indians, though they gave the corresponding title Asura Medha to more than one god of light.[1] The supreme Indian deities were Indra and Varuna, of whom there is hardly a trace in the Avesta, a tolerably sure proof that the Indian worship of Varuna—the mighty Heaven—was evolved after the separation of the Indians and Iranians.

That this was the case is confirmed by the fact that the agreements between the Indian and Greek mythology, of which so much has been made, are nominal rather than real.

Both in India and Greece we have the common linguistic germs of the later mythological conceptions, but the mythology itself is plainly a later growth. The names of Uranus and Varuna are etymologically identical, as are those of Zeus and Dyaus, but this is all that can be affirmed. Indra and Varuna in the Vedic hymns completely take the place and offices of Zeus in the Homeric poems. Varuna is the mighty deity who rules the universe, who listens to human prayers, who does the right, and decides the destinies of men; while Indra, like Zeus, is the wielder of the thunderbolt. Nor does the Greek Uranus correspond more closely to Varuna. As Ludwig has observed, such Homeric phrases as οὐρανὸς ἀστερόεις show that in the oldest literature of the Greeks the word Uranus

[1] Duncker, *History of Antiquity*, vol. v. p. 145.

designated only the physical vault of heaven, and it is not before the time of Hesiod that Uranus is personified, and becomes the spouse of the Earth and the ancestor of Zeus; whereas in India, at a much earlier time, Varuna has become the supreme administrator of the universe, and is never identified with physical phenomena.[1] Dyaus, however, in the Veda is still what Uranus was in Homer, and has not yet become what Zeus was among the Greeks.

It is true that the Indian Dyaus is the same word as the Greek Zeus, while the Latin Ju-piter, the Teutonic Tiu or Ziu, and the Celtic *duw* are names of kindred origin. Hence by far the strongest case is that of Zeus, since this is the only divine name which is found in any considerable number of Aryan languages. But even this wide-spread appellation is not universal. It is not found among the Iranians and the Slaves, and where it is found the mythologic equivalence is questionable.

In the first place, if Dyaus had been recognised as the highest god, or even recognised as a god at all, by the undivided Aryans, or if he had occupied among the Indians the supreme position which Zeus held among the Greeks, it is difficult to understand how every trace of the worship of such a mighty being should have disappeared among the Iranians, whose separation from the Indians was so late, and who agree with them so closely in their religious observances and their mythological beliefs.

While the name of Dyaus does not even appear in the Avesta, in the Rig Veda he occupies a wholly subordinate position, completely overshadowed by Varuna. Indeed he can hardly be called a god; he

[1] See Cook, *Origins of Religion and Language*, p. 66.

is little more than the sky, the physical germ of a mythological conception, just as Uranus was at first among the Greeks. Indra is called a son of Dyaus, a child of heaven, in the same way that Zeus is said to have been one of the grandchildren of Uranus; but Dyaus can hardly be said to have been an object of worship among the Indians any more than Uranus was among the Homeric Greeks. Far less can Dyaus be claimed as the supreme Heaven god, which Zeus was among the Greeks.

It is easier to believe that Zeus was elevated by the Greeks themselves to his exalted position, and that the personification of Dyaus was later than the separation of Indians and Iranians, than to hold with Professor Max Müller and others that the lofty Greek conception had belonged to the half-savage Aryans before the linguistic separation, and that this great primeval faith had almost died out in India, and that in Persia it had altogether disappeared.

But if we once admit that before the separation of the Aryans they had a common name for the sky, as well as for the water and earth, all the difficulty disappears. Not only did the word *dyaus* mean little more among the Indians than the mere physical sky, but even among the Greeks and Romans there are linguistic survivals which prove that the development of the mythological idea was still comparatively recent. When the Greeks said Ζεύς ὕει, "the sky pours down rain," there was still an evident consciousness in the ancient phrase that the word *zeus* had once meant the physical sky and nothing more. That the same was the case among the Romans is shown, among other instances, by the well-known line of Horace, "Manet sub jove frigido venator" (the huntsman abides under the chill sky). Plainly among both Greeks and Romans Zeus and Jove had not altogether ceased to be regarded, like the Indian Dyaus, as the over-arching heaven.

All therefore that we can safely conclude is that before their linguistic separation the Greeks and Indians had common names for the sky, Dyaus and Varuna, and that the mythologic significance of these names may date from a later period, and have been independently evolved.[1]

There is a further difficulty in supposing that Zeus was the god of the undivided Aryans. Not only is the name wanting in the Iranian and Slavo-Lettic languages, but in Celtic, which is so closely related to the Latin, we find only the germ from which such a conception might have been developed. In the Celtic languages no god bears this name, but we find words derived from the same root, *div*, to "shine," from which we get the Sanskrit *diva* and *divasa*, day; the Armenian *div*, "day"; the Latin *dies*; and the Celtic *diu*, *dieu*, and *dyw*, "day." This root is also the source of the Latin *divus* and *deus*, and of the Celtic *duw* and *dia*, a god.[2] To the same source we may attribute the Iranian *daeva*, which denoted a demon or evil spirit.

The fortunes of this word in the Teutonic languages are of more importance. So much has been made of the supposed identity of the Sanskrit Dyaus and the Teutonic Tiu or Ziu, and the identity, if it

---

[1] In like manner, when in the later Greek mythology Uranus had been at last personified, the Iranian *asman*, the heaven, became among the Greeks Ἄκμων, the father of Uranus.

[2] Rhys, *Hibbert Lectures*, p. 119, maintains that the Celtic word never acquired the force of a proper name.

could be established, would have such far-reaching consequences in its bearing on the primitive culture of the undivided Aryans, that the question must be examined in some detail.

Of the German mythology we know little, but the mythologic lore of the Scandinavians has come down to us in considerable amplitude, and since the Low German Tiu and the High German Ziu was undoubtedly the same deity as the Scandinavian Tyr, it will suffice to inquire whether Tyr can be identified with Zeus, or whether he was an independent mythological creation.

Now, in the earliest Scandinavian literature *tyr* (plural *tivar*) is only a divine appellation, meaning simply "a god." Thus Thor is called Reidi-tyr, the car-god, Odin is Hanga-tyr, the gallows-god, or Farma-tyr, the cargo-god. In the plural we have Sigtivar, the gods of victory, and Val-tivar, the gods of those slain in battle. The word *tivar*, remotely related to the Latin *deus*, means properly "the glorious ones," being formed from a root denoting splendour, glory, fame (proto-Aryan *div*, to shine), which is seen in the word *äsc-tir*, spear-fame, or renown in battle.[1]

In the later Scandinavian mythology we find this word appropriated as the proper name of a secondary deity, represented as a somewhat comic personage, whose arm was bitten off by the wolf Fenris, whose wife was unfaithful to him, and who is mocked for his misfortunes by the other gods, like Hephæstus in the Greek mythology.[2] He is simply the glorious one,

[1] Kemble, *The Saxons in England*, vol. i. p. 353.
[2] See the "Loka-Senna" in Vigfusson and Powell's *Corpus Poeticum Boreale*, vol. i. p. 106.

the one-armed god of victory, in no way corresponding in his place or functions to the Greek Zeus, but rather to Mars or Ares. That he was thus identified by our forefathers is shown by the fact that the Teutonic Tues-day is not Jeudi, *Dies Jovis*, but Mardi, *Dies Martis*. The Teutonic Tiu may have a remote linguistic relation to Zeus, but mythologically he corresponds to Ares. In the Teutonic mythology the true analogue to Zeus or Varuna is not Tiu or Tyr, but Woden or Odin,[1] who is the supreme Heaven god, the blessed Father, the Lord of Earth, the All-Father of gods and men, whose consort is Jördh, the Earth, whose all-seeing eye is the sun, the round orb which is also the eye of Ahura Mazda and Varuna, beholding all things upon earth.

Thor, the thunderer, is not the son of Tyr, but *Odins sonr* and *Jardhar sonr*, the son of Heaven and Earth, just as Indra, who answers to Thor, is the son of Varuna. The Anglo-Saxon royal families trace their descent from Woden, not from Tiu, just as noble Greek families did from Zeus. And Frigg, the Mother Earth, is the spouse of Woden, not of Tiu.

If Tiu or Tyr had been mythologically related to Zeus he would in all these aspects have taken the place of Odin. The Baltic tribes possessed the obvious mythological conception of Father Heaven and Mother Earth, but it was wholly independent of the Jupiter and the Demeter of the Mediterranean nations. The mythologists have been led astray by the similarity of the names to infer an identity of Tiu and Zeus which in reality has no existence.

[1] See *Corpus Poeticum Boreale*, vol. ii. pp. 459, 460.

The real "Lesson of Jupiter" is the lesson that philology by itself may be a misleading guide.

But though the All-Father of our Teutonic ancestors was Woden and not Tiu, it has been urged in the article to which reference has just been made that the identification of Zeus and Dyaus is made complete, since we find Dyaus designated as Dyaush-pitar in the Veda, which corresponds to the Latin Diespiter, or Jupiter, and to the Greek Ζεύς πατήρ (vocative Ζεῦ πάτερ). This doubtless is plausible and tempting, but it is by no means certain that such designations belong to the primitive period, and may not have arisen independently. We have no trace of such a compound appellation as Dyaush-pitar or Jupiter among Celts, Lithuanians, Iranians, Slaves, or Teutons; whereas, granting that Dyaus or Zeus was a primitive name of the sky, the notion of regarding Heaven and Earth as the parents of gods and men is so obvious and universal that there is no difficulty in supposing that it may have arisen independently among Indians, Greeks, and Latins. In fact we find the same idea in almost all mythologies. In New Zealand the Maoris regard Rangi, the Heaven, and Papa, the Earth, as the universal parents of all things.[1] The Peruvians, the Caribs, the Aztecs, the Red Indians, the Finns, the Lapps, and the Anglo-Saxons all spoke of Mother Earth, and sometimes the Sun, or more usually the Sky, was regarded as her spouse. Among the Finns, Ukko and Akka are the names given to Father Heaven and Mother Earth.[2] Among the Greeks it was sometimes Uranus and Gæa, sometimes Zeus

[1] Tylor, *Primitive Culture*, vol. i. p. 290; Lang, *Custom and Myth*, p. 48.   [2] Castrén, *Finnische Mythologie*, pp. 32, 86.

and Demeter who were so regarded. So also in the Rig Veda, Dyaus, who is the physical heaven, is called Dyaush-pitar, Father Sky, who with Prithivi-matar, Mother Earth, are the parents of the supreme god, the mighty Indra.

It may, therefore, be questioned whether Dyaus was ever the supreme heaven god of the undivided Aryans. They clearly had two words for the sky—the bright sky of day was called Dyaus "the shining," and the over-arching canopy of night was called Varuna, the "coverer" or "concealer." From these physical conceptions the names of the supreme deities may well have been independently evolved. In the dark West and the cold North the daylight sky was reverenced as the supreme source of good; in the burning and torrid Eastern lands the covering sky of night, and Indra the lord of rain, were rather looked up to and invoked as the blessers of mankind.

In India and in Greece, just as among Red Indians and Maoris, Father Heaven and Mother Earth were regarded as the primeval parents of all things, or the sun and moon were looked upon as brother and sister, or as a wedded pair; or the sun would be pictured as an ardent youth, chasing a fair maiden, the flying dawn. The chariot of the sun, the winds—the invisible messengers of heaven—would be images occurring independently to the poets of both nations; and since the words denoting the sky, and the dawn, and the heavenly bodies would be related words, the few coincidences in mythological names may be explained without the hypothesis of a primitive Aryan mythology, invented in remote neolithic times, and handed down in recognisable form from

THE ARYAN MYTHOLOGY.

the far distant period when the Aryan peoples parted.

But though the common origin of the Greek and Indian mythology, once so confidently asserted, has wholly, or in great part, to be surrendered, we are able to see more clearly what it was that was really common to Greeks and Indians. In India, as in Greece, there was the same over-arching sky, the sun and the moon and the stars, the storm-clouds and the wind, the same succession of day and night, of summer and winter, and all the mysterious phenomena of nature. And there were the elements of a common speech; there were men calling all these things by related names, thinking the same thoughts, speculating in the same way as to celestial phenomena, so that as culture progressed among Indians and Greeks, Teutons, Celts, and Latins, nature myths, with features essentially the same, but underived, were independently evolved, as an attempt to explain the aspects of the world.

But if the Aryans started without mythological beliefs, and merely with common words for day, sky, and brightness, it is easy to see how these words should have independently become the names of the supreme heaven-gods. From the root *div* or *dyu*, to shine, we obtain a whole series of Aryan words, denoting day, and noon, and sky, heavenly and divine, god and 'goddess; and finally the names of specific deities were evolved. Such are, in Greek and Latin, the names Διαίνη and Διώνη, Divania and Diana, Djanus and Janus, Djovis and Jovis, Zeus; and such words as *hora meri-diana, jove diano, sub dio,* ἐν δῖος, at noon, *deus, divus,* δῖος, divine; in Welsh *dyw*, a day, and *duw*, a god; in Irish *diu*, a day, *dia*, a god, and *de*, a goddess; and in Armenian *div*, day.[1]

But even if we admit the identification of the Greek Zeus with the Indian Dyaus—and this is by far the strongest case—we may affirm with Professor Rhys that the so-called Science of Aryan Comparative Mythology which started so long ago with this identification cannot, in all these years, be said to have advanced much further, and it seems doubtful whether even this identification is of the genuine mythologic order, and not merely linguistic.

It is surely easier to believe that rude, uncultured nomads, still in the stone age, should not have risen to the conception of the Hellenic Zeus than that such a conception, if it had existed, should, as they rose in culture, have been degraded to the mere physical conception; and it is equally difficult to understand how the name and worship of the supreme heaven-god should have been lost utterly among the Iranians and the Slaves.

As Professor Rhys remarks—"If the Aryans had attained to the idea of so transcendent a god ... there would be a difficulty in understanding how, as the Dyaus of Sanskrit literature, he should have become comparatively a lay figure, that as Tiu he should have been superseded by Woden and Thor among the Teutons, and that among the Gauls his pre-eminence should at any time have been threatened by a Mercury."[2] Ideas may be the same, and language may be identical, but we cannot affirm that the undivided Aryans were in possession of a common mythology. It is more probable that out of

[1] See Rhys, *Hibbert Lectures*, p. 116.
[2] *Ibid.*, p. 110.

the same common words, and the same thoughts, the Aryan nations, after their separation, constructed separate mythic tales, whose resemblances are apparent rather than real.

Another factor has also to be taken into account. Much of the culture formerly attributed to the undivided Aryans is due, as we have seen, merely to borrowing, and so also it is probable that there has been an extensive migration of myths from tribe to tribe. In many cases this has been proved to be the case. We know that a large portion of the Greek mythic tales were in reality derived from Semitic sources, that the Latin poets transferred Greek myths to unrelated Italic deities, that the Teutons appropriated Celtic deities, while even the mythology of the Edda turns out to be largely infected with ideas which can be traced to Christian sources, and supposed Hottentot traditions of a universal deluge prove to have been obtained from the dimly-remembered teaching of Christian missionaries.

Religious myths, like folk-tales and popular fables, have an astonishing faculty for migration. Sacred legends of the Buddhist priests found their way from India to Bagdad, from Bagdad to Cairo, from Cairo to Cordova, and are now enshrined in the pages of La Fontaine, having been translated by wandering professional story-tellers from Pali into Pehlevi, from Pehlevi into Arabic, from Arabic into Spanish, from Spanish into French and English.

It is more probable that any divine myths which may ultimately be identified in the Aryan languages may have thus migrated at some early time, than that, as the Comparative Mythologists assume, they formed part of the common Aryan heritage in the barbarous and immensely remote period before the linguistic separation. In any case it is clear that the sweeping conclusions which were in vogue thirty years ago as to the nature and extent of the primitive Aryan mythology are based upon assumptions as unwarranted as the theories of the successive migration of the Aryan nations from the East.

The work of the last ten years has been mainly destructive. The work of the previous half-century has been revised, and ingenious but baseless theories have been extensively demolished, and the ground cleared for the erection of more solid structures.

While on the one hand science has been specialised, on the other it has been shown that the correlation of the prehistoric sciences is as intimate as the correlation of the physical sciences. The whilom tyranny of the Sanskritists is happily overpast, and it is seen that hasty philological deductions require to be systematically checked by the conclusions of prehistoric archæology, craniology, anthropology, geology, and common sense.

INDEX.

Ablative, 259, 294
Achilles, 300
Acorns, 167
Adam, M., 286
Adelung, 9
Adonis, 302
Agglutination, 284
Agni, 312
Ahlqvist, 290, 296, 297
Ahura Mazda, 318, 320, 321
Ainos, 109
Alba Longa, 173, 176
Albanian, 268
Albinism, 42, 43
Algeria, 200, 202
Amazons, 302
Ambigatos, 234
Ammianus Marcellinus, 77
Anderson, 279, 290, 291
Andromeda, 303
Anglo-Saxon, 102
Anna Comnena, 245
Anthropology, 19, 63
Aphrodite, 302, 306
Apollo, 304
Aquitani, 93, 110, 223
Arabic, 207, 211
Arcelin, 60
Archæology, 25
Ares, 303
Armenian, 52, 195, 267
Arrows, 151
Aspatria, 244
Arnold, Matthew, 245
Artemis, 302, 310
Aryans—the name, 2; race, 19, 31, 38, 197-250; migrations, 4, 12, 17, 26, 48, 125, 272; language, 40, 251-298; origin, 8, 18, 30, 52, 53; civilisation, 125-196; mythology, 299-332.
Asman, 324
Ass, 161
Astarte, 301
Athena, 305
Aurora, 311, 315
Autumn, 163, 187
Auvergnats, 113, 119, 218, 221
Avesta, 14, 16, 176, 190, 211, 320
Aztecs, 202

Bacmeister, 256
Bactria, 10, 14, 16
Balkash, Lake, 29
Barley, 165
Barrows, long, 67, 75, 78, 94
Barrows, round, 68, 69, 70, 75, 78, 112, 238
Basques, 19, 80, 94, 139, 205, 215, 217-226, 296
Batavodunum, 256
Bateman, 183
Beddoe, Dr., 68, 84
Beech, 16, 25, 26, 28, 49, 62
Belgæ, 110
Belgium, 6, 204, 225
Benfey, 14, 24, 54
Bengali, 5
Bhaga, 258, 273, 318
Bienne, Lake of, 169
Bits for horses, 160
Black race, 64, 65
Blau, 268
Boadicea, 76
Boats, 177
Bogu, 267
Bohemond, 245
Boii, 77, 84

INDEX.

Boiodurum, 256
Bopp, 1, 3, 270
Borreby, 104, 105
Brachycephalic, 64, 80
Breeches, 172
Brennus, 136, 150
Britain, races of, 66
Broca, 6, 42, 65, 94, 95, 101, 110, 113, 197, 215, 218, 241
Bronze, 128, 138-142, 148
Bronze age, 56, 58, 126, 127
Bulgarian, 281
Burgundians, 103, 244
Busk, 96
Butterwick, 128

Cæsar, 110, 242, 249
Caledonians, 77
Calori, Dr., 87, 98, 241
Calpurnius Flaccus, 109
Camel, 25, 162
Camulos, 308, 315
Cannibalism, 101, 109, 183, 224
Canstadt race, 105-107
Capercailzie, 62
Carniola, 238, 256
Catholicism, 248
Cattle, 151-163
Caucasian languages, 2
Caves, sepulchral, 78, 174
Caves, Cefn, 67; Chauvaux, 93; Engis, 106; Furfooz, 116; Genista, 96, 123; Victoria, 60; M. Tignoso, 90; Sclaigneaux, 81; Caverne de l'Homme Mort, 93; Caverna della Matta, 90
Celt, copper, Sipplingen, 141
Celts, 7, 34, 38, 48, 70, 73, 76, 78, 80, 81, 92, 110, 112, 120, 147, 192, 201, 205, 214, 221, 223, 226, 233, 238, 257
Celtic deities, 307, 314
Celtiberians, 223
Cereals, 127, 164, 237
Cesnola, 141
Cevennes, 222
Chalcis, 140
Chamblon, 58
Chariots, 160
Chavée, 227
Cheese, 168
Chinese, 276

Cimbric, 7, 70
Constance, Lake of, 128, 141, 257
Cook, Canon, 4, 8
Colours, 156
Cooking, 167
Copper, 137-142
Coritavi, 76, 77
Corsicans, 95, 97
Counting, 187
Couvard, 184
Cow, 155
Craniology, 18, 63
Croll, Dr., 55
Cro-Magnon, 69, 95, 96, 100, 116
Cronus, 306
Cuno, 30, 33, 164, 290, 291
Cyprus, 141

Dacians, 236, 268
Dahn, 163
Danes, 84, 104
Darius, 180
Darwin, 66, 261
Daughter, 185
Dawkins, Professor, 60, 101, 122, 128
Declensions, 285
De Belloguet, 77
Delbrück, 38
Delitzsch, 40
Denmark, 27
De Quatrefages, 66, 109, 120, 215
Dialects, 36, 261
Diefenbach, 79, 290
Dio Cassius, 76
Diodorus Siculus, 77
Dionysus, 304
Dioscorides, 267
Diseases, 202, 203
Disentis type, 121
Dodona, 27, 310
Dog, 130, 156, 240
Dolichocephalic, 64, 80
Dolmens, 119, 177
Doors, 174
Dravidian, 259, 274; dress, 171
Druids, 249
Dual, 287, 288
Dutch, 200
Dyaus, 189, 317, 322-329
Dyaush-pitar, 327

INDEX. 335

Ecker, 102
Edda, 331
Egypt, 200
Engis skull, 244
English language, 37, 276, 280
Eos, 311
Erinyes, 315, 317
Etruscan, 126, 144
Europa, 302
European languages, relations of, 21, 22, 252-260, 268-273
Evans, Dr., 141, 145, 148, 149

Family, the, 186
Fick, 24, 270
Fimon, Lake of, 88, 127
Finnic languages, 32, 279, 282-298
Finnic civilisation, 296
Finnic theory, 125, 213, 217
Finns, 91, 115, 122, 278
Firbolg, 78
Fish, 168, 237
Fjörgyn, 317
Fligier, 44
Folk tales, 331
Food, 167
Formatives, 292
French, 277
Frigga, 308, 326
Frisians, 103, 243, 244
Furfooz race, 116
Future tense, 280

Galatians, 77
Gandharvas, 305, 315, 317
Gauls, 66, 77, 81, 207, 221, 224, 228
Geiger, 26, 28, 29
Gender, 289
Germans, 226, 228
German dialects, 289
Gibb, 274
Gibraltar, 96, 123
Gilliéron, Prof., 58
Glacial period, 19, 55
Glück, 221
Goat, 157
Gold, 135
Goths, 46, 201, 204, 210, 249
Grassmann, 270
Grave mounds, 86
Greek, 34, 35, 98, 194, 209, 260

Greek deities, 307
Greenwell, Canon, 67, 71, 79
Grenelle race, 115
Grimm, Jacob, 11
Griquas, 199
Gristhorpe, 76, 91
Guanches, 94, 96, 97, 220

Hale, Dr., 9
Half-breeds, 198
Hamites, 41, 219, 224
Hainault, 118
Hair, 65
Halle, 85
Hallstadt, 85, 169
Harits, 300
Hehn, 23, 39, 40, 43, 189, 268
Helbig, 59, 87, 126, 127, 144, 163, 173, 222
Helen, 300
Helvetii, 86, 121
Heracles, 305, 306
Hercules, 306
Hermes, 315
Herodotus, 184, 236
Hesiod, 145
Hestia, 313
Hissarlik, 60, 99, 144, 182
Hodgkin, Dr., 210
Höfer, 39
Hohberg type, 244
Homer, 145, 182
Homme Mort, Caverne, 93
Hommel, 40
Horse, 130, 152, 158-161
Hovelacque, 286
Human sacrifice, 183
Humboldt, 219
Hunting, 152
Husbandry, 163, 194
Huts, 78, 174
Hut urns, 176
Huxley, Prof., 81, 122
Huzaras, 207
Hyksos, 159

Iberians, 68-78, 92-101, 213-225, 282
Idols, 309
Ilderton, 83
Illyrian, 268
Index, Orbital, 65

INDEX.

Index, Cephalic, 64
Indians, 200, 212
Indian deities, 307, 312-323
Indian languages, 2, 259
Indo-European languages, 2
Indo-Iranians, 23, 35, 49
Indra, 190, 300, 312
Inflections, loss of, 37
Iranian languages, 2, 257
Iron, 143-147
Isdhubar, 306
Istar, 301

Japhetic languages, 2, 8, 17
Jews, 246
Jones, Sir William, 1
Jördh, 308, 326
Jubainville, 233
Jupiter, 310, 322, 326

Kabyles, 99
Keller, 59
Kiepert, 39
King Lud, 315
Kitchen Middens, 60, 61, 105, 131, 153, 169, 239, 241
Klaproth, 10
Kühn, 315

Ladino dialects, 265
Laibach, 166, 237
Lake dwellings, date of, 58, 59
Lang, Andrew, 316
Language, mutability of, 45, 204-213
Languages, Aryan, 40, 251-294
Languages, Semitic, 40, 283
Language and Race, 5, 41, 45, 273-281
Langue d'oc, 265
Lappanoide, 113
Lapps, 113, 115
Lassen, 10
Latins, 32, 192, 209, 257, 259, 271, 277
Latin dialects, 264, 265
Latham, Dr., 20
Latovici, 238
Law, 186
Lead, 147
Lenormant, 138, 304
Leskien, 36
Lesse, 116, 240

Ligurians, 90, 110, 113, 214
Lindenschmit, 43
Lion, 25
Lissauer, 104
Lithuanians, 15, 20, 228, 231, 258, 260, 271, 284, 291
Livy, 77
Loke Senna, 325
Lubbock, Sir J., 149
Lucan, 108
Lugdunum, 256

Mahometans, 246
Mamelukes, 275
Man, antiquity of, 55, 57
Manilius, 77
Mannhardt, 316
Marne, R., 119
Marriage, 185
Mars, 304, 316
Martial, 109
Maruts, 304, 316
McFirbis, 78
Mead, 170
Medicine, 186
Melicertes, 305
Metals, 127, 133, 149
Mithra, 320
Mommsen, 9
Money, 154
Mongols, 65, 70, 91
Möringen, 153
Morlot, 59
Morris, 53
Mortar, 175, 177
Mortillet, 57, 227
Mortimer, 79
Mouse, 164
Mulattoes, 199
Müller, F., 41, 283
Müller, Professor Max, 3, 11, 27, 53, 155, 215, 282, 284, 299, 300, 305, 315, 316, 319, 323.
Mycenæ, 144, 170
Mythology, Aryan, 299-332

Neanderthal skull, 101, 106
Negroes, 199, 202, 203, 208
Neolithic age, 56, 57
Neptune, 306, 315
Nerthus, 308
Nidau, 153, 169

INDEX.

Niebuhr, 228
Nilsson, 105
Numidians, 219

Oars, 178
Odomanti, 179
Oliphant, K., 280
Olmo skull, 90
Oppert, 251
Orthocephalic, 64, 228
Oxus, 11, 13
Ox wagon, 179

Paladru, 160
Palæolithic age, 55, 57, 93
Pamir, 41
Parietal angle, 114
Passive, 273
Paul, Professor, 36
Pauli, 270
Pausanias, 97
Penka, 37, 44-47, 197, 230, 232, 234, 246, 294
Perkunas, 317
Perseus, 303
Persian, 15, 258
Peschiera, 126
Phœnicians, 135, 196, 301
Phonetic tests, 275-277
Phrygians, 267, 318
Pictet, 12
Pidgin English, 276
Piètrement, 29, 39
Pile dwellings, 86, 131, 152, 171, 176, 179, 235, 236, 309
Pile dwellings, Swiss, 51, 59, 126, 141, 153, 160, 176
Pile dwellings, Italian, 59, 87, 127, 144, 163, 169, 175, 259
Pit dwellings, 174
Pliny, 222
Plough, 166
Plural formation, 288, 293
Polygamy, 184
Pont de la Thièle, 58
Population, density of, 51, 61
Pösche, 42, 77, 197, 200, 227, 246
Pott, 10, 270
Pottery, Art of, 79, 181
Poultry, 162
Prakrits, 258
Pramantha, 313

Prithivi, 308
Procopius, 109
Prognathism, 64
Prometheus, 313
Pronominal Suffixes, 292
Protestantism, 247
Prüner Bey, 70, 113, 214
Prunière, 119
Pyrites, 140

Race, permanence of, 45, 198 203
Races, Northern, 226, 245
Rangi, 327
Rawlinson, Professor, 6
Razor, 173
Reindeer, 117
Religion, 190, 246, 299-332
Rendell, Professor, 230
Retzius, 214, 216, 218
Rhætians, 121
Rhode, J. G., 9
Rhys, Professor, 53, 80, 230, 281, 284, 317, 330
Rice, 28
Rig Veda, 176, 190, 312, 319
Rokitno Swamp, 42, 47
Rolleston, 69, 82
Romans, 204, 307
Round barrow race, 295
Row graves, 42, 86, 102, 201, 228, 244
Russians, 90, 278
Rye, 28

Sails, 179
Salt, 148
Sanskrit, 14, 15, 20, 35, 50, 259, 291
Sarama, 315
Saturn, 306
Savagery, 183
Sayce, Professor, 13, 14, 52, 210, 219, 230, 287, 303
Scandinavians, 46, 102, 213, 229
Scandinavian deities, 325
Schaffhausen, 104
Scherzer, 198
Schlegel, 10
Schleicher, 13, 270
Schliemann, Dr., 60, 98, 114, 131, 144, 145

338 INDEX.

Schmidt, 33-36, 272-274, 255, 269, 300
Schrader, Dr., 45, 48-52, 139, 163, 189, 285, 289, 290
Schussenried, 152, 166, 169, 236
Sclaigneaux Cave, 81
Sea, the, 187, 191
Semele, 304
Semitic languages, 40, 41, 283
Seneca, 97
Shakespeare, 276
Sheep, 157
Shibboleth, 275
Shields, 151
Sicilian Vespers, 275
Sicily, 97, 159
Sidonius Apollinaris, 244
Silius Italicus, 77
Silures, 68, 78
Silver, 142, 143
Siret, M. M., 141
Skene, 78
Skins, 172
Slaves, 90, 190, 191, 195, 104, 257, 272
Slavonic deities, 307
Slavonic languages, 34, 281
Smith, George, 300
Smith, the, 133, 137
Social life, 182
Skulls—Rudstone, 71, 72; Cowlam, 71, 72; Sherburn, 74; Ilderton, 75; Borreby, 83, 104; Sclaigneaux, 82; Sion type, 86, 87; Theodorianus, 89; Caverne de l'Homme Mort, 93-95, 119; Genista Cave, 96, 123; Hissarlik, 98, 114; Neanderthal, 101, 106; Trou de Frontal, 117; Furfooz, 116, 122; Grenelle, 115, 117; Disentis type, 121; Rodmarton, 123; Spanish Basque, 220; Row Grave, 103; Roman, 88, 89; Canstadt, 105, 108, 116; Stængenæs, 105, 240; Engis, 106; St. Mansuy, 108; Robert Bruce, 108; Auvergnat, 111; Cro-Magnon, 69; Eguisheim, 106; Olmo, 90
Skull form, 63-65
Solutré, 130, 158
Sonne, 270

Sow, 157
Spaniards, 200, 202, 206, 222
Spiegel, 41, 42, 47, 270, 274
Stængenæs, 105, 240
Stammbaum theory, 33-35
Starnberg, Lake of, 237
Steenstrup, Prof., 62, 240
Stonehenge, 177
Strabo, 76, 77
Swords, 150

Tacitus, 68, 77, 109
Tammuz, 302
Tancred, 245
Tartars, 50
Tattooing, 173
Teutons, 42, 44, 46, 102-109, 190, 259
Teutonic deities, 307, 314, 325
Thomsen, Dr., 290
Thor, 314, 325, 326
Thousand, 255
Thracian, 268
Thurnam, Dr., 70, 80, 92, 122
Time, computation of, 187
Tinière, 59, 121
Tiu, 138, 322, 326
Todas, 109
Tombs, 135
Topinard, 7
Toutiorix, 315
Trades, 180
Triton, 306
Troyon, 126
Tuatha Dé Danann, 78
Tuesday, 326
Turanian, 70, 80, 85, 92, 123, 215
Tyr, 325

Ugrians, 225, 286
Ujfalvy, 226, 227
Ulphilas, 276
Umbrians, 27, 87, 126, 163, 175, 256
Uranus, 303, 319, 321
Ushas, 311

Vambéry, 91, 297
Van Eys, 219
Varuna, 307, 319, 321, 328
Veda, 155, 169, 172, 176, 190, 211, 299, 308, 312, 316, 319-323, 327

Venus, 306, 310
Verbal roots, 290-292
Vesta, 312, 313
Victoria Cave, 60
Vikings, 183
Vinson, 219
Virchow, 82, 98, 103, 106, 241, 243
Vocalic harmony, 286

Wallace, 151
Wauwyl, 153
Wave theory, 269
Weapons, 150, 194
Weaving, 171
Welsh, 277

Weske, 290
Wheel, 179
Whitney, Professor, 12, 24
Williams, Monier, 41
Wine, 170
Winter, 164, 187
Woden, 273, 308, 314, 326, 327
Wool, 172
Wotiaks, 91

Yama, 320
Year, 187

Zend, 15, 258
Zeus, 310, 321, 326
Zeuss, 238

Printed by WALTER SCOTT, *Felling, Newcastle-on-Tyne.*

THE
Contemporary Science Series.

Edited by HAVELOCK ELLIS.

Illustrated Volumes, containing between 300 and 400 pp.

THE CONTEMPORARY SCIENCE SERIES will bring within general reach of the English-speaking public the best that is known and thought in all departments of modern scientific research. The influence of the scientific spirit is now rapidly spreading in every field of human activity. Social progress, it is felt, must be guided and accompanied by accurate knowledge,—knowledge which is, in many departments, not yet open to the English reader. In the Contemporary Science Series all the questions of modern life—the various social and politico-economical problems of to-day, the most recent researches in the knowledge of man, the past and present experiences of the race and the nature of its environment—will be frankly investigated and clearly presented.

The first Volumes of the Series are:—

THE EVOLUTION OF SEX. By Prof. PATRICK GEDDES and J. ARTHUR THOMSON. With 90 Illustrations, and about 300 pages. [*Ready.*

"A work which, for range and grace, mastery of material, originality, and incisiveness of style and treatment, is not readily to be matched in the long list of books designed more or less to popularise science. . . . The series will be, if it goes on as it has begun, one of the most valuable now current."—*Scottish Leader.*

"The book is the opening volume of a new Scientific Series, and the publishers are to be congratulated on starting with such a model of scientific exposition."—*Scotsman.*

ELECTRICITY IN MODERN LIFE. By G. W. DE TUNZELMANN. With 88 Illustrations. [*Ready.*

Among the contents of this volume are:—What we know about Electricity—What we know about Magnetism—Magnets and Conductors traversed by Electric Currents—Sources of Electricity—Magneto and Dynamo Electric

Machines—Overland and Submarine Telegraphs—The Telephone—Distrib
tion and Storage of Electrical Energy—Electric Lighting—Electro Metallur
—Electricity in Warfare—Medical Electricity, etc. This volume will be
interest not only to the specialist engaged in different applications of Ele
tricity, but to all who care to know something of the theory and application
the force which is creating so many transformations in the modern worl
While being both copious and explicit in detail, the subject is treated in su
a way as to appeal to the general reader.

THE ORIGIN OF THE ARYANS. By Dr. ISAAC TAYLO
    With numerous Illustrations.   [*Read*

The last ten years have seen a revolution in the opinion of scholars as to t
region in which the Aryan race originated, and theories which not long a
were universally accepted as the well-established conclusions of science no
hardly find a defender. The theory of migration from Asia has been di
placed by a new theory of origin in Northern Europe. In Germany sever
works have been devoted to the subject, but this is the first English wo
which has yet appeared embodying the results recently arrived at by phil
logists, archæologists, and anthropologists. This volume affords a fresh a
highly interesting account of the present state of speculation on a high
interesting subject.

PHYSIOGNOMY AND EXPRESSION. (Illustrated.)   F
    P. MANTEGAZZA.   [*Read*

This work, by Professor Mantegazza, a brilliant and versatile author, a
the leading Italian anthropologist, has already being translated into sever
European languages. Professor Mantegazza, whose name is well known
readers of Darwin, has co-operated in the present English edition of his wo
by writing a new chapter specially for it. This volume will be among t
most popular and interesting of the present series.

EVOLUTION AND DISEASE. (130 Illustrations.) By
    BLAND SUTTON.   [*Read*

THE VILLAGE COMMUNITY IN BRITAIN. By G.
    GOMME. Numerous Illustrations.

Other volumes to follow at short intervals, including "Bacteria and the
Products," "The Evolution of Marriage," "The Development of Electr
Magnetic Theory," "The Science of Fairy Tales," "Capital and Interest
"Sanity and Insanity," "Manual Training," "Industrial Development
"The Criminal," etc.

The following Writers, among others, are preparing volumes f
this Series:

Prof. G. F. Fitzgerald, Prof. J. Geikie, E. C. K. Gonner, Prof. J. Jastro
(Wisconsin), E. Sidney Hartland, Prof. C. H. Herford, Dr. C. Mercie
Sidney Webb, Dr. Sims Woodhead, Dr. C. M. Woodward (St. Loui
Mo.), etc.

IBSEN'S PROSE DRAMAS.

EDITED BY WILLIAM ARCHER.

Crown 8vo, Cloth, each $1.25.

The Norwegian dramatist, Henrik Ibsen, is at this moment one of the most widely-discussed, if not the best known, of European writers. His writings have given rise in Germany (to say nothing of the Scandinavian kingdoms) to a whole literature of books, pamphlets, and reviews; while France possesses translations of his most noted dramas. His name has been made famous throughout the English-speaking world by the production of *A Doll's House* in London, New York, Boston, and Melbourne. In each of these cities it excited an almost unprecedented storm of controversy. Hitherto, however, there has existed no uniform and authoritative edition in English of the plays of which so much has been said and written. An arrangement has been concluded with Henrik Ibsen, under which will be published a uniform series of his prose plays. Most of them will be translated and all will be carefully revised by Mr. William Archer, author of the translation of *A Doll's House*, performed in June 1889 at the Novelty Theatre, London.

VOL. I.

With Portrait of the Author, and Biographical Introduction
by William Archer.

This volume contains—"A DOLL'S HOUSE," "THE LEAGUE OF YOUTH" (*never before translated*), and "THE PILLARS OF SOCIETY."

VOL. II. *Ready 25th April, Containing*

"GHOSTS," "AN ENEMY OF THE PEOPLE," AND "THE WILD DUCK."

Among the Prose Dramas included in further volumes will be Lady Inger, The Warriors at Helgeland, The Pretenders, Rosmersholm, The Lady from the Sea etc. The sequence of the plays *in each volume* will be chronological; and the set of volumes comprising the dramas will thus present them, when complete, in chronological order. The issue will be bi-monthly.

New York: Scribner & Welford.

GREAT WRITERS.
A NEW SERIES OF CRITICAL BIOGRAPHIES.
Edited by Professor ERIC S. ROBERTSON, M.A.

LIBRARY EDITION.—Printed on large paper of extra quality, in handsom binding, Demy 8vo, price $1.00 each.

VOLUMES ALREADY ISSUED.

Balzac.
"A finished study, a concentrated summary, a succinct analysis o Balzac's successes and failures, and the causes of these successes and failures, and of the scope of his genius."—*Scottish Leader.*

Brontë, Charlotte. By Augustine Birrell.
"Those who know much of Charlotte Brontë will learn more, and thos who know nothing about her will find all that is best worth learning i Mr. Birrell's pleasant book."—*St. James' Gazette.*

Bunyan. By Canon Venables.
"A most intelligent, appreciative, and valuable memoir."—*Scotsman.*

Burns. By Professor Blackie.
"The editor certainly made a hit when he persuaded Blackie to writ about Burns."—*Pall Mall Gazette.*

Carlyle, Thomas. By Richard Garnett, LL.D.
"This is an admirable book. Nothing could be more felicitous an fairer than the way in which he takes us through Carlyle's life and works.'—*Pall Mall Gazette.*

Coleridge. By Hall Caine.
"Brief and vigorous, written throughout with spirit and great literar skill."—*Scotsman.*

Congreve. By Edmund Gosse.
"Mr. Gosse has written an admirable and most interesting biography o a man of letters who is of particular interest to other men of letters."—*Th Academy.*

Crabbe. By T. E. Kebbel.
"No English poet since Shakespeare has observed certain aspects o nature and of human life more closely. . . . Mr. Kebble's monograph i worthy of the subject."—*Athenæum.*

Darwin. By G. T. Bettany.
"Mr. G. T. Bettany's *Life of Darwin* is a sound and conscientiou work."—*Saturday Review.*

Dickens. By Frank T. Marzials.
"Notwithstanding the mass of matter that has been printed relating t Dickens and his works . . . we should, until we came across this volume have been at a loss to recommend any popular life of England's mos popular novelist as being really satisfactory. The difficulty is removed b Mr. Marzials's little book."—*Athenæum.*

Emerson. By Richard Garnett, LL.D.
"As to the larger section of the public . . . no record of Emerson' life and work could be more desirable, both in breadth of treatment an lucidity of style. than Dr. Garnett's."—*Saturday Review.*

Goethe. By James Sime.
"Mr. James Sime's competence as a biographer of Goethe, both in respect of knowledge of his special subject, and of German literature generally, is beyond question."—*Manchester Guardian.*

Goldsmith. By Austin Dobson.
"The story of his literary and social life in London, with all its humorous and pathetic vicissitudes, is here retold, as none could tell it better."—*Daily News.*

Heine. By William Sharp.
"This is an admirable monograph . . . more fully written up to the level of recent knowledge and criticism of its theme than any other English work."—*Scotsman.*

Hugo, Victor. By F. T. Marzials.
"Mr. Marzials's volume presents to us, in a more handy form than any English, or even French handbook gives, the summary of what, up to the moment in which we write, is known or conjectured about the life of the great poet."—*Saturday Review.*

Johnson, Samuel. By Colonel F. Grant.
"Colonel Grant has performed his task with diligence, sound judgment, good taste, and accuracy."—*Illustrated London News.*

Keats. By W. M. Rossetti.
"Valuable for the ample information which it contains."—*Cambridge Independent.*

Lessing. By T. W. Rolleston.
"Mr. Rolleston has written on Lessing one of the best books of the series in which his treatise appears."—*Manchester Guardian.*

Longfellow. By Professor Eric S. Robertson.
"A most readable little work."—*Liverpool Mercury.*

Marryat. By David Hannay.
"We have nothing but praise for the manner in which Mr. Hannay has done justice to him whom he well calls 'one of the most brilliant and the least fairly recognised of English novelists.'"—*Saturday Review.*

Milton. By Richard Garnett, LL.D.
"Within equal compass the life-story of the great poet of Puritanism has never been more charmingly or adequately told."—*Scottish Leader.*

Mill. By W. L. Courtney.
"A most sympathetic and discriminating memoir."—*Glasgow Herald.*

Rossetti, Dante Gabriel. By Joseph Knight.
"Mr. Knight's picture of the great poet and painter is the fullest and best yet presented to the public."—*The Graphic.*

Schiller. By Henry W. Nevinson.
"Presents the leading facts of the poet's life in a neatly rounded picture, and gives an adequate critical estimate of each of Schiller's separate works, and the effect of the whole upon literature."—*Scotsman.*

New York: SCRIBNER & WELFORD,

Scott. By Professor Yonge.
"For readers and lovers of the poems and novels of Sir Walter Scott, this is a most enjoyable book."—*Aberdeen Free Press.*

Shelley. By William Sharp.
"The criticisms . . . entitle this capital monograph to be ranked with the best biographies of Shelley."—*Westminster Review.*

Smith, Adam. By R. B. Haldane, M.P.
"Written with a perspicuity seldom exemplified when dealing with economic science."—*Scotsman.*

Smollett. By David Hannay.
"A capital record of a writer who still remains one of the great masters of the English novel."—*Saturday Review.*

The following Volumes will shortly be Issued :—

LIFE OF GEORGE ELIOT.   By Oscar Browning.
LIFE OF JANE AUSTEN.   By Goldwin Smith.

Complete Bibliography to each volume, by J. P. ANDERSON, British Museum.

Volumes are in preparation by Goldwin Smith, Frederick Wedmore, Oscar Browning, Arthur Symons, W. E. Henley, H. E. Watts, Cosmo Monkhouse, Frank T. Marzials, W. H. Pollock, John Addington Symonds, Hon. Roden Noel, Stepniak, Moncure Conway, Prof. Wallace, etc., etc.

Quarto, cloth elegant, gilt edges, emblematic design on cover, $2.25. May also be had in a variety of Fancy Bindings.

THE MUSIC OF THE POETS·
A MUSICIANS' BIRTHDAY BOOK.
EDITED BY ELEONORE D'ESTERRE KEELING.

This is a unique Birthday Book. Against each date are given the names of musicians whose birthday it is, together with a verse-quotation appropriate to the character of their different compositions or performances. A special feature of the book consists in the reproduction in fac-simile of autographs, and autographic music, of living composers. The selections of verse (from before Chaucer to the present time) have been made with admirable critical insight. English verse is rich in utterances of the poets about music, and merely as a volume of poetry about music this book makes a charming anthology. Three sonnets by Mr. Theodore Watts, on the "Fausts" of Berlioz, Schumann, and Gounod, have been written specially for this volume. It is illustrated with designs of various musical instruments, etc.; autographs of Rubenstein, Dvorâk, Greig, Mackenzie, Villiers Stanford, etc., etc.

"To musical amateurs this will certainly prove the most attractive birthday book ever published."—*Manchester Guardian.*

"One of those happy ideas that seems to have been yearning for fulfilment. . . . The book ought to have a place on every music stand."—*Scottish Leader.*

New York : SCRIBNER & WELFORD.

Printed in Poland
by Amazon Fulfillment
Poland Sp. z o.o., Wrocław